Springer Series

FOCUS ON MEN

Daniel Jay Sonkin, Ph.D., Series Editor
James H. Hennessy, Ph.D., Founding Editor

Focus on Men provides a wide range of books on the major psychological, medical, and social issues confronting men today.

P. Lynn Caesar, Ph.D., is a licensed psychologist in private practice and Director of Training and Education for the Center for Family Development in Beverly, Massachusetts. Her practice includes psychotherapy with children, adolescents, adults, couples, and families, and she trains clinicians and students in family therapy. Dr. Caesar received her doctorate in clinical psychology from the California School of Professional Psychology-Berkeley in 1985 and has received extensive training in family therapy. She is a cofounder and past president of the Central Vermont Shelter Project, Inc., a private, non-profit grass roots organization for battered women and their children. Dr. Caesar has presented papers at professional conferences and authored an article on her research on men who batter. Her professional interests include bridging family-systems ideas with clinical work with families where there is violence.

L. Kevin Hamberger, Ph.D., received his doctorate from the University of Arkansas in 1982. Currently an Associate Professor of Clinical Family Medicine at the Medical College of Wisconsin, he is also the founding member and chairperson of the Kenosha Domestic Abuse Intervention Project. Dr. Hamberger is the coauthor, with Jeffrey M. Lohr, of *Stress and Stress Management* and author of several articles on his research.

Treating Men Who Batter:
Theory, Practice, and Programs

P. Lynn Caesar, Ph.D.
L. Kevin Hamberger, Ph.D.

Editors

Springer Publishing Company
New York

Springer Publishing Company, Inc.
536 Broadway
New York, New York 10012
89 90 91 92 93/5 4 3 2 1

Library of Congress Cataloging-in-Publication Data

Treating men who batter: theory, practice, and programs / P. Lynn
   Caesar, L. Kevin Hamberger, editors.
      p.   cm. — (Springer series, focus on men; v. 5)
   Includes bibliographies and index.
   ISBN 0-8261-6340-8
   1. Wife abuse—Treatment. I. Caesar, P. Lynn. II. Hamberger, L.
Kevin. III. Series: Springer series, focus on men; 6.
RC569.5.F3T74 1989
616.85′822—dc20   89-6369
                                                     CIP

Printed in the United States of America

To Peter and Nancy

Our loving partners in nonviolence

Contents

Foreword

Treating Men Who Batter: Theory, Practice, and Programs gives much-needed shape and form to the proliferation of batterer counseling programs. Batterer programs were founded in the late seventies largely in collaboration with the battered women's movement to complement the work of nearly 1,000 women's shelters. With more recent promptings from the criminal justice system and the advent of family service efforts, some 200 batterer programs have been established, and many more are being developed. The great diversity of approaches and techniques has, however, brought controversy as well as confusion to the field.

Lynn Caesar and Kevin Hamberger, the editors of *Treating Men Who Batter*, have identified the prevailing approaches to batterer treatment: feminist, cognitive-behavioral, family systems, and integrative approaches. And they have enlisted distinguished spokespersons to describe each of these approaches. As seasoned batterer counselors and researchers in their own right, Caesar and Hamberger also supply a historical backdrop and pinpoint the current issues. The result is a welcome dialogue among experts of the field —people with commitment, experience, and knowledge. In the process, *Treating Men Who Batter* implicitly mends fences and builds bridges toward a more comprehensive way to stop violence toward women.

Treating Men Who Batter provides a showcase of model batterer programs for any practitioner working in the field of domestic violence and for those simply with a concern about what is being done to alleviate violence in the home. For those new to batterer counseling, this book demonstrates that all counseling is not the same. It gives pause to the knee-jerk public reaction, "Send them to counseling." *Treating Men Who Batter* helps the novice begin to differentiate "counseling" and press toward a specific kind of counseling.

This book should be particularly instructive to those expanding their practice to batterers, as many substance abuse and mental health counselors are doing. The book presents the prevailing options in a way that offsets tunnel vision and challenges biases. Well reasoned adaptations of popular clinical theory, like family systems and cognitive-behavioral psychology, appear alongside the founding feminist perspective and integrative approaches.

For the veteran of batterer counseling, *Treating Men Who Batter* offers a kind of refresher course. It gives us several measuring rods to assess our own assumptions and techniques. It can help us see the distinctiveness of our own approaches, as well as the contribution of some other approaches. In the process, we are likely to refine and develop the theoretical foundations of our own work.

The primary purpose of this book is not to referee the debate over approaches or to recommend some synthesis. It is, furthermore, much more than a handbook of state-of-the-art programming or a simplistic "how to" book. This book is in fact a challenge for all of us to more seriously consider the relationship of theory and practice. Its chapters instruct us in this regard by example. The authors thoughtfully put theory behind their practice. They discuss the assumptions underlying batterer counseling, the procedures and techniques that logically follow from them, and the evaluation procedures that might help substantiate their approach. Moreover, these different approaches juxtaposed one to another make the theoretical issues of the field more apparent, as the concluding chapter of the book aptly points out.

In the rapid emergence of newer batterer programs or in the long-standing prominence of others, theory has sometimes fallen by the wayside. The pressured crisis orientation of batterer intervention, and human services in general, understandably pushes aside the reasoning, justification, and philosophy of our work. As *Treating Men Who Batter* makes apparent, we need to continually sharpen our definition of battering, explanation for its cause, and identification of the processes that stop it.

A program's identity, direction, and purpose are built on its theoretical foundation. It is theory that guides a program through expansions, uncertainties, and problems. Having a well established theory provides a decisive and discernible message to "clients." Batterers, for instance, are more likely to know what is expected of them and how to get there if the program has a well developed theory behind its practice.

Theoretical development is, moreover, similarly important in a program's dealings with other community agencies. With the increasing demand to coordinate batterer counseling with the courts, substance abuse programs, and mental health agencies, we have to represent and defend what we stand for amid sometimes competing interests. We also have to be more informed about the different approaches in order to more effectively collaborate with other programs in the field.

There remains, nevertheless, an outstanding dilemma that must be considered, regardless of theoretical clarity. How do we account for the sometimes divergent assumptions and techniques of batterer programs? Are some more "right" than others? There are several possibilities a reader might consider in weighing this important question.

One possibility is that a diversity of approaches is warranted to address such a complex and extensive problem as woman abuse. We may need a variety of ways to interrupt men's violence and bring safety to women. Perhaps different treatments would work better for different types of men. Those batterers in deep denial and resistance to change may be more likely to respond to the didactic confrontation of the feminist approach. Additionally, different approaches may be more appropriate for men at different points in their change process. The couples' counseling advocated by the family systems approach may be effective after a batterer has accomplished substantial behavioral change promoted in the cognitive-behavioral programs.

A second possibility of the diversity may be that all of the approaches reasonably reinforce men motivated to change. A consistent message that the men must take responsibility for the abuse, that the abuse must and can be stopped, and that alternatives to the abuse exist may be what is at work in all the approaches described in *Treating Men Who Batter*. The group process, the role model of the counselors, and the monitoring of behavior and attitudes may be the common—albeit implicit—means of instruction.

A third possibility is that one approach is superior to the others. One particular approach may encompass the contributions of the others or have the least risk, if not the most success. Perhaps the one best possibility is a factor of our own training and expertise and the resources available in our community. Given that most communities do not have the luxury of a variety of batterer programs, if they have one at all, this is a possibility that presses at many of us.

The answer to the diversity of programs, it would seem, is in the evaluation results of the respective approaches. Many sticky questions unfortunately plague our evaluation efforts, as is noted in the conclusion of this book and in several of its chapters. How do we determine the long-term effect of counseling? Some highly touted alcohol programs and delinquency programs have, for instance, had dramatic success rates in the short-term, only to be discredited by long-term failures. How much and what kind of failure can be tolerated? The infamous Willie Horton case, for instance, has now put prison furlough programs on hold, despite their documented successes. There may similarly be some batterer programs that are more prone to drop-outs, "con" games, or serious relapse.

Research in related fields, such as the treatment of depression, alcoholism, or eating disorders, suggests that these possibilities and problems are not unique to batterer intervention. For instance, substantial debate continues between Alcoholics Anonymous (A.A.) advocates and cognitive-behavioral alcohol counselors. There are also those who attempt to combine the sociological components of A.A. with the psychological aspects of cognitive-behavioral treatment. Moreover, much of the outcome research on individual and couples' counseling shows similar outcomes regardless of approach. Clinical trials of depression treatment likewise suggest that cognitive treatment, interpersonal counseling, and antidepressant drugs have comparable success in reducing symptoms, at least in the short-term.

The possibilities for a diversity of batterer programs, nevertheless, cannot be taken lightly. The controversy and sometimes heated debate over batterer counseling is motivated by more than self-interest or bias. The stakes are particularly high. Battered women are much more likely to return to their batterers if they seek counseling. Therefore, batterer counseling, while attempting to lower the man's violence, is at the same time putting a woman more at risk.

There is, furthermore, no established way to predict the reoccurrence of violence. Both counselors and potential victims must remain on guard despite the professions of the batterer or apparent "successes." Those of us involved in batterer counseling must consequently make doubly sure we know what we are doing.

In any case, the presentations in *Treating Men Who Batter* go a long way in offering a blueprint for a less violent society. They suggest not only why men are abusive and violent toward women but also ways in which this violence might be stopped. In essence, the editors have assembled the results of the first decade of experimentation in batterer counseling. Granted, we have a long way to go, but this book shows us that we have made substantial progress.

EDWARD W. GONDOLF
Author of *Men Who Batter* and
Battered Women as Survivors

Preface

The question of what kind of help should be offered to men who beat their wives is a controversial one. All of us who have worked with, known, or been battered may question why a man who violates the civil liberties of a woman in a violent, humiliating, and dehumanizing fashion should engender empathy, concern, or special attention. To offer help to a man who beats his wife suggests that we will share the problem. Assisting a man who rapes, beats, and infringes upon the rights of his female partner arouses strong emotions within anyone who cares enough about the problem of wife battery to get involved. To feel moral outrage when a battered woman reveals her blackened eyes but to contain the anger to get close enough to the batterer to whom the woman may soon return is, at times, an exercise in emotional gymnastics. The women and men who have contributed to this book have not only allowed themselves to experience such discomfort, but have also committed themselves as political and social activists, feminist scholars, psychologists, psychotherapists, researchers, and academicians to advance our knowledge in working with men who batter women.

We are psychologists who have conducted research on men who batter and provided therapy for batterers and battered women. Our backgrounds and interest guided us to edit this book emphasizing theory and practice of counseling interventions for batterers. We recognize that there are other forms of interventions for men who batter that are valid and important and that should be pursued, for example, necessary reforms in the criminal justice and legal systems.

Law enforcement interventions reflect another level at which the problem of wife beating needs to be addressed. However, we realize that some batterers may never come to the attention of these agencies and that those who do are often referred to therapy or psycho-educational programs.

Furthermore, because of strong evidence that the number of batterer treatment programs are proliferating, the importance of examining theory as it relates to practice is a timely undertaking. One needs only to have attended any number of domestic violence conferences in recent years to have observed the polemical and, at times, vituperous exchanges between proponents of different approaches. Not infrequently, such exchanges generate more heat than light on how to treat male batterers and stop spousal violence. When we begin to critically think about the relationship of theory to practice, a context is created for questioning, examining, testing, confirming, and modifying our assumptions and behaviors in such treatment settings.

It is our contention that all helpers of wife beaters and battered women need to inform themselves about the problems, as well as to question their own assumptions and methods of intervening. Given the epidemic proportion of marital violence (Straus, Gelles, & Steinmetz, 1980), the emotionally charged nature of the issue, the documented serious injury factor to women (Berk, Berk, Loseke, & Rauma, 1983; Straus, 1980), and the potential for death to batterers (Browne, 1987), it is essential to critically examine our response from many disciplines.

The people who try to help batterers are as similar and different as the batterers themselves. That is partially what this book is about. Though research on batterers in the 1980s has focused upon seeking profiles of the typical wife beater, it appears that men who batter are indeed a heterogeneous group (Caesar, 1986; Barnett, 1986; Hamberger & Hastings, 1986).

Batterers also bring with them implicit or explicit premises regarding how they understand their violence. Men who batter bring contextually shaped family relationships, life histories, personality styles, emotional responses, psychobiology, value systems, strengths, weaknesses, educational and occupational opportunities, and cultural, racial, and religious backgrounds.

Helpers also have differing assumptions, beliefs, and theories about battering. These assumptions may be reflected in the language used to describe the problem, the philosophy of the intervention model, and the way in which the helper relates to the battered woman. The premises underlying the counseling program or format may be explicit or implicit. Some therapists may collaborate with others around shared assumptions. Some may feel polarized regarding differences of opinion. Men (and the women they batter), exposed to the scrutiny of outside interventions, will most certainly be sensitive to the belief systems of helpers and the cooperative or polarized climate of help.

Our interest in examining diverse counseling methods in working with men who batter evolved from two concerns. What seems to have emerged in the field of services to batterers, as well as to battered women, is a schism between professional and paraprofessional, scientist and practitioner, social control agent and humanitarian, activist and provider. The 1987 Third National Family Violence Research Conference sponsored by the University of New Hampshire conducted separate conferences for practitioners and researchers. Dialogue among individuals assuming different roles within the battered women's movement often led to debates that further polarized the field. Consequently, we are concerned that there are few opportunities for cross-fertilization to occur among those who are investing their hard work into furthering research, social and political activism, and psychotherapeutic practice related to advances in working with men who batter. Because there has been so much division in the field, we are also concerned that the intervention models being developed lack a "self-reflective" process that examines ideology, theory, methodology, and evaluation of success and failure.

The primary goal of the book is to provide the reader with a variety of theoretical and practical perspectives about counseling interventions with male spouse abusers. As such, this book is designed to assist the reader in understanding the theoretical rationale that underpins specific, different approaches to the treatment of male batterers. Hence, chapters are organized to address theory first, followed by discussion of how technique is guided by theory and how outcome (and therefore theory) can be assessed. Furthermore, each theoretical orientation is presented in its own right, not in reaction to competing orientations. With debate or polemics reduced, the reader is left to evaluate the merits of the various orientations as they are presented by the various proponents. We encourage readers to try to glean some new information from each chapter, no matter how divergent the approach may be from their own. We hope the following chapters will stimulate thought about the compatibility of the various perspectives with readers' own assumptions, theories, and work settings.

This book shares the work of leading experts who, thoughtfully and carefully, detail their different conceptualizations in working with men who batter. The four approaches represented in this volume, feminist, cognitive-behavioral, family-systems, and integrative, were chosen for several reasons. The first three of these modalities are most represented in the literature and in surveys of batterer programs (Eddy & Myers, 1984; Feazell, Mayers, & Deschner, 1984; Pirog-Good & Stets-Kealey, 1985; Roberts, 1984). We chose integrative approaches to represent models that borrow from two or more conceptual frameworks. In addition to selecting the chapter sections, we believe that our choice of authors provides the reader with a rich cross-section of contemporary research, service-provision, psychotherapeutic approaches, and sociopolitical ideas represented in the field of intervention programs for batterers.

Each contributor offers a unique vantage point from which to examine the problem and intervene. The authors offer a richly detailed method of working with batterers, which is rooted in a particular theory, set of theories, and/or assumptions. Drawing from feminist, social learning, and general systems theories; cybernetics; behaviorism; reality therapy; rational-emotive therapy; community mental health perspectives; and empirically based findings on batterers, each author presents a comprehensive system of working with men. This includes definitions of violence based upon their frameworks or the guiding principles behind their models. Each chapter develops a rationale for its approach and describes the level at which the intervention is directed. For example, based upon the conceptualization of the issue of wife beating, the contributors may direct their program at the sociopolitical, interpersonal, and/or intrapersonal level. Finally, the authors make recommendations for evaluation studies that can measure the effectiveness of their approaches.

The book is divided into four parts. The first section, "Feminist Approaches," contains chapters by David Adams and Ellen Pence. David Adams's chapter describes profeminist educational programs for battering men based upon his collaborative work at Emerge in Cambridge, Massachusetts. Ellen Pence presents a model, developed in Duluth, Minnesota, in which police and human service agencies' responses to domestic assault are coordinated and monitored. Rehabilitation programs for offenders are secondary to and part of a much larger community intervention strategy.

The second section encompasses cognitive-behavioral approaches. Kevin Hamberger and Jeffrey Lohr develop the theoretical foundation behind language functions and the behavior of battering. Daniel Saunders describes the application of cognitive-behavioral treatment.

The third section, "Family Systems Approaches," offers two versions of family therapy with violent couples. Robert Geffner, Carol Mantooth, Dawn Franks, and Loretta Rao present the Family Preservation Project based in Tyler, Texas, in which psychoeducation and couples' therapy are combined to reduce spouse abuse. Gerry Lane and Tom Russell from Atlanta, Georgia, describe a model of therapy with couples' violence based upon second-order systemic ideas.

The fourth section includes two chapters presenting integrative models of therapy. Coauthors Alan Rosenbaum and Roland Maiuro present two models of intervention with batterers that integrate empirically based findings on men with community mental health, social learning, profeminist, and family therapy premises. Anne Ganley offers a historical perspective in her chapter, which integrates social learning analyses of aggression with feminist theory.

We recognize that labeling the type of interventions in this book as counseling or therapeutic interventions may be inaccurate. Proponents within the battered women's movement have raised our consciousness about the danger of using labels, pointing, for example, to the deleterious effects when members of the psychiatric profession have misdiagnosed battered women and battering men as mentally ill. Does offering counseling to men or women, then, imply that the roots of violence lie in the psychological or psychiatric realm? Some feminist models and family systems approaches of intervention are not based upon traditional psychological theories but offer a coherent, circumscribed approach to reducing male violence. The answers are not simple. Our goal in this book is to raise questions for the readers to ponder, reflect, and discuss.

References

Barnett, O. (1986, August). Sex role perceptions and masculinity of male spouse abusers. In L. Kevin Hamberger (Chair), *The male batterer: Characteristics of a heterogeneous population.* Symposium conducted at the annual meeting of the American Psychological Association, Washington, DC.

Berk, R. A., Berk, S. F., Loseke, D. R., & Rauma, D. (1983). In D. Finkelhor, R. J. Gelles, G. T. Hotaling, & M. A. Straus (Eds.), *The dark side of families: Current family violence research* (pp. 197-212). Beverly Hills, CA: Sage.

Browne, A. (1987). *When battered women kill.* New York: Free Press.

Caesar, P. L. (1986, August). Men who batter: A heterogeneous group. In L. Kevin Hamberger (Chair), *The male batterer: Characteristics of a heterogeneous population.* Symposium conducted at the annual meeting of the American Psychological Association, Washington, DC.

Eddy, M. J., & Myers, T. (1984, August). *Helping men who batter: A profile of programs in the U.S.* Austin, TX: Texas Department of Human Resources.

Feazell, C. S., Mayers, R. S., & Deschner, J. (1984). Services for men who batter: Implications for programs and policies. *Family Relations, 33,* 217-223.

Hamberger, L. K., & Hastings, J. E. (1986, August). Personality characteristics of spouse abusers: A controlled comparison. In L. Kevin Hamberger (Chair), *Men who batter: Characteristics of a heterogeneous population.* Symposium conducted at the annual meeting of the American Psychological Association, Washington, DC.

Pirog-Good, M., & Stets-Kealey, J. (1985). Male batterers and battering prevention programs: A national survey. *Response, Summer,* 8-12.

Roberts, A. R. (1984). *Battered women and their families: Intervention strategies and treatment programs.* New York: Springer.

Straus, M. (1980). Victims and aggressors in marital violence. *American Behavioral Scientist, 23*(5), 681-704.

Straus, M. A., Gelles, R. J., & Steinmetz, S. K. (1980). *Behind closed doors: Violence in the American family.* New York: Doubleday/Anchor.

Acknowledgments

To Ola Barnett, Ph.D., we are grateful for her inspiration and support of the idea of writing a book on batterers. We are indebted to the Central Vermont Shelter Project and Delta and to the Kenosha Domestic Abuse Intervention Project, to the women and men whose volunteer efforts to educate the community and provide services for battered women and batterers influenced our professional work in profound ways. We are also appreciative of Daniel Sonkin, Ph.D., Springer's Men's Series editor, whose encouragement, editorial help, and support for our autonomy to pursue this particular subject enhanced our jobs as volume editors. We are most thankful to Barbara Watkins, vice president and senior editor of Springer Publishing Co., for her superb editorial comments, which shaped and added polish to the final manuscript. We are appreciative of Peter Roden's technical assistance, managing the manuscript using computer technology. His expertise enhanced our efficiency and helped us translate a monumental job into a completed product of which we are proud. Finally, we are indebted to the women and men who wrote the chapters in this volume. Without their dedication, creativity, and commitment to the field of marital violence, this volume truly would not have been possible.

Contributors

David Adams, M.Ed.
Ed.D. Candidate
President, Emerge, A Men's Counseling Service on Domestic Violence
Cambridge, Massachusetts

Dawn Franks, B.S.
Executive Director
East Texas Crisis Center
Tyler, Texas

Anne L. Ganley, Ph.D.
Licensed Psychologist
Domestic Violence Program and Family Therapy Program
Seattle Veterans Administration Medical Center
Private Practice
Seattle, Washington

Robert Geffner, Ph.D.
Associate Professor
Department of Psychology
University of Texas at Tyler
Director, Family Violence Research and Treatment Program
University of Texas at Tyler
Director, Counseling and Testing Services
Private Practice Clinic
Tyler, Texas

Gerry Lane, A.C.S.W.
Director of Clinical Training
Families First
Atlanta, Georgia

Jeffrey M. Lohr, Ph.D.
Associate Professor
Department of Psychology
University of Arkansas
Fayetteville, Arkansas

Roland D. Maiuro, Ph.D.
Associate Professor
Department of Psychiatry and Behavioral Sciences
University of Washington School of Medicine
Director, Harborview Anger Management Program
Seattle, Washington

Carol Mantooth, M.S.
Instructor of Psychology
University of Texas at Tyler
Licensed professional counselor
Private practice
Tyler, Texas

Ellen Pence
Training and Technical Assistant Coordinator
Domestic Abuse Intervention Project
Duluth, Minnesota

Loretta Rao, M.S.
Ph.D. Candidate
East Texas State University
Tyler, Texas

Alan Rosenbaum, Ph.D.
Associate Professor
Department of Psychiatry
University of Massachusetts Medical School
Worcester, Massachusetts

Tom Russell, M.S.S.W.
Director, Northeast Unit for Counseling
Families First
Atlanta, Georgia

Daniel G. Saunders, Ph.D.
Assistant Scientist
Department of Psychiatry
University of Wisconsin
Madison, Wisconsin

Introduction: Brief Historical Overview of Interventions for Wife Abuse in the United States

P. Lynn Caesar
L. Kevin Hamberger

Legal Precedents of Wife Beating

As early as 1641, the Massachusetts Body of Liberties ruled that wife beating was illegal (Pleck, 1987). This was the first American reform against family violence. However, according to Pleck, Puritan courts valued family preservation over the physical protection of victims. Puritans intervened in the family only to restore family harmony. Enforcement of laws against domestic violence threatened the stability of the family. Consequently, the Puritan laws against marital violence were less likely to enforce punishment of abusers. Rather, Pleck maintains, such laws served as a guide to the community's moral principles.

As the state gradually relinquished its commitment to enforcing morality, exceptions to the Massachusetts Body of Liberties were made (Pleck, 1987). In 1824 the Supreme Court of Mississippi granted a husband the right to chastise his wife (Dobash & Dobash, 1979). Similar decisions were made in Maryland and Massachusetts. This treatment of wives was based upon English common law, which gave husbands the right to chastise their wives with a stick no thicker than a thumb (Davidson, 1977).

According to Pleck (1987), the 2 decades following 1870 represented a high point of feminist interest in crimes against women, not again attained until the 1970s. The women's movement of that earlier era challenged male dominance, and female organizations grew. In addition, the Civil War had led to more public acceptance of state intervention in the family. It is not surprising, according to Pleck, that legal interventions against wife beaters began to be initiated in the late 19th century. For example, in Baltimore in 1884, wife beaters were publicly whipped, sometimes by their wives' brothers or fathers. This form of social humiliation was believed to contribute significantly to the decline in the number of arrests for wife beating in Baltimore ("Whipping and Castration," 1899). It was during this era that wife beating was again repudiated by the courts. In 1871 in Alabama and Massachusetts and in 1894 in Mississippi, laws were enacted ruling wife battery illegal (Walter, 1982).

Pleck's (1987) scholarly feminist analysis depicts the evolution of reforms against family violence since 1640. She traces the history of civil and criminal reforms and the influence of psychiatry and mental health practitioners on the community's perception of wife beating. Pleck's book (*Domestic Tyranny*) gives thorough coverage to the assumptions underlying the reforms that occurred over time. What is striking is the way in which history repeated itself. Pleck points out that each generation of reformers condemned the practices of the previous one. Consequently, there was rarely the opportunity for each group to build upon what had been learned during the previous generation of changes. Observations have been made today that many staffers of domestic violence programs are often unaware of the existence of other similar programs (Star, 1983). Staff often feel as if they are working in a void. Such isolation and tunnel vision occur when staff are not only providing direct services but having to keep the intensity of the issue alive in the social and political sphere. Pleck maintains that if family violence loses its emotional salience, its appeal as a social issue begins to fade.

The antirape movement in the early 1970s provided the feminist ideology, methodology, and public acceptance of victim advocacy necessary for the emergence of the battered women's cause (Pleck, 1987). As spouse abuse became more visible in the public eye and more women began seeking relief from assaults at home, battered women's advocates became instrumental in lobbying for legislative changes that would protect women from further violence. Slowly, new legal remedies for battered women emerged, which began to affect the course of interventions for men. As of April 1980 (*Response*, 1980), at least 27 states had enacted laws making civil protection orders available to battered women seeking relief from abuse. According to the Center for Women's Policy Studies (*Response*, 1980), a judge can order an abuser to leave his residence shared with his partner, to avoid all contact with his wife, to abstain from further abuse, or to participate in counseling. In other cases, a temporary restraining order can award custody of the children to the woman and can require the man to pay child support or restitution for injuries suffered.

Often, an abuser who is served with a civil protection order may, for the first time, be exposed to the scrutiny of the court and outside agencies. What had been a privilege within the sanctity of his home is suddenly labeled deviant. The man becomes an "offender," and his wife a "victim."

Along with civil protection orders that may direct batterers into counseling, domestic violence diversion programs that order battering men into therapy have also emerged. Sonkin, Martin, and Walker (1985) report on such a domestic violence diversion program established in California in 1980. When a person is arrested in California on charges that constitute domestic violence (battery, disturbing the peace), that person can be diverted from the criminal justice system into a counseling or education program lasting from 6 months to 2 years. If the person completes the program, charges are dropped, and the record is expunged.

Historically, diversion programs have been established to "divert" first-time offenders, either juvenile or adult, from the criminal justice system (Burkett, 1972). Drug and alcohol diversion programs existed before domestic violence programs. The primary aim of such programs is to avoid stigmatizing first-time offenders who may, in fact, have committed a crime because of other problems, such as substance abuse or emotional instability (Burkett, 1972). The existence of such a diversion program for marital violence implies that emotional instability and substance abuse are the "underlying causes" of wife battery. Although such programs may have been designed to shift the legal system's victim-blaming focus to one of holding the batterer more accountable, assumptions were made that "treating" the man's emotional problems and substance abuse would "cure" his violence. These assumptions have not yet been confirmed empirically.

The Controversy Surrounding Interventions for Batterers

The specialized counseling programs that have evolved for batterers are, in part, a response to a complex interaction between battered women, their advocates, the criminal justice system, law enforcement agencies, legislative bodies, and mental health professionals. Many of the counseling programs that have been established for violent men evolved out of the shelter movement for abused women. Battered women's advocates identified inadequacies within the mental health and criminal justice systems' responses to the needs of victims. Feminists expressed concerns about battering men who were not held accountable for their actions when they came to the attention of mental health professionals and criminal justice agencies. Instead, the women they battered either became mental health "clients" who were subjected to analyses of their masochistic strivings or single-handedly had to convince the criminal justice system that something "also" had to be done with their husbands in order to ensure the women's own protection.

According to proponents within the battered women's movement, reforms were needed, along with the development of alternative services. Mental health professionals, many of whom were trained and employed in settings in which the medical model was followed, were not considered to be sufficiently trained in the sociopolitical roots of violence. Of the specialized counseling programs for batterers that began to flourish in the early 1980s, self-help groups have led the way (Watts & Cowtois, 1981). This self-help concept followed on the heels of similar models used by feminist groups and rape counseling centers.

Many battered women's self-help groups emerged initially, in part, to empower women to help women in an egalitarian, nonpatriarchal context. The outgrowth of the comparable self-help male collectives in the mid to late 1970s provided a context for men to take responsibility for male violence while experimenting with nonhierarchical organizational structures (Emerge, 1980). Toch (1965) maintains that many self-help groups have, by definition, an inherent antiprofessional bias. Pattison (1974) has also noted that many self-help groups adhere to ideological, rather than scientific, theories. Schechter (1982) identified that self-help battered women's advocates were seen as organizers, consciousness-raisers, and educators, not as providers. They emphasized a politicized understanding of violence toward women, not psychologically based definitions that are more likely to be held by human service's providers.

As services for men and women evolved, however, the realities of funding sources gave more traditional social service agencies and professionals a stronger position in the field. Conflict grew between professionals and nonprofessionals and between activists and providers (Schechter, 1982), and there was little, if any, cross-fertilization of ideas between those polarized groups. The provision of services became a highly controversial issue. The language of mental health and social services began to permeate descriptions of battered women and batterers. Feminists and grass-roots organizers were concerned about "cooptation" of the battered women's movement by government-funded social agencies whose programs did not emphasize the sociopolitical roots of wife battering (Morgan, 1981; Pleck, 1987; Schechter, 1982).

As the horror of wife beating is becoming more publicly acknowledged, and as the mass media have assumed more responsibility to raise social consciousness about the issue, the hard work of grass-roots organizers and service providers continues. However, the direction of research and practice in the field is beginning to shift from what it has been during the past 2 decades. More journal articles are appearing examining batterer characteristics and outcome studies of batterer treatment programs. Psychology is beginning to earn new respect among feminists who previously found psychological theories to be limiting to any sociopolitical understanding of wife beating and to have contributed to victim blaming. Service providers are beginning to leave the sanctity of the office and become involved in community work to expand their understanding of the problem.

As the controversy within the field evolves to a new stage, it appears that service providers who work with batterers are faced with an enormous responsibility not only to remain current within whatever discipline they are practicing but also to draw from other disciplines and areas of specialization. Contributions from psychology, sociology, feminist studies, criminology, law, social work, medicine, and psychiatry are being made to inform those working to develop programs designed to interrupt the cycle of violence.

Development of the Counseling Movement

It is not known precisely how many programs for counseling male batterers exist. Roberts (1984) indicated that as of 1975, there were only two batterer counseling programs in the United States. By 1981 there were an estimated 80 treatment services. By 1985 Pirog-Good and Stets-Kealey (1985) estimated that there were in existence about 89 programs for men who batter.

Roberts (1984) noted that in the overall history of the batterer counseling movement, the establishment of programs for batterers had not paralleled the proliferation of shelters and services for battered women. A primary reason cited by Roberts for this delay is that battering men are much less likely to view themselves as having a problem. Indeed, in a study of treatment acceptance, Hamberger and Hastings (1986) found that only 16% of identified batterers followed through on obtaining treatment, even when it was offered for no fee.

Another reason that the development of batterer treatment programs has lagged behind that of women's programs is based on the paramount value placed upon victim safety at all levels of community planning, including resource allocation. Specifically, many men's programs have developed only after programs were developed to provide safety, support, and empowerment to battered women. Moreover, men's programs typically have agreements with women's programs to not compete for financial resources. As noted by Roberts (1984), such noncompetition, coupled with a less organized men's movement, could account for the relative dearth of batterer counseling programs.

E. W. Gondolf (personal communication, March 1988) has suggested that the important question is not "how many" programs exist but what do we mean by "batterer programs"? For example, there are at least two sources of batterer counseling programs: those that exist exclusively to counsel and treat male batterers and those that constitute one component of a larger mental health or family service delivery system. Consistent with Gondolf's observation, Feazell, Mayers, and Deschner (1984) also identified two basic agency types: special programs and service agencies.

Feazell et al. (1984), as well as Gondolf (1985), suggest that specialized programs may differ from "service agency" batterer programs in basic philosophy, which, in turn, may be reflected in the general types of services offered to abusive men. For example, Feazell et al. found in their survey that specialized programs saw proportionately more physically abusive men than did service agency programs. In contrast, service agency programs reported seeing more emotionally abusive men than specialized programs. Similarly, Gondolf noted that service agency programs are more likely to address the problem of spousal violence through individual, couples', and family therapy than are specialized batterer counseling programs. Hence, different treatment formats between specialized and agency-based programs may reflect differences in missions and goals, which, in turn, reflect different theoretical orientations. A specialized program that evolves directly from a battered women's program will view battering behavior as the primary problem. A violence abatement program evolving within a mental health center or family service organization may view battering as symptomatic of some underlying personal or family pathology (Feazell et al., 1984).

Feazell et al. (1984) identified 17 different treatment approaches among the 90 programs they surveyed. Similarly, Roberts (1984) reported a variety of theoretical and treatment formats. In particular, Roberts reported that 60% of the programs surveyed relied primarily on group counseling approaches, while 25% of the programs utilized primarily individual and couples' formats, without the use of groups. Feazell et al. also found that self-help groups and peer counseling were preferred by specialized treatment programs, compared to agency-based models. Both Feazell et al. and Roberts, as well as a survey conducted by Pirog-Good and Stets-Kealey (1985), found several commonalities between programs as well. Specifically, training in communication and conflict resolution skills were found to be prevalent in most programs. Various cognitive-behavioral approaches to reducing or controlling stress and anger were also prevalent, as were relaxation training and the use of time-outs. The treatment format and the specific methods used, then, may reflect the agency's or counselor's theoretical orientation regarding battering and the treatment of male abusers.

The considerable heterogeneity in batterer treatment approaches suggests a diversity of theoretical conceptualizations of the causes and interventions for wife abuse. The majority of batterer counseling programs are quite new (Eddy & Myers, 1984; Feazell et al., 1984; Pirog-Good & Stets-Kealey, 1985; Star, 1983). As such, there is little information about the relative effectiveness of one approach over another. It is appropriate and timely, therefore, to begin a careful consideration of the specific theoretical assumptions and principles that guide the behavior of the domestic violence practitioner doing abuser counseling. Such consideration serves at least three purposes. First, it forces us to clarify our thinking about what it is we do when "treating" spouse abusers. Second, by clearly enunciating our basic assumptions about the causes of and interventions into domestic violence, we begin to see how our approach is similar to or different from that of others. Such observations can lead to the formulation of relevant research inquiry. Third, formulation of questions through use of research methodologies provides the opportunity to examine assumptions and principles. Through this method, assumptions, theory, and, subsequently, interventions can be refined, advanced, and reexamined.

Theory and Practice

How a therapist chooses to intervene in counseling wife beaters is determined by how the therapist views the problem. Why are there so many theories of the causes and treatment of wife battering? It stems from the reality of battering as a complex and multifaceted phenomenon that occurs in a multidetermined matrix.

According to Bruner, Goodnow, and Austin (1956), conceptual categories, which are the building blocks of theory, function to reduce the complexity of a particular set of stimuli through identification and ordering. Furthermore, what and how sets of stimuli are categorized is a function of perception and experience. That is, the particular sets of phenomena that the person has observed, directly or indirectly, comprise the "stuff" that is categorized. Such categories are therefore best viewed as fluid and dynamic, subject to change as the person's experiences and perceptions change. Because battering is complex, it is possible for different theorists to simultaneously observe, classify, and categorize different aspects of it and thus develop different sets of principles or assumptions. These are, however, subject to inquiry and change through research methods of observation and experimentation.

Unfortunately, theories often are, by default, accepted as "fact" or "law." Indeed, Gelles (1980) stated that concerning wife beating, certain concepts based on highly qualified findings have been, over time, accepted as unquestioned facts, despite there being little in the way of empirical support for them.

Theory, as it relates to wife beating, is very important. It is theory that guides the behavior of the activist, the researcher, the clinician, and the policy-maker. Such behaviors include messages that are communicated to the men who batter and to the women who are beaten. Such messages include statements about how battering is caused, who is responsible for it, and how to stop it. On the level of public policy-making, for example, it was at one time theorized that what went on in a family was private. This resulted in inaction by legislators, police, and criminal justice officials. On a psychological level of analysis, it was once thought that women brought on their own victimization through underlying masochistic strivings. Both social movements and feminist scientific inquiry have discredited both of the latter theories.

An important lesson learned from such past experiences is that it is paramount for workers in the field of wife abuse to be keenly aware of their personal theoretical assumptions and to hold such assumptions as dynamic and open to change and refinement as they are tested or challenged. In addition to holding their preferred theories up to ongoing scrutiny and revision, domestic violence workers need to carefully monitor their own theory-guided behaviors as they influence the thousands and even millions of victims and perpetrators of violence, and the societal matrix in which such violence occurs. In the field of domestic violence, such actions can literally make the difference between life and death.

References

Bruner, J. S., Goodnow, J. J., & Austin, G. A. (1956). *A study of thinking*. New York: Wiley.

Burkett, S. R. (1972). Youth, violence and alcohol. In *Proceedings of the Joint Conference on Alcohol Abuse and Alcoholism* (pp. 1–8). College Park, MD: Department of Health, Education and Welfare.

Davidson, T. (1977). Wifebeating: A recurring phenomenon throughout history. In M. Roy (Ed.), *Battered women: A psychosocial study of domestic violence* (pp. 2–23). New York: Van Nostrand Reinhold.

Dobash, R. E., & Dobash, R. (1979). *Violence against wives: A case against the patriarchy*. New York: Free Press.

Eddy, M. J., & Myers, T. (1984, August). *Helping men who batter: A profile of programs in the U.S.* Austin, TX: Texas Department of Human Resources.

Emerge. (1980). *Organizing and implementing services for men who batter. Emerge: A men's counseling service on domestic violence.* Pamphlet available from: Emerge, 280 Green Street, Cambridge, MA 02139.

Feazell, C. S., Mayers, R. S., & Deschner, J. (1984). Services for men who batter: Implications for programs and policies. *Family Relations, 33,* 217–223.

Gelles, R. J. (1980). Violence in the family: A review of research in the seventies. *Journal of Marriage and the Family, 42,* 873–885.

Gondolf, E. W. (1985). *Men who batter: An integrated approach for stopping wife abuse.* Holmes Beach, FL: Learning Publications.

Hamberger, L. K., & Hastings, J. E. (1986). Characteristics of spouse abusers: Predictors of treatment acceptance. *Journal of Interpersonal Violence, 1*(3), 363–373.

Morgan, P. (1981). From battered wife to program client: The state's shaping of social problems. *Kapitalistate, 9,* 17–39.

Pattison, E. M. (1974). Rehabilitation of the chronic alcoholic. In B. Kissin & H. Beggleiter (Eds.), *The biology of alcoholism: Vol. 3, Clinical pathology* (pp. 587–658). New York: Plenum Press.

Pirog-Good, M., & Stets-Kealey, J. (1985). Male batterers and battering prevention programs: A national survey. *Response, Summer,* 8–12.

Pleck, E. (1987). *Domestic tyranny.* New York: Oxford University Press.

Response. (April-June, 1980).

Roberts, A. R. (1984). *Battered women and their families: Intervention strategies and treatment programs.* New York: Springer.

Schechter, S. (1982). *Women and male violence.* Boston: South End Press.

Sonkin, D., Martin, D., & Walker, L. (1985). *The male batterer: A treatment approach.* New York: Springer.

Star, B. (1983). *Helping the abuser: Intervening effectively in family violence.* New York: Family Service Association of America.

Toch, H. (1965). *The social psychology of social movements.* Indianapolis: Bobbs-Merrill.

Walter, P. D. (1982). Expert testimony and battered women. *Journal of Legal Medicine, 3,* 267–294.

Watts, D., & Cowtois, C. (1981). Trends in the treatment of men who commit violence against women. *Personnel and Guidance Journal, 60*(4), 244–249.

Whipping and castration as punishments for crime. (1899). *Yale Law Journal, 8,* 371–386.

I
FEMINIST APPROACHES

1

Feminist-Based Interventions for Battering Men

David Adams

Testimony from both battered women and feminist writings has informed the development of profeminist educational programs for men who batter. Feminist-based programs distinguish themselves from conventional psychological approaches in their perception of wife beating as a sociopolitical problem. The interventions they provide and their methods of evaluation are consistent with that analysis. A brief explication of feminist formulations will lay the groundwork for describing profeminist batterer programs.

There are two elements to the feminist definition of wife beating, one describing its physical manifestations and the other ascribing political meaning to it. The political meaning of interpersonal behavior is the effect of such behavior on the balance of power among the individuals involved (Arendt, 1961; Dobash & Dobash, 1987). Violence is any act that causes the victim to do something she does not want to do, forces her to do something she does not want to do, or causes her to be afraid. It need not involve physical contact with the victim, since acts of intimidation, such as punching walls and making verbal threats, can achieve the same results.

But wife beating is more than seemingly disconnected violent or frightening acts. It is a coherent pattern of coercive controls that includes acts of economic, sexual, and psychological abuse (Schechter,

1982). Battered women's testimony reveals that they are frequently subjected to sexual and verbal assaults. Schechter cites the following examples: "'You are the dumbest woman I ever met"; "You can't do anything right"; "How could I have married a pig like you!" Verbal assaults and accusations are particularly powerful when combined with physical violence, since covert controls serve to subliminally remind the victim of the potential for repeated violence (Adams, 1988; Arendt, 1961).

Wife beating, as a pattern of coercive acts, is behavior with a distinct meaning and purpose. Its purposes are to intimidate and undermine the victim. Dobash and Dobash (1979) elaborate on the purposeful nature of batterers' violence in their empirical study of 109 battered women:

> The altercations relate primarily to the husband's expectations regarding his wife's domestic work, his possessiveness and sexual jealousy, and allocation of the family resources. . . . When a husband attacks his wife he is either chastising her for challenging his authority or for failing to live up to his expectations or attempting to discourage future unacceptable behavior. (p. 122)

Schechter (1982) rejects the notion that wife abuse is spontaneously irrational behavior. She observes that men's violence serves to gain compliance from their wives and that as a form of intimidation it "signals that the man's way will prevail even when the woman struggles against it." The fear of future attacks, adds Schechter, leaves many battered women in a constantly vigilant state. The battered woman's doubts that she will not be able "to make it on her own" are instilled and reinforced by her husband's repeated insults to her intelligence and independence (Dobash & Dobash, 1979).

Deeper examination of the coercive patterns of wife abuse reveals that the physical violence is accompanied and reinforced by other forms of abuse, as follows:

Psychological Abuse. This wide range of behaviors includes criticism, ridicule, accusations, sexual degradation, the withholding of compliments and other forms of emotional support, infidelity, and ignoring. Acts of psychological abuse serve to erode the battered woman's sense of self-worth and to increase her dependence on her partner. The withholding of praise and other forms of validation, for example, is known to be a particularly effective means of control (Adams, 1988; Henley, 1971). The abusive husband puts his wife in the position of having to strive even harder to gain his approval by making his expressions of positive attention rare and contingent on her "good" behavior. The man's withholding of approval, especially when it is accompanied by routine verbal and physical punishment, puts him in a parental role in relation to his wife. By providing little attention beyond his anger and disapproval, the battering man retains the power to validate (or invalidate) his partner and the authority to give (and take back) permission for her actions.

Economic Abuse. The battering man often maintains tight control over the money, the family car, and other economic resources. Walker (1984) found that 27% of the 400 battered women she interviewed did not have access to cash from their partners, and 34% did not have access to a checking account. This compared to 8% of her nonbattered control sample not having access to cash from their husbands and 26% not having a checking account. Moreover, it is common for the battering man to threaten to withhold alimony and child support should his wife leave him. Testimony from battered women who have left the relationship reveals a common pattern of financial withholding, as well as other attempts to sabotage the women's economic independence. These include harassing a woman at her place of employment and disrupting her job or school plans. For instance, one battering man attempted to have his wife fired from her new job by reporting to her employer that she had pilfered a small amount of office supplies.

Demands of Domestic Services. Battered women are subjected to the same kinds of normative sex role expectations as nonbattered women. As with most wives, it is expected that they will provide childrearing and housekeeping as well as sexual and emotional support. Battered women, however, undoubtedly feel less free to refuse services or to demand reciprocity from their husbands because of the presence of physical and psychological coercion (Mederos, 1987).

Social Isolation. Battered women frequently find themselves socially isolated from neighbors, friends, co-workers, and relatives. This happens for two major reasons. First, it is embarrassing to be beaten, and many battered women are therefore hesitant to reveal that they live with a man who abuses them. Battered women are sometimes afraid that others will disbelieve or blame them, since their husbands often maintain a more respectable and credible public image. This is particularly true in cases when the battering husband is a white-collar professional. Second, battering men often actively restrict their wives' social lives. Many battered women report that their husbands react to their contacts with friends with jealous accusations, attempts to embarrass them in public, and refusal to provide childcare during their nights out (Martin, 1976; Pagelow, 1981; Schechter, 1982). In surveying formerly battered women on their past and current social lives, Walker (1984) found that the women visited neighbors twice as frequently as they did when they lived with an abusive partner.

Detailing men's patterns of abuse helps to show that men derive real benefits from their violence. Coercive controls help the battering man to maintain double standards and unilateral privileges in relation to his partner. He may maintain active social (and even sexual) relations with others but restrict hers. He may make or change plans without consulting her, but she cannot. He may criticize her behavior and raise other grievances, but she cannot do likewise without being seen as a "provocative nag." In short, his verbal and physical assaults serve to keep her on the defensive and to give him the last word.

Profeminist Programs for Battering Men

Profeminist Philosophy

The profeminist sees battering in terms of its purposeful utility rather than its psychological etiology. Because power and control are seen as the fundamental issues, an educational process is provided that challenges the abusive man's attempts to control his partner through the use of physical, psychological, and economic abuse. Peer group education is the preferred format since it is believed to best reinforce the message that wife abuse is learned behavior that has its roots in patriarchal social norms rather than in individual or interactional pathology. A dialectical educational process, in particular—one that combines didactic material with open discussion—enables men to take responsibility for their own behavior and at the same time to critically examine the social context in which battering occurs (Adams & McCormick, 1982; Pence & Paymar, 1986).

Profeminist programs for batterers have much in common with other psychoeducational or cognitive-behavioral approaches to violence. All are influenced by social learning theory, which holds that violence is socially learned and self-reinforcing behavior (Edleson, Miller, & Stone, 1983; Novaco, 1978; Rimm, 1977). Psychoeducational programs for batterers vary, however, according to whether they provide a gender analysis of wife beating. Whereas some programs include discussion of sex roles and sexist attitudes, others avoid discussion of gender altogether. Those programs that do not address issues of sexism view battering more as a skill deficit or a stress management problem than an abuse of power problem (Adams, 1988; Gondolf, 1985). This notion of wife abuse as being essentially a skill deficit problem is reflected by such terms as "anger management," "conflict containment," "stress control," or "family education" in program descriptions. The majority of interventions are aimed at helping abusers to better manage their anger, cope with stress, and improve their communication skills.

The anger-management approach misnames the problem, however. When interventions are too broadly aimed at reducing stress or improving interpersonal skills, the critical power and control dimensions to wife abuse are minimized or ignored (Adams, 1988; Gondolf, 1986). The existence of external stress or poor coping skills cannot explain why *women* are often the sole targets of men's abuse, unless gender politics are also considered (Ptacek, 1984; Schechter, 1982). Nor can this theory account for the evidence that many men who lack basic interpersonal and stress-coping skills *do not* beat their wives.

Closer attention to gender politics reveals that how each man copes with stress, communicates his feelings, and attempts to resolve conflicts is situation-specific. It appears to depend as much on the gender and status of those with whom the man is interacting as it does on his social skill level. For instance, some research has shown that men are better listeners to male co-workers and friends than to female co-workers or their own spouses (Eakins & Eakins, 1976; Henley, 1971; Spender, 1980). The management of anger and the ability to cope with conflict are other skills in which battering men are said to be deficient (Sonkin & Durphy, 1982). Yet abusive men's interactions with bosses, neighbors, police officers, and others outside the family often reveal that they are capable of responding in a conciliatory or assertive manner when they perceive such responses to be in their best interests.

These discrepancies between the battering man's public and private behavior suggest that rather than simply lacking certain social skills, he may possess two sets of skills—cooperation skills and control skills. The battering man may not lack cooperation skills as much as the *motivation* to negotiate in a noncontrolling and equitable manner with his partner. He may not want to relinquish the prerogative of having the last word. Although profeminist educational programs for abusive men recognize the need to provide basic education to batterers about cooperative communication and caretaking skills, they also see it as essential to confront the sexist expectations and attitudes that diminish men's motivation to consistently use these skills in a noncontrolling manner.

Antisexist Education: Steps of Interventions

Profeminist educational programs have adopted goals that extend beyond improving the abusive man's psychological well-being and strengthening his communication skills. The goals are to eliminate all behaviors on his part that serve to undermine the woman's rights as an individual and as a partner. Moreover, the battering man is expected to respect her rights to leave the relationship, to seek protective orders, or to pursue criminal complaints, should she decide to do so. He is expected to respect her right to be ambivalent and to make decisions about her participation in the relationship in a manner that does not expose her to further abuse or coercion. Finally, he is expected to respect her rights to pursue grievances and to demand fairness within the relationship.

The initial interventions of profeminist batterer programs are primarily devoted to ensuring the safety of the battered woman. Men are expected to make "safety plans" that will minimize the possibility for continued violence (C. Norberg, personal communication, July, 1986). Safety plans include full compliance with court protective orders, respecting the battered woman's wishes about visitations, leaving when asked to, eliminating drug or alcohol use if it has accompanied violent behavior, and ceasing any intimidation or pressure tactics intended to disrupt the woman's plans. Some batterer programs make separate contact with the battered woman to inform her about available support, advocacy, and emergency shelter services. In other cases, this contact with the victim is made by the local battered women's program. The battered woman is validated in her efforts to make the safety of herself and her children the first priority. She is also advised against holding false hopes that her partner will end his abusive behavior by participating in the batterer program. Information from the battered woman helps the batterer program to keep current about the man's patterns of abuse and to formulate safety plans that are compatible with the woman's wishes. The information obtained from the battered woman is kept confidential unless she prefers to make it known to her partner or others.

Beyond safety planning, initial interventions in profeminist batterer programs include educating men about the effects of abusive behavior and confronting their attempts to deny or minimize responsibility for their violence. Batterers excuse or minimize their violence by projecting blame onto their partners, claiming "loss of control," blaming alcohol or drug use, or citing good intentions (Adams & McCormick, 1982). Group members at Emerge, a counseling program for batterers, are expected to list their common excuses and to recognize how each excuse dilutes men's responsibility for their own choices. The claim of "loss of control," for example, is challenged on the basis that men are quite selective in *how* and *to whom* they are violent (Adams & McCormick; Ptacek, 1984). Some men grab but never hit their wives, some slap but never punch, and some punch but don't use weapons. One battered woman observed that her husband took his rings off before punching her. This man had claimed that "it happened so fast, I didn't know what I was doing" (Emerge, 1986).

Educating men to the short- and long-term effects of their violence is another early intervention of profeminist batterer programs. This is effective for two reasons. First, ignorance about the consequences of violence helps the battering man continue to focus on his "good intentions" rather than the battering's damaging impact on her. These programs make it clear to the man who batters that he is responsible for the consequences of his violence, regardless of whether it was well intended. Violence and other forms of abuse are inevitably harmful to the physical and psychological well-being of the victim. Further, violence in an intimate relationship inevitably erodes trust, security, and closeness. Ironically, this makes it impossible for the batterer to have some of the very things he says that he wants in the relationship. The man is asked, "How can she trust you and feel close to you as long as you continue to abuse her?"

A second reason for identifying the destructive effects of violence on the victim is that it helps to expose their hidden benefits to the perpetrator. It is convenient for the battering man to claim ignorance about the impact of his violence and to remain only partially aware of the benefits that he derives from it. Learning theorists have observed that it is much more difficult for individuals to maintain destructive behaviors once they are seen as deliberate (Ellis, 1970; Novaco, 1975).

Education that identifies other forms of male coercion is also provided because of the tendency for abusive men to replace physical violence with more subtle forms of abuse. Usually the battering husband wants a "quick fix" to his conflict with his wife. He wants to restore the status quo and to lose as few privileges as possible. There is often an implicit expectation on his part that she must reward him for his nonviolence. His initial changes are often provisional and cosmetic (for appearances only). The battering man continues to bargain with his violence to bring about concessions or changes on his partner's part (Adams, 1988b). His bargaining behavior often includes attempts to pressure or intimidate his partner into changing her plans or ending any doubts she may have about the relationship. He may also withhold financial support, make accusations or threats of infidelity, issue ultimatums or deadlines for her to make up her mind, use the children as allies against her, and accuse her of not appreciating his efforts to change. Such continued pressure tactics indicate that he still does not accept her right to live apart from him or to demand more rights within the relationship.

One key technique that is used by several profeminist educational programs for batterers is the assignment of "control logs," weekly diaries of their abusive and controlling behaviors. With this exercise, men are expected to develop critical awareness of their own controlling behaviors, as well as the attitudes and expectations that give rise to them. The Domestic Abuse Intervention Program in Duluth uses videotaped portrayals of various types of abusive behavior in order to sensitize men to their own patterns of abuse. Men are asked to identify the purpose behind the coercive acts they witness and to apply this understanding to their own situations (Pence & Paymar, 1986). The Batterer's Program of the Marin Abused Women's Services in Marin County, California, uses psychodrama to have men reenact their abusive behavior and receive critical feedback from other group members (Sinclair, 1987).

Once the batterer has demonstrated willingness to abstain from violent and abusive behaviors, attention is increasingly directed to the attitudes, expectations, and feelings that accompany such behavior. Ganley (1981) reports that most men's violence is preceded by irrational and anger-arousing "self-talk" that distorts their perception of their partners' actions and leads them to overreact. A critical element in this internal dialogue is the batterer's ability to label his partner's behavior in a manner that justifies or gives permission for his violence. Such is the case, for instance, when the man labels his wife's behavior as "intolerable" or "provocative." This is quite similar to the well recognized tendency of the man who commits rape or incest to diminish responsibility for his actions by saying that the victim was "asking for it" or behaving in a "seductive" manner (Groth, 1979; Hermann, 1981). Dobash and Dobash (1983) call attention to the sexist assumptions that belie these characterizations by citing research that shows that virtually any behavior on the battered woman's part is likely to be deemed "provocative" by her husband. For example, the batterer may see her as inciting violence for talking too much on some occasions and for not talking enough on others.

Contradictory as it is, the batterer's self-talk usually has distinctly negative themes that reflect a desire to devalue and denigrate his wife rather than a desire to respect her (Adams, 1988). In educational groups, this is evident in the ways that the battering man reports interactions with his partner. Rather than reporting what his partner has actually said or done, he typically characterizes her words or actions in a mocking, trivializing, or otherwise denigrating manner. Comments like "She was in a bitchy mood," "She went on and on about nothing," and "There was no pleasing her" are common.

When a man has a desire to respect rather than a desire to devalue his partner, his responses to her are quite different. If he does not understand a resentment she has expressed, for example, he is more likely to ask her to clarify her feelings than to accuse her of being "impossible to please." His confusion inspires questions rather than accusations. When his respect for her is lacking, he is likely to dismiss or trivialize her concerns and grievances rather than to devote the time and energy necessary to better understand them.

The battering man is often able to find active support from the other men in the group for his negative pronouncements about his partner. The tendency for men to support and reinforce one another's negative stereotypes about women is called *male bonding* (Hart, 1987). This devaluation process is seen by feminists as an essential part of the abuse and oppression of women (Adams, in press; K. Carlin, personal communications, 1985; Schur, 1984). Devaluation serves as an ideological justification for violence since it creates and strengthens negative attitudes about victimized groups (Adorno, Frenkel-Brunswick, Levinson, & Sanford, 1950). Shared negative beliefs about the oppressed create opportunities for oppressors to blame the victims and to affirm group identity (Hart, 1987; Memmi, 1965; Ryan, 1973).

Profeminist facilitators take an active role in interrupting the devaluation process as it occurs in groups for abusive men. The goal is to build peer pressure and support among men for more respectful attitudes and behaviors toward women. The following group dialogue illustrates this (Emerge, 1986):

JIM: We should have a class about what the women do; I'm not justifying my violence or anything, it's just . . . like last night, I come home, I'm tired, but the minute I'm in the door she's all over me, blah, blah this, blah, blah, that. I mean, I could have . . .

RALPH: I know exactly what you mean! My wife's exactly the same. She can't understand my needs when I get home. For her, it's just "Here's someone I can dump my shit on." (Laughter from the other group members.)

HAL: Yeah, why are they like that?

FACILITATOR: What was Betty mad about, Jim?

JIM: That's another thing—she calls me at work. Now, I've told her so many times: Don't call me at work. I've got people milling around my desk, people waiting to use the phone, and I'm on trying to look like everything's cool, you know, and I'm saying to her, "Betty, I can't talk now, I can't talk," and she keeps on and on, and I say I'm going to hang up, and she keeps on, so I finally just hang up. I've already lost time because of this thing, and you know how things are, it's a small office, everybody knows everybody's business.

HAL: Right, that's what I'm saying. Why do they do that? Jim's right, there should be a class for women so they can know what sets us off, it's two people. My wife knows there are certain things . . .

FACILITATOR: So Jim, Betty was upset that you hung up on her. Was there anything else? Why did she call you up at work?

JIM: Oh, Tracy wasn't back from school. She calls up all hysterical cause Tracy runs away, supposedly. She's done this before, mind you. She'll get upset and feel like she's not getting what other kids are getting, and she stays at a friend's house; it just happened last week-end. So I told her (Betty), she's probably at her friend's house, but she keeps going on about how if I wasn't so mean to her, how I mistreat her, and meanwhile I'm saying, "Not now, Betty, I got to get off," and she keeps going.

FACILITATOR: So Betty was upset because Tracy hadn't come home from school, and she'd run away a week before. And was she back when you got home?

JIM: No, she stayed out at a different friend's. The mother called around midnight, and we came and got her the next morning.

FACILITATOR: Let me get this straight. Betty calls you at work because your daughter has run away. You put her off, and then you hang up on her. Then, when you get home, your daughter's still missing, and she's probably worried sick. But the way you told the story, Betty was just going on and on about nothing and wasn't letting you unwind from work. Ralph, you've got teenagers—does that sound like nothing to you?

RALPH: No, I can understand how she'd be worried. And you [Jim] did kind of put her off there. Maybe she had stayed at a friend's before, but you never know nowadays.

FACILITATOR: But what I want to know is, why weren't the rest of you more concerned about what Jim wasn't saying; why weren't you more curious about what Betty was mad about?

RALPH: Well, it seemed like from what Jim was saying he was upset. I didn't want to get him more upset.

FACILITATOR: And you, Marvin, why didn't you speak up?

MARVIN: At first, it seemed like a situation where Jim wasn't allowed to settle down after work; it seemed like his wife wasn't being sensitive to that. But I can understand her being upset, especially with him hanging up on her like that.

FACILITATOR: Hal, you were pretty quick to jump in and agree with Jim; why didn't you ask him some questions?

HAL: I thought he was saying like it was. I didn't feel it was my place to ask what he wasn't saying.

FACILITATOR: But is this helping Jim? And what about the rest of you? When you're so quick to sympathize and you don't ask questions, Jim's mad and we treat him with kid gloves just like Betty has to. Is this the kind of help you need?

The men in this group were progressively better in the following weeks about asking astute questions and confronting one another's excuses. Moreover, they showed greater sensitivity and respect for their partners' positions. Men in this group were no longer able to bond with each other at the expense of women.

Battering men in many profeminist educational programs are expected to become advocates for change once they have been violence free for a designated period. Advocacy of this kind is believed to help men consolidate and deepen their own commitment to nonviolence (Sinclair, 1987). Peer support and pressure among men for respectful attitudes toward women cut against the grain of how most men are socialized. For this reason, the profeminist educational curriculum helps men to recognize that their attitudes, expectations, and behaviors toward women are not unique. They exist in a social context that restricts the freedom of women, gives unfair advantages to men, and promotes misogynistic attitudes (Rich, 1979; Rose, 1986). Battering men are expected to develop a critical awareness of these normative arrangements while continuing to take responsibility for their own participation in them. Antisexist education challenges men to explore the relationship between their values and their behavior and to think more critically about their lives. This process, according to Pence and Paymar (1986), "encourages men to think on a deeper level than they are used to in their daily interactions with the world. They are asked to become actors rather than reactors—to step back from their lives, to examine the basis for their behavior, and to understand how it acts against their own human desires to have a trusting, intimate relationship."

The battering man's acceptance that he cannot control his partner's feelings, thoughts, and actions signals that he has entered a more mature stage of growth. Whether the relationship has continued or ended, he respects the woman's right to be her own person and to pursue her own interests. Moreover, he is more self-motivated to confront his own controlling behaviors and his self-centered thinking. He does not see his growth as a finished product but is determined to continue learning. Men at this stage also have a deeper commitment to helping others, something that is continually reinforced by profeminist educational programs. As was mentioned earlier, many profeminist programs encourage men to become advocates for social change within their communities. They may be trained as volunteer hotline counselors or group facilitators or enlisted in community education and institutional change projects (Sinclair, 1987). These activities provide opportunities for the formerly abusive man to sharpen his critical awareness about sexist social norms and to engage in meaningful and cooperative work with other men and women.

Whether the abusive man progresses to this level of change depends a great deal on the kinds of legal, social, and social service interventions he encounters along the way. Interventions that allow men to minimize their violence, divert attention to other issues, or bargain for concessions from their partners reinforce men's resistance to change. Since men's resistance to giving up their controlling behaviors is strong, it is not likely that counseling or education alone will be effective. Clear legal sanctions against wife beating are essential. Recognizing this, profeminist educational programs do not help battering men to circumvent the legal consequences of their violence. Profeminist programs in several cities have been successful in helping to bring about more consistent criminal justice responses. Comprehensive intervention projects such as those in Seattle, Duluth, San Francisco, and Minneapolis have established pro-arrest policies that include court advocacy for victims and mandatory counseling/ education for offenders (Brygger & Edleson, 1986; Pence & Paymar, 1986). Convicted batterers in these cities are sentenced, placed on probation, and required to attend educational groups. Their sentences are stayed pending their successful completion of the batterer program. Probation is revoked when men commit new acts of violence or fail to comply with other requirements of the program.

Profeminist batterer programs work jointly with battered women's advocates to bring about more effective community-wide responses to wife beating. Often this has meant refuting popular myths and sensitizing people about wife beating. Battered women have also organized community groups to hold men accountable for their violence while also providing safety *and justice* to battered

women. Battered women must not be expected to give up economic
rights in order to guarantee their freedom from continued violence.
Profeminist batterer programs therefore seek direction and regular
supervision from local battered women's programs in establishing
interventions that do not compromise the safety and rights of battered women. This helps to ensure their accountability to the goals
and efforts of the battered women's movement (Hart, 1987).

Evaluation

Profeminist batterer programs evaluate their impact on battering
men, but their evaluations neither start nor stop there. Profeminist
programs also evaluate their impact on battered women and their
communities. Considering their impact on communities is consistent
with the feminist philosophy that change must occur at the societal
as well as the individual level. Evaluating their impact on battered
women reflects their commitment to making women's liberation
from physical, psychological, and economic control their first priority. Changes in the battering man and the community are measured
against this primary goal.

It should be noted that contact between a batterer program and
battered women varies from program to program. Some programs
make direct telephone contact with battered women in order to learn
about violent and abusive behaviors, to inform women about the
batterer program, and to refer them to shelter and support services
(Emerge, 1986). Others have no direct contact with victims but
utilize information that has been gathered by victim advocates (with
victim consent) and police reports. *What* information is to be obtained from victims and *who* obtains it are matters that are mutually
agreed upon by profeminist batterer programs and their local battered women's programs.

Feminist-based batterer programs evaluate their success according to the following questions, which relate to battered women,
battering men, and the community.

Impact of the Program on the Battered Woman

- Is she fully informed about the goals and methods of the
  batterer program? Is she informed that the man's violence is

purposefully controlling behavior that is not the result of alcohol use, insanity, temporary insanity, stress, anger, or poor communication skills?

- Is she given the clear message that the man is entirely responsible for his violence and that she in no way shares in this?

- Is she informed about the limitations of counseling/education, advised that change is a long-term process, and encouraged to pursue her own and her children's safety and rights independently of the man's short-term progress in ending violence?

- Is she given specific information about support, shelter, and advocacy services and encouraged to make use of them?

- Is she given informed consent about how the information she gives is to be used? Are her confidences and privacy protected at all times?

- Is she informed about the man's noncompliance or failure to complete the batterer program? Is she immediately informed of any threats he makes and apprised of any special concerns that batterer programs have about his potential dangerousness to her?

- Is she asked about psychological, sexual, and economic abuse?

- Is she treated in an empathetic, respectful, and consistent manner?

- Does the information she obtains from or about the batterer program validate her right to live free from violence, to pursue justice, and/or to demand equality within the relationship?

- Is she told that she has the right to nonviolently express anger and to raise grievances without being blamed for the man's violence?

Impact of the Program on the Battering Man

Has the batterer program provided the man with:

- identification of the various forms of violence and abuse, including his own?

- identification of the short-term and long-term effects of violence on the victim?

- confrontation of his own and other men's common excuses for violence?

- redefinition of violence as purposefully controlling behavior?

- identification of the verbal, nonverbal, and somatic cues that precede his violence? With identification of his negative and sexist self-talk?

- formulation of a safety plan that entails steps he must take to minimize the possibility for future violence?

- identification and discussion of men's sexist expectations of women and men's attempts to devalue their partners?

- information about positive communication, reciprocity within intimate relationships, caretaking responsibilities, and emotional support?

- interruption of male bonding between group members and of attempts by men to devalue and complain about their partners?

- information about self-care responsibilities to be fulfilled in a manner that respects the rights of others?

- sensitization to the cultural norms that promote violence against women, discrimination against women, and sexist beliefs?

- a process in which interaction, critical self-awareness, and vulnerability are encouraged and supported?

- a process in which men are expected to confront and support one another in making and maintaining changes in their attitudes and behaviors toward women?

- specification of men's accountability to their partners and to the criminal justice system for past and continued acts of violence?

- minimum standards relating to men's compliance with safety plans, attendance, group participation, abstinence from drugs and alcohol, and cessation of violence?

- clear feedback and evaluation pertaining to the above standards?

- suspensions from the program and notification of partners (and probation officers, if this applies) in cases where the man fails to meet these standards?

- provisions for ongoing support, referrals for other services, and long-term follow-up to prevent regression and to assess long-term progress?

Impact of the Program on the Community

- Does the batterer program operate in a manner that is consistent with the wishes and goals of the battered women's programs?

- Is it giving the same messages to the community about the individual and social causes of wife beating? Do its interventions reflect this *to the satisfaction of the battered women's programs?*

- Does the batterer program help make the community more aware of men's responsibility for their violence against women?

- Does the batterer program consistently affirm the primary importance of shelter and support services for battered women?

- Does the batterer program publicize the limitations of counseling or education alone for batterers? Does it help make the criminal justice system aware of its responsibility to hold men accountable for their violence? Does it help build public awareness of the need for preventive education?

- Does the batterer program help eliminate sexist and racist institutional practices that hinder women's ability to avoid and escape violence?

- Does it actively support social change efforts to promote equal rights for women?

Summary

Men's violence toward their partners exists in a societal context that has a very uneven commitment to equal rights and liberty for women. Men's individual expectations, attitudes, and feelings, which serve to rationalize, excuse, and project responsibility for their violence toward women, are sanctioned and reproduced by our social and economic institutions. Traditional psychological theories about men's violence reflect these biases. They have reduced men's motives for violence to intrapsychic issues and, more critically, obscured the connections between patriarchal norms and individual actions.

Profeminist programs for battering men have established an educational process that helps men recognize the undermining effects and sexist precipitants of their violent and abusive behavior. Further, by emphasizing the similarities rather than the differences between battering and nonbattering men, these programs help battering men to critically identify the common social context that gives men permission to think, feel, and act in ways that devalue women (Adams, 1988; Hart, 1987; Mederos, 1987). Profeminist programs reinforce men's respect for the rights and freedom of women by educating men about how respect and disrespect are manifest in their behavior.

Individual men as well as society have proven to be quite resistant to ceasing sexist violence and to extending equal rights to women. Such resistance, however, does not indicate that feminist efforts to call attention to the enforcers of gender inequality are wrong. Neither does it mean that resistance on either level should be accommodated. Evaluations of feminist-based strategies should not lose sight of their long-term goals. Change efforts at all levels, efforts that name rather than obscure the problem, must be strengthened.

References

Adams, D. (1988). Counseling men who batter: A profeminist analysis of five treatment models. In M. Bograd & K. Yllo (Eds.), *Feminist perspectives on wife abuse* (pp. 176–199). Beverly Hills, CA: Sage.

Adams, D. (1988). Stages of anti-sexist awareness change for men who batter. In L. Dickstein & C. Nadelson (Eds.), *Family violence* (pp. 63–97). Washington, DC: APPI Press.

Adams, D., & McCormick, A. (1982). Men unlearning violence: A group approach. In M. Roy (Ed.), *The abusive partner: An analysis of domestic battering* (pp. 170–197). New York: Van Nostrand Reinhold.

Adorno, T., Frenkel-Brunswick, E., Levinson, D., & Sanford, R. (1950). *The authoritarian personality*. New York: Harper & Row.

Arendt, H. (1961). *What is authority? In between past and future*. New York: Viking Press.

Brygger, M. P., & Edleson, J. (1986). *The Domestic Abuse Project: A multi-systems intervention*. Unpublished manuscript. (Available from the Domestic Abuse Project, 2445 Park Ave. S., Minneapolis, MN 55404.)

Dobash, R., & Dobash, R. (1979). *Violence against wives*. New York: Free Press.

Dobash, R., & Dobash, R. (1983). Unmasking the provocation excuse. *Aegis: Magazine on Ending Violence Against Women, 37*, 57–68.

Dobash, R., & Dobash, R. (1987, July). *Responding to wife abuse in the United States and Britain*. Paper presented at the Third National Family Violence Research Conference, University of New Hampshire, Durham, NH.

Eakins, B., & Eakins, G. (1976). *Verbal turn-taking and exchanges in faculty dialogue*. Paper presented at the Conference on the Sociology of Languages of American Women, San Antonio, TX.

Edleson, J., Miller, D., & Stone, G. (1983). *Counseling men who batter: Group leader's manual*. Unpublished manuscript. (Available from the Men's Coalition Against Battering, PO Box 6447, Albany, NY 12206.)

Ellis, A. (1970). *The essence of rational psychotherapy: A comprehensive approach to treatment.* New York: Institute for Rational Living.

Emerge (1986). *What you should know about your violent partner.* (Pamphlet available from Emerge, 280 Green St., Cambridge, MA 02139.)

Ganley, A. (1981). *Court mandated counseling for men who batter: A three-day workshop for mental health professionals.* Washington, DC: Center for Women's Policy Studies.

Gondolf, E. (1985). *Men who batter: An integrated approach for stopping wife abuse.* Holmes Beach, FL: Learning Publications.

Gondolf, E. (1986). The case against anger control treatment programs for batterers. *Response, 9*(3), 2–5.

Groth, N. (1979). *Men who rape: The psychology of the offender.* New York: Plenum Press.

Hart, B. (1987). *Advocacy for women: Monitoring batterers' programs.* Pennsylvania Coalition Against Domestic Violence, 524 McKnight St., Reading, PA.

Henley, N. (1971). *Body politics: Power, sex, and nonverbal communication.* Englewood Cliffs, NJ: Prentice-Hall.

Hermann, J. (1981). *Father-daughter incest.* Cambridge, MA: Harvard University Press.

Martin, D. (1976). *Battered wives.* San Francisco: Glide.

Mederos, F. (1987). *Men who abuse women and "normal men": Theorizing continuities and discontinuities.* Unpublished manuscript. (Available from Emerge, 280 Green St., Cambridge, MA 02139.)

Memmi, A. (1965). *The colonizer and the colonized.* Boston: Beacon Press.

Novaco, R. (1975). *Anger control.* Lexington, MA: Lexington Books.

Novaco, R. (1978). Anger and coping with stress: Cognitive-behavioral interventions. In J. Foreyt & D. Rathjen (Eds.), *Cognitive behavior therapy: Research and applications.* New York: Plenum Press.

Pagelow, M. (1981). *Women-battering: Women and their experiences.* Beverly Hills, CA: Sage.

Pence, E., & Paymar, M. (1986). *Power and control: Tactics of men.* Unpublished manuscript. (Available from Minnesota Program Development, 206 West Fourth St., Duluth, MN 55806.)

Ptacek, J. (1984, August). *The clinical literature on men who batter: A review and critique.* Paper presented at the second national conference for family violence researchers, University of New Hampshire, Durham, NH. (Available from Emerge, 280 Green St., Cambridge, MA 02139.)

Rich, A. (1979). *On lies, secrets, and silence.* New York: W. W. Norton.

Rimm, D. (1977). Treatment of anti-social aggression. In G. Harris (Ed.), *The group treatment of human problems: A social learning approach* (pp. 101–113). New York: Grune & Stratton.

Rose, H. (1986). Women's work: Women's knowledge. In J. Mitchell & A. Oakley (Eds.), *What is feminism?* (pp. 166–183). New York: Pantheon Books.

Ryan, W. (1973). *Blaming the victim.* New York: Vintage Books.

Schechter, S. (1982). *Women and male violence: Visions and struggles of the battered women's movement.* Boston: South End Press.

2

Batterer Programs: Shifting from Community Collusion to Community Confrontation

Ellen Pence

A Picture of an Abusive Relationship

Nancy was 19 years old, 3 months pregnant and married only 6 months when her husband first hit her. She was stunned. In their 2 years of dating, Bill had talked many times about how his father had hit his mother, so she felt particularly safe with him. His disgust for that kind of violence was somehow reassuring.

He didn't beat her, he slapped her and shoved her down. He left the house crying. She was afraid for him, for her unborn child, and for herself. What was going wrong? Why so soon? This was not supposed to happen.

She went to her mother. She needed to figure this out. Her mother saw the signs of a new marriage under stress, her daughter struggling with the challenge of being a wife to a man, a boy really, with the worries of a man not yet secure with who he was in the world. She cautioned her daughter against a rash decision. It's a hard world out there for a single woman with a child—welfare, the stigma of a divorce, the type of man who would now be attracted to her. She advised that Nancy's best bet was to work it out, to figure out what she could do to restore a sense of balance to the relationship. It was the first big test; she should be cautious.

Nancy adjusted. She hashed and rehashed that single blow until it made sense, until it no longer represented a threat to everything she was building.

Bill adjusted, too. He made excuses for his violence. He explained it to her. He talked about why they both had to work it out. He took responsibility, sort of, but mostly he blamed the outside world. He believed himself. It made it easier. He swore he'd never touch Nancy again, but he knew she was changed by the episode. She was more compliant, more tuned into his moods, but also more distant—and something he wanted from her was being withheld. She had taken a piece of herself away from him and put it somewhere he couldn't reach.

He obsessed over that piece.

Their baby was born. She was a mother. He was a father. Another piece of her was taken from him and given to their daughter, another piece that didn't belong to him.

He obsessed over that piece.

A phase of their relationship was over, the phase in which she had centered her life around him, his phone calls, their dates, his dreams. They lived together now. There was the baby. There was a renewed tie with her mother and her sister, who also had a baby. There were pieces of her that were separate from him.

He obsessed over those pieces.

He had become more moody, more demanding. He wasn't violent toward her, but he knew that certain outbursts of anger drew her total attention to him.

Sara was Nancy's best friend. He hated that relationship. One night at a Halloween party, he made a pass at Sara. Suddenly that relationship wasn't so threatening. Now he was in it. In fact, he was in the middle of it. He felt Nancy's jealousy, and he felt the split between Sara and Nancy. He knew he had succeeded. He could stop obsessing about one thing.

On their daughter's first birthday, it happened again. The room was filled with guests—her mother, her sister, her friends and their kids. He came into the room and told her to fix him a sandwich. He had been working on the car, and he was hungry. She put him off, telling him, "I'll fix it later."

He grabbed her by the arm and threw her into the kitchen. "You'll fix it now. I'm hungry now." The party broke up. The tension stayed on. That night when she screamed at him in outrage, he hit her first with an open hand and then with a fist. He walked out.

She was pregnant again, but she hadn't told anyone. Her world was shrinking. Her friend was gone; her sister and her mother were disappointed in her withdrawal from them.

He came home drunk. He decided to tell her the truth about how he was jealous of the baby, her mother, her friend, how he didn't deserve her, how he was scared of being a father like his own. She comforted him. She told him the news, and they held each other and committed themselves once again to love each other above all else.

He became preoccupied about how she would react to his last act of violence. He wanted to know her every thought. Had she talked to her mother? Her sister? Was she attracted to other men? Of course she was. Was she sleeping with someone? He hated the power she had over him. She was making him feel this way on purpose.

He told himself he would never hit her again, but she would have to see how life would be without him. She's stupid, she wouldn't make it without him, she'd never get custody of the kids if she left him. He reminded her of these truths daily.

She wanted things to be different. She feared him, she fought with him, she told him what he wanted to hear, she begged him, she screamed at him, she ignored him, she got drunk with him, she started to slip. She started to merge with him. His thoughts and opinions became hers, his truths became hers. She was losing herself, and she knew it. She hated herself.

She had no real friends, and her relationships with her mother and sister were strained. She had tried going back to school, but he put a stop to that. She was trapped.

In the spring, he beat her again. This time she was afraid as she had never been before. She called the police. She was bleeding from her mouth, and the kids were crying. He was meaner than she'd ever seen him. As the police pulled up to the house, he grabbed her by the hair, pulled her face up to his, and whispered, "Someday I know I'm going to have to kill you."

The police came. "What happened? Why did you hit her?" "What do you want, lady?" "Is this your husband?" "If you want to press charges, call the city attorney." They warned him, "Another trip out to this address tonight will land you in jail." They left.

The next night he comes home, kicks off his shoes, throws his paper down. He is angry. She doesn't know why, and she really doesn't care. She tells him to leave if he's going to bring all that shit in the house. The kids leave the room. They know when to leave the room now. They're old enough to figure these things out but not old enough to know why—why the constant fear, the hatred, the names, the attacks.

She backs off when she sees the danger signs. He tells her to make his dinner, she complies. He tells her he wants her to go out with him to a party. She declines the offer.

It isn't an offer.

She doesn't have a babysitter.

"Get one."

She doesn't feel good.

"You never do for me. You must save it for someone else."

She senses what's about to happen. She picks up the phone, he grabs it.

"Forget it. Maybe you would rather go out with your boy-friend."

She tries to change the subject.

He wants to know who "he" is.

"There isn't anyone."

"You're lying. Tell me who he is."

She's fed up. She's sick of the whole thing. She's exhausted, she's scared, she tries to gather her energy to find the right words, as she has so many other times. Words that will divert his attention, change his energy. Her mind is racing but she senses the futility. She keeps talking, talking, talking.

Finally he leaves the house.

A reprieve—something worked, she doesn't really know what it was.

Grabbing her out of a sound sleep, he grasps her neck hard. "Tell me who he is."

She can't breathe. What's going on? There's that familiar smell. Booze and rage. It's 2, maybe 3 A.M. She struggles to free herself, but she can't move under the weight of his body.

"Tell me who he is."

She's shaking her head. Gasping for air. "There isn't anyone."

The veins in his neck are bulging. His eyes are burning with hatred. "Tell me who he is."

She's grabbing at him, scratching at his face. With one hand he holds her down, with the other he pushes his fingers into her rectum as hard as he can.

She screams in pain and humiliation.

"Whoever he is, he can have you."

She pleads with him to stop.

He pulls himself up and leans over her. "You wanted it to come to this. You always wanted it to come to this."

She's sobbing.

He still doesn't have those pieces of her that she's kept for herself, but at this point she doesn't either.

The Response to Abusive Men

To have even a remote chance of stopping the violence of millions of Bills in this country, we must first ask ourselves, "Who is he? Where did he come from? Why does he do these terrible things to a woman he claims to love?"

Since the first battered women's shelters opened in 1974, activists in this social movement have been asked, "What about the men? What are you doing for them?" It was asked by reporters, judges, police officers, community board members, members of countless audiences, funders, and more and more often through the years by battered women.

For years that question was answered by some with a cold stare, by others with a cynical quip, by still others with a return question: "What would you suggest?" But many programs worked to offer real solutions: arrest, detention, prosecution, expulsion from the home. From the mid-1970s to the present, women's organizations in all 50 states have struggled to provide concrete tools for communities to answer constructively the question "What about the men?"

Most states now have arrest laws that provide police officers with expanded powers of arrest in domestic abuse cases. These laws were passed in response to the repeated claims of police officers that their hands were tied in these cases when the officer doesn't see the assault and the woman won't press charges. A few states mandate that officers arrest in certain domestic situations, such as those involving felony assaults, assaults resulting in injury to the victim, or threats with a weapon. But the overwhelming majority of police officers legally empowered to make arrests still failed to do so, now arguing that arrest without successful prosecution is meaningless.

Prosecutors, on the other hand, claimed that placing immediate legal sanctions on wife beaters was difficult in the cumbersome and painfully slow criminal court system. Still recovering from legislative battles around arrest, advocates for battered women, many of whom were battered themselves, were again in the halls of state legislatures seeking and in many states winning civil court orders of protection. These new laws provided a speedy remedy to exclude batterers from the homes of those they abused. But as the violence continued, women now legally entitled to police protection waved their civil court orders in front of apathetic officers.

More laws were passed to close the loopholes and tend to the more technical aspects of the legal system. Specialized criminal justice reform projects cropped up in cities such as Minneapolis, Seattle, San Francisco, and Miami. As these projects successfully pushed for more effective court and police intervention, thousands of "Bills" came into the courts, with an equal number of "Nancys" asking for a just and safe resolution.

By 1980 there was a sinking feeling across the country that the question, "What about the men?" was bigger than the solution of arrest and jail. Judges and probation officers asked, "How are you going to help them?" They meant "rehabilitate." Suddenly the battered women's movement was asked to fix batterers in exchange for women's protection.

Before 1980 there were only a handful of programs working on developing counseling/educational interventions for batterers. Most of those were operating with primarily volunteer labor. As the courts began to mandate batterers into chemical dependency programs, counseling agencies, and self-help groups, the mental health profession responded to the "new client on the horizon." As group, individual, and couples' counseling involving batterers spread across the nation, young Ph.D. candidates worked tirelessly for more established researchers, picking apart and analyzing these acts of hitting, biting, slapping, kicking, gun waving, hair pulling, stabbing, and killing. A national debate ensued. Is Bill the problem, or is it alcohol, or is it his background, or is it his anger, or is it the relationship? After all, two out of three women don't get beaten. Why was Nancy one of the ones who did? Who or what should we study?

Battered women's programs spanned the range of reaction to the growing number of programs. Some ignored them completely, others engaged in a time-consuming monitoring process. Still others, hoping to ensure that the men's programs in their communities were run properly, started their own.

And so the question of what to do with the men became a more immediate question: "What are we doing with the men?"

It was at this point in 1980 that the Domestic Abuse Intervention Project (DAIP) was organized by women in Minnesota who had for the past 5 years been actively involved in the shelter movement. Its goal was to test an emerging theory that coordinating police and human service agencies' responses to domestic assault cases, through developing uniformly applied procedures, would drastically reduce the acts of violence against women seeking help from the system. Simply put, if everyone did his or her job well, most women wouldn't keep getting beaten. Of course, this forced the community to ask some basic questions: "What is the job of the police when intervening in a case of wife beating? What is the role of a therapist or any representative of a community institution when confronted with this issue? What does it mean to collude with batterers?"

The Duluth Response

The Duluth response, like all other efforts, is limited in its total vision. This program has, however, made some key contributions to the national search for an intervention and prevention strategy. First, the goal of the project is the protection of battered women, not the fixing of batterers. The rehabilitation of abusers is a component of a much larger intervention strategy beyond the DAIP. Second, the project assumes that battering is not an individual pathology or a mental illness but rather just one part of a system of abusive and violent behaviors to control the victim for the purposes of the abuser.

In 1980 and 1981 the DAIP negotiated written agreements with the police, prosecutors, probation officers, family and criminal court judges, jailers, and the women's shelter, all designed to place increasingly harsh legal sanctions on abusers who continue to threaten or harm their former or current partners. A rehabilitation program is offered as an alternative to jail for offenders who are convicted for the first time and to second-time offenders after serving some jail time.

The following is a synopsis of how a typical assault case would be handled in this system.

The intervention process begins when the police are called to the home of the victim and the assailant. An assault has occurred during the evening, and police have been called by the victim. Upon arrival, the officers take statements from both the assailant and the victim. The officers learn (for the sake of this illustration) that the couple are married, and the wife states that her husband hit her in the face following an argument that occurred an hour earlier. Officers observed bruises on the victim's face. The assailant is informed that he is being arrested for fifth-degree assault. The victim is told that a women's advocate from the intervention project will be contacting her. The assailant is then transported by police to the county jail.

At the jail an officer calls the shelter to inform shelter staff of the arrest and provide information on the assailant and victim. Shelter staff use a beeper system to contact the on-call women's advocate. Women's advocates work alone or in teams of two. Information on the assailant and victim is given to the advocates, and they immediately visit the victim at her residence.

Meanwhile, the assailant has been jailed and is held until court, normally the following day. During the early morning, the shelter calls the volunteer on duty and informs him of the arrest. At 8:00 A.M. the volunteer visits the assailant in jail. He explains the intervention program and informs the assailant that a counseling/educational program is available for stopping violent behavior.

At the arraignment, the assailant enters his plea. In this illustration, the assailant pleads guilty to a misdemeanor assault. Had a not-guilty plea been made, the trial process would have begun, and until the case was resolved, there would have been no further DAIP-initiated contact with the assailant.

A pre-sentence investigation is next completed by a probation officer. The probation officer interviews the assailant and consults with the on-call advocate or the victim and anyone else thought necessary in arriving at a sentencing recommendation to the judge. The probation officer, following the agreed-upon sentencing guidelines, recommends (1) a jail sentence, (2) a jail sentence partially served and participation in counseling, or (3) a stayed jail sentence with counseling. The recommendation is based on the assailant's (1) prior convictions, (2) willingness to follow through on counseling, (3) past record in following through on counseling, and (4) the appropriateness of the counseling to the individual. In this case, the judge accepts the probation officer's recommendation and sentences the assailant to 30 days in the county jail. The jail sentence is stayed, and the assailant is placed on probation for 1 year. Probation conditions mandate the assailant to comply with the DAIP and frequently require completion of a chemical dependence program prior to entering DAIP.

Following sentencing, the assailant meets with a DAIP staff member who explains the assailant's obligation to the DAIP and assigns him to a group. If the assailant re-offends or does not meet DAIP obligations, the assailant is reported to the probation officer. The result is normally a violation of probation charge and an imposition of a portion of the original jail sentence with an order to once again participate in the DAIP.

A DAIP staff member interviews the partners of men mandated to groups, preferably in person. Women are encouraged to attend two DAIP-sponsored groups that explain the theory and process of abusers' groups and the process for reporting new violence. In addition, a shelter advocate keeps in contact with the women, offering childcare and transportation to enable them to attend one of three weekly neighborhood-based groups. Counselors, probation officers, advocates, and DAIP staff all encourage women to report further acts of violence.

Today the primary functions of the DAIP are to monitor the compliance of professionals in the community with agreed-upon protocols and to monitor individual batterers' compliance with court orders. Monitoring the response of police, prosecutors, and other agencies involved is done through a continual review of their records, attendance at all civil protection order hearings, and periodic interviews with victims. Monitoring individial batterers is similarly done by monitoring the records of counseling agencies and frequent contacts and interviews with their partners. Bimonthly meetings are facilitated by DAIP staff for probation officers, counselors, and shelter advocates.

In order to allow for communication among intervening agencies and to comply with confidentiality laws, all abusers court ordered to a rehabilitation program are ordered directly to the DAIP, which enters into specific agreements with assailants and assigns them on a rotating basis to one of eight ongoing groups conducted by three community mental health agencies.

The Importance of Community-Wide Coordination

The monitoring and coordinating role of the DAIP is intended to prevent community collusion with abusers. First, it ensures that individual police officers, probation officers, therapists, prosecutors, judges, advocates, or jailers are not screening cases out of the system based on misinformation provided by the abuser, lack of information, or race, sex, or class biases. Such screening is one of the most prevalent ways communities collude with batterers. Since the establishment of closely monitored procedures and protocols in 1981, annual arrests are 10 times higher than those of prepolicy years, the percentage of minority males arrested has dropped from 33% to 11%, and the arrest of women has increased from 0% to 8%. The number of women filing and following through on protection orders has tripled. Conviction rates in domestic assault cases have significantly increased, and the number of assailants brought back to court for failure to comply with civil or criminal court orders has risen tenfold.

A second form of community collusion is the victim blaming that permeates our thinking, our language, and our reactions to victims of domestic violence. Perhaps no issue has caused as much tension and conflict within the network of agencies in Duluth as that of eliminating victim-blaming practices and acknowledging the relationship of these practices to collusion with batterers. One of the most important functions of the DAIP is to maintain open communication among the many intervening agencies and individuals connected with these cases. To coordinate a community effort that involves a paramilitary, male-dominated police force and a nonhierarchical female-dominated shelter staff with nine other agencies is no easy task. But no sustained change will take place if such an effort is merely based on having the political power to enact policies and protocols. At some point, those practices must reflect each agency's intervention role.

For example, an advocacy group can use the media, contacts with community leaders, public opinion, and friends in the court system or city government to secure a mandatory arrest policy. Such a policy forces police officers to act otherwise than they would if given personal discretion. However, unless officers eventually accept the need for these policies, such policies will be sabotaged by a disgruntled front line at the police department. Many communities have seen their police departments' arrest policies used against women and minorities by officers resisting commands from above. In the state of Washington, for example, where all departments were mandated by law to arrest abusers, entire departments resisted, resulting in scores of women being arrested, emergency meetings, and, finally, amendments to the law.

In addition, the DAIP offers participating agencies a constant forum for reflection. Everything a community does—naming groups, developing an intake process, using jail, excluding abusers from their homes, implementing a group rehabilitation process—communicates a message to those battering and those being battered. An independent organization strongly influenced by formerly battered women that provides a forum for open discussion greatly reduces collusion with batterers. If collusion is the secret cooperation with something questionable or wrong, then the intervention process used in the Duluth program is its opposite. When the project functions properly, each case is open to scrutiny. Each case can be held up for examination and approval. This creates a context that is not conducive to collusion.

In the first 3 years of organizing the DAIP, a series of agreements were reached. Most notably, police and court administrators and participating therapists agreed with victim advocates that the act of violence must be made the sole responsibility of the person using it. In other words, the police would no longer base the decision to arrest an assailant on what the victim said or did to contribute to the argument that preceded the assault. The judge would not order a woman to counseling with her abuser to learn how she could communicate with him differently to avoid his beatings. A probation officer would not rest easy that a client was not being violent simply because he has been ordered not to have contact with the woman he was convicted of assaulting. A therapist would not provide marriage counseling to a couple when violence was present. The collective community message to batterers must be clear: When you beat your partner, you are not the victim, you are the aggressor. Either stop it or lose increasing amounts of your personal freedom.

Second, the agencies agreed that their contact with batterers was to be a part of a community effort to confront their use of violence and not to advocate for them. When batterer counseling programs are not tied to a much larger community system of controls and accountability, they are used by abusers to get back into their homes, to win court and custody battles, to avoid criminal and civil court sanctions and proceedings, and to convince their partners that they are changing when, in fact, there has been no true altering of the power dynamics in the relationship.

General agreements or statements must ultimately be applied to real people's lives. In many ways, Bill is very much like the majority of men who are mandated to the DAIP. His acts of violence, if analyzed as separate and unrelated events removed from the context of all his other abusive and controlling behaviors, may appear to be uncontrolled bursts of anger releasing days or months of built-up tension. He may be seen as impulsive, having poor stress or anger control skills, insecure, codependent. Surely there is a piece of the truth in each of these observations, but from another view he is very much in control of his anger. After all, he chose when and where and how severely to hurt Nancy. At times it seems that he felt very secure. For example, when the police arrived, Nancy was intimidated enough by Bill's threat to kill her that she protected him from the law enforcement officer. His threat served to mobilize her to get the police to back off. The DAIP has attempted to build a coordinated community-wide program that involves literally hundreds of people, each with his or her own biases and perspectives on battering. The primary function of the DAIP is to draw those separate perspectives together under a common intervention strategy.

It is in a community utilizing its institutional powers to confront batterers that the DAIP conducts the men's groups discussed below. To conduct such classes without first insisting on police and court reforms is not only shortsighted but can also be, in the long run, dangerous to battered women. Ninety-two percent of the abusers in Duluth convicted of assaulting their partners are court mandated to the DAIP. Twelve percent also serve some jail time. Ninety-seven percent of all civil protection orders granted in cases where there are minor children involved also carry a requirement that the abuser participate in educational classes conducted by the DAIP. Approximately 92% of abusers mandated to the DAIP are male, and 8% are female.

The Rehabilitative Process

The Duluth court requires abusers who have been convicted or who have had orders for protection issued against them to participate in a 26-week counseling and educational program coordinated by the DAIP. The first 2 weeks consist of orientation sessions teaching men the rules and concepts of group process and the underlying assumptions of the program.

The next 12 sessions are conducted by therapists in one of three community mental health/counseling programs. These groups focus on confronting men's minimization and denial of their violence, with the goal of stopping the violence through anger management training. Following 12 weeks of counseling, the men enter a 12-week course taught by community activists trained by DAIP staff. Facilitators use a curriculum designed by the DAIP staff. Men are encouraged to remain in the program beyond the total 26 weeks of required sessions. They may choose to remain in the classes or to join an ongoing support group. In addition to court-required groups, voluntary relationship counseling is offered by participating therapists, but only if the batterer has completed the initial 12 weeks of the program and has remained nonviolent.

The description below focuses on the 12-week curriculum developed by the DAIP, because it best demonstrates the integration of theory with practice.

Assumptions of the Curriculum

Men who batter use a system of abusive tactics to control their partners. Violence is rarely used to the exclusion of other controlling and abusive tactics. Figure 2.1 presents a chart developed by the DAIP based on interviews and discussions with over 200 battered women, which depicts nine of their abusers' most controlling and abusive tactics. The use of physical attacks, whether frequent or sporadic, reinforces the power of other tactics such as emotional abuse, isolation, sexual abuse, and threats of taking the children.

These behaviors are not unintentional. Each abusive act can be traced back to an intention of the abuser's. For example, an abuser will frequently increase his use of degrading names prior to an assault in order to depersonalize his partner. Once he has objectified her, he hits the object he has created rather than the person he lives

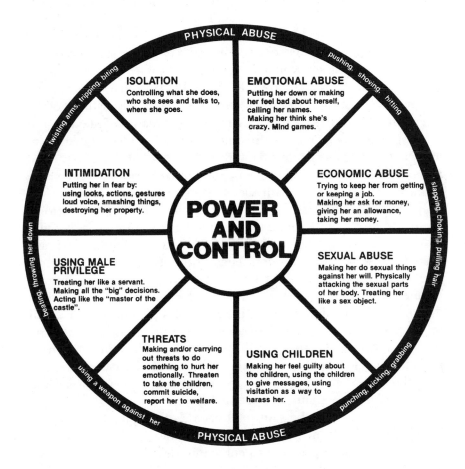

Figure 2.1 Abusers' most controlling and abusive tactics.

with. The tactics used by abusers reflect tactics used by many groups or individuals in positions of power in our culture. These men mirror the worst of our society's norms. Each of the tactics depicted on the chart is typical of behaviors used by groups of people who dominate others. They are the tactics employed to sustain racism, ageism, classism, heterosexism, anti-Semitism, and many other forms of group domination. The men learn these tactics not only in their families of origin but also in their experience of the dominant culture in this society.

They, like those who intervene to help, have been immersed in the consciousness of oppressiveness. This consciousness is rooted in the assumption that, based on differences, some people have the legitimate right to master others. This relationship is seen as beneficial to both the master and the one who is "guided" by the master. Afrikaners dominating South African blacks claim that the technical advancements of that nation resulted from this relationship; Southern whites proclaimed segregation to be God's plan carried out in the interest of Southern blacks; the Soviet Union invades Afghanistan, and the United States, Grenada, for the "benefit" of those countries. Elaborate systems are constructed to legitimize various relationships of mastery. Community institutions are used by those in control to shape the consciousness of all within the system. Extensive efforts are made to obtain a general acceptance of the premises that the hierarchy is natural and that those who are at the bottom of it are there because of their own deficiencies or defects.

The consciousness of separateness prevails. Differences among people are not celebrated and treasured but used as a reason to dominate. The dominant culture then becomes the norm to which all others are forced to assimilate unless they prefer to exist on the fringe of a more "sophisticated" society. Individuals mirror these national and global relationships in their own interpersonal dealings with the world. Abusers operate from deeply held beliefs regarding their gender-based rights in relationships.

Consciousness is the sum total of one's thoughts, feelings, and world view. To be in this world with a critical consciousness, one must be allowed to question, to enter into debate, and to challenge much of the "mystical thinking" this culture promotes. Mystical thinking fails to distinguish between the laws and forces of nature and human-made laws and forces of culture.

Men, operating from a submerged consciousness, vigorously defend their beliefs as absolute truths: "Somebody has to be in charge"; "You can't have two captains to one ship"; "If I don't control her, she'll control me"; "God made man first, which means men are supposed to rule women."

The consciousness of both men and women in this society is shaped by their experiences of this system and all of the forces that work within it. Yet not all men batter women, even though all men have been socialized in a society that grants them certain gender privileges. Likewise, not all white people commit violent acts of

racism, yet all whites have been exposed to powerf
experiences that tell them they are superior to people

There are different reasons why men feel the n___ ___
the women they live with. Each man brings to a group his own
history. It is often a history that has included abuse as a child,
exposure to men who have demonstrated hateful attitudes toward
women, exposure to a myriad of woman-hating environments, alcoholism, racial and class oppression, or the denial of love and nurtu-
rance as a child. These individual experiences become both an explanation of why he batters and his excuse to continue his violence. To
change long-held patterns, men must acknowledge the destructive
nature of their present behaviors and accept responsibility for their
actions. They are not, however, responsible for creating the many
forces that have shaped their consciousness. While men are not
victims of sexism as are the women they beat, they are dehumanized
by their socialization.

Not all batterers are the same. Some are mentally ill, some have
seemingly no remorse for their violence, and others are, if not
motivated to change, at least miserable enough to want their situations to change. Still others are truly appalled at their behavior. The
rationalizations of abusers for their behaviors, like those of other
individuals and groups who dominate through force, often result in
the men's not only portraying but also in some sense believing
themselves to be the victims of the women they beat. This delusion is
reinforced by the practices of police, judges, social workers, clergy,
educators, reporters, and other representatives of society's institutions, who collude with an abuser's claim of being the victim.

Batterers are capable of personal transformation, and many
men will make very powerful changes if certain conditions exist.
These include a community that holds them fully accountable for
their use of violence by making and enforcing consequences of
continued acts of abuse and by providing an environment that is
nonviolent, respectful of women, and nonjudgmental in which to
make those changes. In addition to these conditions, the individual
must be willing to work on a long process involving self-reflection,
self-respect, painful honesty, and accountability to his victim. Men
who batter do not often reflect about how they are living their lives
and frequently are guided by mystical thinking. Such thinking prevents a critical consciousness and contributes to men's engaging in
self-destructive behavior and, even more intensely, in behavior with

brutal and terrorizing effects on the women and children they dominate.

The use of these tactics results in the abuser's domination of his
partner physically, sexually, emotionally, and spiritually. Women
subjected to these acts of terror experience severe physical, psychological, and spiritual trauma. When a battered woman manifests
characteristics of being traumatized or fights back, she is labeled
defective by the abuser and by the system that colludes with him. The
victim is labeled by the abuser as provocative, a whore, a drunk or
junkie, a bitch, a bad mother, violent, a liar, a man hater, a thief, out
to get him, clinging, and a host of other negative things. She is
labeled by the community as an enabler, codependent, nonassertive, a
poor mother, a drug or alcohol abuser, violent, self-destructive, and
provocative. Like any person or group at the bottom of an abusive
hierarchical order, she is thought to be there because of some defect
or weakness. He defines her this way, and the system backs him up in
both subtle and blatant ways. She is studied by countless Ph.D.
candidates in her postvictimized state and is typically judged to be
lacking. She's compared to "nonbattered women" in test after test,
and the difference between the two is defined as the cause of her
problem. The question of why this woman is the one who gets hit is
answered by academic and professional theories that sound suspi-
ciously like the claims of her batterer. She lacks certain skills, certain
attitudes, and her behavior is not quite right. He is reinforced; she is
revictimized. He becomes a more cooperative client; she becomes
more problematic. In such a system, he is no longer challenged to
change.

A system that attempts to help batterers change and avoid these
victim-blaming practices is difficult to establish. It is, however, possible to create a supportive environment in which men can make
changes without our collusion with them, without abandoning the
goal of establishing a community safe for women.

Finally, the DAIP and its curriculum are based on the assumption that there is no such thing as a neutral educational or change
process for men who batter or for the women they abuse. Every
aspect of the class, from the seating arrangement to the evaluation
form, either supports or challenges the consciousness of domination. To teach a man who has beaten his wife how to get what he
wants without violence without ever asking him, "Is what you want
fair?" is neither neutral nor moves toward a more just and non-

violent relationship. The implication of this assumption is far-reaching. It calls for each teacher to join with the men in the process of self-reflection. It brings the facilitator into process with the men, because it ultimately acknowledges that the consciousness of the abuser, which presupposes a right to impose his values and needs on his partner, is a consciousness shared by most people in this culture. With this recognition and a commitment to making personal change, the facilitator can stand in process with him, without judgment and without collusion, while standing equally in the process of liberation with the women he has hurt.

Curriculum Design

Each of the nine tactics of control depicted on the chart in Figure 2.1 is discussed over a 2- or 3-week period for a total of 18 weeks. The first stage of discussion of each topic focuses on six aspects of the use of a particular tactic. The group examines these aspects by answering a series of questions relative to their last or most powerful use of a certain tactic. These questions are

1. Exactly how do I use this tactic and how does my use of this tactic interact with other abusive tactics?
2. What is my intent in using this tactic, and specifically, what did I want to have happen the last time I used it?
3. What are some underlying belief statements that seem to be in operation when I use this tactic or feel justified to obtain the goal I've set with abusive tactics?
4. How have I minimized or denied my use of this tactic and the effects of my using this abusive behavior on others?
5. What effects has my use of this tactic had on me, on my partner, on my children, on my relationship, and on others?
6. What is the relationship of my past use of violence to continuing incidents in which I still use this tactic of control or abuse?

During the second stage of discussion on a particular tactic, the group explores noncontrolling and nonviolent behavior they could have used in situations in which they have previously been abusive. The facilitator teaches skills lacking in some of the men, for example, assertiveness rather than aggressiveness, letting go of needing to win, negotiating, fighting fairly, anger management, relaxation, empathizing, compassion, and expression of feelings. If, for example, Bill, whose story was told earlier, was a class participant in the 2- or 3-week period covering physical abuse, the following would occur: The group begins by watching a short videotape depicting physical abuse. Bill is then asked to role play or discuss in detail with one of the other group members a situation in which he used physical violence. He chooses the day of the Halloween party. The facilitator assists in getting as real a reenactment or description of Bill's emotions and behaviors in that situation as possible. Bill's experience and the short videotape are now group experiences. They become "codes" or a common framework for the class. The class now decodes the scenes step by step.

Week 1 of Each Tactic

Naming Actions. First, the men name each controlling or abusive tactic Bill used in this situation or that they viewed in the videotape. Although the scene involved physical abuse as the primary tactic, Bill also used gestures and language that employ other tactics (i.e., emotional abuse, threats, isolation).

The men are asked to examine the relationship of various tactics to one another. They observe not only which tactics were used but also how Bill shifted tactics throughout the scene. This discussion dispels the myth of the "blown fuse." The men are able to see the skillful use of different tactics at different times for different results. Although it is acknowledged that Bill felt out of control, he also faces the reality of how much control he was intuitively using.

Intentions and Beliefs. Next, the discussion moves to an examination of Bill's intent—what did he want in this situation? What did he think would be different if he employed these tactics? If the men are going to stop thinking of themselves as victims and therefore powerless to change, they must face the reality that each of their abusive behaviors is intended to change how their partners act, think, or feel. This realization comes and goes from week to week as the men come face to face with themselves in these scenes.

Why did Bill do this in front of her family? Why didn't he just fix himself a sandwich? Why did he get so angry? What did he gain by this? Intent is rooted in belief. If, for example, his intention was to keep her from being with her family, then he must believe something about that. "If she hangs around with her sister and mother, she will leave me." "She's supposed to take care of me first." "If she has other interests outside of me, it means she doesn't care about me." A major goal of this educational process is to help the men act in the world in a reflective way. Most of the men hold strong opinions about whose role it is to do the money-making, the housework, the childcare, the decision making. These long-held beliefs are reported by the men as laws of nature, as God's way. The men are continually confronted in these discussions with the possibility that these "truths" are perhaps created by people. They are cultural, not laws of physics, and therefore, they are alterable situations. This discussion frequently traces the source of these "truths" in the individual and collective cultural experiences of the men.

Feelings. After exploring the tactics of power used by Bill, along with his intentions and his underlying beliefs, the group goes on to examine the relationship of Bill's feelings to his actions. Bill first identifies how he was feeling (for example, hurt, jealous, angry, lonely). Next, Bill and the group make the connections between what he wanted, what he believed, and how he felt. In this phase of the discussion, the group comes to understand that feelings are not free-floating entities separate from who we are; they are extensions of how we see ourselves in the world. Many of an abuser's negative, hostile, and angry feelings are inextricably tied to who he believes he is and who he believes his partner is in the world. For example, through the reflective group process, Bill may articulate that Nancy was with her family, or her children. They were having a birthday party, and he didn't fit in. He wasn't central to that activity; therefore, he felt excluded.

The curriculum is not designed to teach men that by expressing their feelings to their partners, they will be less abusive. In fact, quite the opposite may be true. If an abuser's perceived right to control his partner, to shape who she is, what she does, and how she feels, is not first challenged, then teaching him to talk about or express his feelings may only increase the pressure on his partner to comply to his wishes. Now, not only does he feel jealous, but he has also shared this feeling with her. He has become more vulnerable to her and may expect her to respond by fixing his feelings. For example, if Bill is told that an alternative to his abuse would have been to come in the house and call Nancy aside and say, "I feel excluded," what does that mean Nancy should do? Ask her mother and sister to leave? Try to bring him into the group? Go outside and be with him? He must first give up the expectation that she must make all his negative feelings go away before the expression of these feelings to her will be healthy for either of them.

Minimizing and Denying. From this discussion, Bill, again with help from the group, lists methods he used to minimize and deny his actions or to blame Nancy or others for the abusive behavior. The group looks at the intents and effects of his denial. Once again, this discussion counters the almost universal claim of the abusers that they are victims of the women that they batter. This discussion will often focus on the self-talk practices of the men. It is the almost universal experience of the men that they turn everything around in their minds so much that a simple phone call to her friend is seen as total disloyalty to him. During this self-talk, many belief statements come pouring out. Getting Bill to role play all his self-talk aloud to the group sets the stage for a meaningful discussion of this aspect of abuse.

Effects of Behaviors. In order to motivate the men to change these behaviors, the discussion focuses on the effects of Bill's behaviors on himself, his partner, and their relationship. This discussion clearly demonstrates that these acts of abuse often work to gain her compliance to what he wants. However, the men also see that these behaviors have the long-term effect of alienating them from their partners, their children, their friends, and their families.

Past Use of Violence. The first phase of discussion of this topic ends with the group's naming the ways in which Bill's past use of violence affected Nancy in this situation. The group may also discuss how men's violence and aggression toward women in general affects Nancy. Each group ends with a brief acknowledgment that the effect of past violence toward women in relationships and in society is always there and provides a foundation for a woman's response to an abuser.

Week 2 of Each Tactic—Alternatives to Abusive Behaviors

The next week the men each bring to group a personal log that analyzes their own use of physical abuse to control a woman's behavior. Bill, with the help of other group members, once again role plays the situation in which he used violence. This time he uses noncontrolling behavior in the same situation. Several men role play or discuss alternatives to the abusive behaviors recorded on their logs during that week. The group explores concrete steps a participant can take to alter these behaviors. What can each man do in the situation that is nonabusive? What must he do in the long run to stop engaging in these behaviors? This is the time to teach men nonviolent relationship skills, including anger control techniques, positive self-talk, and time-out and relaxation techniques. In this part of the discussion, many of the commonly used cognitive-behavioral therapy techniques used in other batterer programs are employed. It is not enough for men to come to the realization that they are using abusive tactics to control their partners. They must be given specific and obtainable tasks and goals to start doing something different.

Figure 2.2 is a control log that each of the men complete by analyzing a specific form of control that they used against their partners. The log is completed and brought to the second phase of the discussion. Four or five members of the group may role play their nonviolent alternatives.

The use of the logs and highly structured group process help facilitators keep the focus of the group on the central issue—the use of abusive tactics to exercise power and control over women.

Evaluation

Since 1980 the DAIP has attempted to measure its successes and failures in a number of ways. Three methods have consistently provided meaningful feedback and have been incorporated in the overall program design.

The first process uses a participant research method to review the effectiveness of policies, procedures, and protocols in protecting women and reducing institutional victim-blaming practices.

In 1984 and 1985, 11 formerly battered women worked with Dr. Melanie Shepard of the University of Minnesota to design two instruments to measure program effectiveness. The first instrument is an extensive questionnaire administered anonymously to a random sampling of women who contacted the police, the shelter, or the

No Log—No Credit
Instructions: Complete each section. Be specific.

Topic: _____ Date: _____ Name: _____

1. Briefly describe the situation and the action *you* used to control (statements, gestures, tone of voice, physical contact, facial expressions).

_____

_____

_____

2. Intent: What did you want to happen in this situation?

_____

_____

_____

3. What feelings were you having?

_____

_____

_____

4. In what ways did you minimize or deny your actions or blame her?

_____

_____

5. Effects: what was the result of your action? Include results of blaming or minimizing.

(on you) _____

_____

_____

(on her) _____

(on the relationship and others) _____

_____

6. It would have been better if I . . . .

_____

_____

_____

7. How did your past use of violence affect this situation?

_____

_____

_____

Figure 2.2 Controlling behavior: weekly logs—educational groups.

courts because of physical abuse. These questionnaires are mailed to women 2 years after their initial contact with the system. They ascertain the women's satisfaction with seven aspects of community intervention: initial police calls, the prosecution of criminal cases, the civil court process, the legal advocacy provided by the shelter, educational groups for women, probation officers' and judicial involvement in criminal cases, and the counseling and education groups for abusers. The questionnaire is designed to measure women's satisfaction with the actions and attitudes of whomever they called upon for protection. The final section of the survey asks women to rate the overall effectiveness of the combined community response in protecting her from further abuse.

A community meeting is called to analyze the results of these surveys. Invitations are sent to all women to whom surveys are sent, as well as to current and former shelter residents, members of neighborhood-based education groups, and DAIP and shelter staff. The results of each section of the surveys are thoroughly discussed, and a series of recommendations are made to improve the system's response. Committees composed of DAIP or shelter staff and battered women are formed to follow up with agency meetings on each recommendation.

The results of this survey in Duluth showed that a majority of the 65 respondents reported that they had had favorable experiences with the police, the shelter, and the court system. They reported less favorable experiences with probation officers and prosecutors. All of the respondents thought that their assailants should have been ordered to attend counseling and education groups, and most felt safer when the assailant was doing so. Eighty-eight percent reported that the combined response of the police, the courts, the shelter, and the counseling and education groups had been helpful or very helpful.

Half of the respondents attended the follow-up community meeting forum, in addition to 25 women who were currently participating in women's groups. The 55 women broke into five groups, each group reviewing the results of a section of the survey and reporting back to the larger group with a list of recommendations. Thirty-one recommendations were made for altering procedures or policies. Forty-two women volunteered to serve on four committees formed to implement the recommendations. Eventually, 23 of the recommendations were implemented.

This evaluation process did more than provide DAIP with an agenda for further work. It pointed out the importance of battered women's organizing on their own behalf. The women's recommendations and their effort to implement them brought the project back to the grass roots, where the battered women's movement began.

The second set of questionnaires is administered at three different intervals to men court mandated to groups and to their partners. This "behavior checklist" was designed by formerly battered women and Dr. Shepard. It is designed to measure the change in the frequency of use of all of the abusive and controlling tactics depicted in Figure 2.1 by abusers over a 12-month period.

The same process was used to design a survey for women to measure the degree to which their freedoms are restored over a 1-year period. This questionnaire attempts to assist women in evaluating how free they are to act without control or restraints from their abusers.

The results of the questionnaire in Duluth showed significant reductions in rates of abuse being reported, particularly during the first 3 months of the intervention process (Novak & Galaway, 1983; Shepard, 1985). Shepard (1986) found that approximately 70% of the victims reported experiencing no recent physical abuse at a 1-year follow-up. Although significantly less psychological abuse was reported, 60% of the women did report having experienced some form of psychological abuse. Evaluation efforts have been limited by the unavailability of comparison groups and difficulty in locating subjects at follow-up. The extent to which different components of the project contributed to program outcomes is unclear. Police and court intervention, as well as the counseling and education program, are important elements of the program. Novak and Galaway (1983) did find that fewer victims reported experiencing violence from DAIP court mandated participants than from those who were not mandated. Studies of other programs have reported a range from 32% to 81% of program participants remaining nonviolent at follow-up periods from 3 months to 1 year. Diversity in treatment and research methods makes it difficult to compare findings.

Finally, DAIP staff and shelter staff collect data on a continuing basis to determine if the procedures, protocols, and policies are consistently applied. Through examination of police, court, shelter, and DAIP records and telephone interviews with women, a fairly accurate assessment of when and how the system breaks down can be determined.

The results of the data show that the level of compliance with the procedures, protocols, and policies varies with the agency. If the role of the agency is very concrete, it is more likely to adhere to the agreements than an agency whose role is more subjective.

These three processes are neither exhaustive nor adequate to evaluate fully this community's response to battering. They do, however, provide three important pieces of information: Are the community agencies doing what they say they are doing? How do battered women experience this system? Does the community response reduce women's vulnerability to continued abuse?

Conclusion

Every aspect of the program, from the police arrest to the group structure, is designed to focus on the batterer as a person in control of his partner, acting in what he perceives to be his best interest at the expense of his partner and children. This does not mean he is in control of himself. In fact, most men feel very out of control on a personal level. To focus literally hundreds of people in a community toward that end is a long process, but one we owe to battered women.

This work begins with commitment. It starts with a commitment to women who are beaten, kicked, pushed, stabbed, held hostage, called names, and subjected to constant attack on their very essence as human beings. It involves a commitment to these men—not to the part of them that unfairly uses another person but to the part of them that is capable of giving and receiving love. Our work must be personal. This work offers each of us the opportunity to examine some of our most basic beliefs about who we are in relationship to our partners, our friends, and our communities. Our culture and society encourage us to see power as the ability to control. The extent to which one is able to influence events, to acquire and control increasing amounts of resources, and to influence the behavior and actions of others is the measure of one's power. Those of us intervening in these cases, as well as the abuser, share in that cultural perspective.

To move from a society in which individuals seek power and its corresponding ability to control to a society in which its members seek collective and personal empowerment and its creative power is a complex process. But what is the role of the individual batterer in the overall scheme of things? If we see him as only the victim of a larger system in which he has no say and as merely a pawn of a sexist society, we take away his individual responsibility, making it difficult for him to change. This program in all its aspects rejects the notion of men as victims of sexism. Any system that gives one group power over another group dehumanizes both those with too much power and those without enough power. However, that does not make those who abuse their access to power innocent victims of the system. Ultimately, each of us must be held accountable for the choices we make. This project challenges men to see their use of violence as a choice—not an uncontrolled reaction to their past, their anger, or their lack of skills, but a choice.

The socialization of men and women in this society teaches us to adhere to rigidly defined roles that in the end separate us from one another. A community confrontation challenges much of what the men believe and in the process challenges those of us who orchestrate the confrontation.

A non-victim-blaming community response to abusers is all about power and can lead to true empowerment in men. It challenges men to take the risk to stop controlling, to stop having all the power. Above all else, it is respectful to each man because it believes that at each man's core is the ability to act in a loving and caring way. It gives men control of themselves and asks them to be in a world as a whole person—a person who feels pain, who sometimes loses, and who doesn't always get to decide. It asks men to give women the choice to love them. Finally, it asks men to respect women, to give up the privileged status our society has given them.

As a community, our ability to successfully intervene with a batterer is directly tied to our understanding of him as a manifestation of a part of all of us. He mirrors the worst in our culture. He is changed by our responding not in collusion with him, not by seeing him as different than us or as mentally ill, but by acknowledging the need for our own personal and institutional transformation to be a part of his.

References

Novak, S., & Galaway, B. (1983). Independent evaluation conducted for the Domestic Abuse Intervention Project.

Shepard, M. (1985). Independent evaluation conducted for the Domestic Abuse Intervention Project.

Shepard, M. (1986). Unpublished doctoral dissertation conducted at the University of Minnesota.

II

COGNITIVE-BEHAVIORAL APPROACHES

3

Proximal Causes of Spouse Abuse: A Theoretical Analysis for Cognitive-Behavioral Interventions

L. Kevin Hamberger
Jeffrey M. Lohr

Introduction

The phenomenon of wife abuse has received close scientific scrutiny for only the past 10 to 15 years, even though it is an age-old problem (Scott, 1980; Westra & Martin, 1981). Several reviews have been published detailing descriptive issues in violent relationships (Goldberg & Carey, 1982; Goodstein & Page, 1981) and sociological formulations of wife abuse (Gelles, 1977; Stahly, 1978; Stark, Flitcraft, & Frazier, 1979; Straus, 1977a). Gelles (1980) has reviewed research on family violence conducted during the 1970s, most of which has focused upon sociological factors. Most of the research reviewed suggests that spouse abuse is rooted primarily in sociocultural, political, and religious traditions (Dobash & Dobash, 1977; Gelles, 1980; Straus, 1976, 1977a, 1977b).

More recently, researchers have mentioned the role of individual factors (Gelles, 1980; Rounsaville, 1978) as part of the constella-
tion of factors associated with wife abuse. Several recent studies have
appeared in the literature that investigate intrapersonal (demographic and personality) characteristics of batterers (Caesar, 1986; Goldstein & Rosenbaum, 1985; Hamberger & Hastings, 1986; Hastings &
Hamberger, 1988; Rosenbaum & O'Leary, 1981; Saunders, 1987).
Yet, in general, individual factors such as personality and psychopathology have, historically, not been considered important for the
understanding of and intervention into wife abuse as a behavior
problem. Both researchers and clinicians alike have suggested that
continued development of effective interventions with batterers will
be contingent upon increased knowledge of batterer characteristics
or subtypes (Geller & Wasserstrom, 1984; Gondolf, 1987; Hamberger & Hastings, 1986; Roberts, 1984; Saunders, 1987). This call
for greater refinement of our understanding of intrapersonal characteristics reflects concern about the negative effects of uniformity
myths (Kiesler, 1966) about patient characteristics (all batterers are
essentially alike) and prevention strategies (because all batterers are
alike, there is a uniform etiology and therefore a preferred, uniform
treatment approach).

We recognize there is much disagreement about including intrapersonal factors in the conceptualization of interventions for
spouse abuse. Indeed, some workers have strongly argued that an
emphasis on such factors is detrimental to sociologic or profeminist
interpretations of spouse abuse (Adams, 1988; Mederos, 1987). It is
not our intention to "psychopathologize" the process, which could be
viewed as a "psychiatric excuse" for a social problem. Our purpose is
to elucidate the manner in which intrapersonal factors may be involved. We hope to show how a social learning analysis can explain
some aspects of the abuse process and explain how the perpetrator of
abuse initiates and maintains the process.

As interest in the definition and conceptualization of spouse
abuse has increased, there has been a concomitant proliferation of
intervention modalities. Some intervention approaches focus upon
sociocultural factors (Pence & Paymar, 1985) and others upon interpersonal factors (Geller & Wasserstrom, 1984). We feel that knowledge of batterer characteristics is also crucial in the determination of
targets for change and the design of interventions. Rather than
readapting an "illness" model, this chapter will present a compre-

hensive theoretical formulation of battering in social learning terms. This analysis will examine how battering is initiated and maintained and how it can be ameliorated through a *cognitive-behavioral* treatment approach. We view the cognitive-behavioral approach as offering the most comprehensive, molecular analysis of *proximal* causes of battering. By "proximal" is meant those factors closest (in space or time) to the battering behavior of the individual batterer. Such behavior may reflect prevailing sociocultural and political norms and practices vis-à-vis women, and hence, the cognitive-behavioral model is viewed as compatible with such conceptualizations. Nevertheless, the broader political and social issues related to violence are viewed as more distal to any *specific instance* of battering, which consists of several covert (cognitive) and overt (behavioral) components. It is the latter set of components that is the primary focus of the present analysis and that is referred to as "proximal."

Dimensions of the Problem

When we use the term "dimensions," we mean "defining characteristics" of battering, and we presume there are several. We feel that an analysis of these dimensions is necessary to show how social learning and cognitive-behavioral approaches can help elucidate the problem. A brief review of spouse abuse definitions may be instructive.

Definition of Battering

The definition of male-to-female violence has not been universally agreed upon. Some authorities focus on the severity of physical beatings, defining abuse in terms of the degree of injury to the victim (Stewart & deBlois, 1981; Rounsaville & Weissman, 1978). Other definitions focus on the frequency of physical abuse. Parker and Schumaker (1977) stipulated that the criteria for battering are repeated attacks (at least three times) resulting in demonstrable injury (at least a severe bruise). Barnett and Wilshire (1987) utilizes a frequency × severity algorithm to define abuse or battering. Specifically, a man is classified as a batterer if he admits to frequent episodes of less severe violence (e.g., pushing, restraining, slapping) or one or more episodes of severe violence (e.g., punching, multiple blows, using a weapon).

Straus (1977b) and Gelles and Straus (1979) define violence as comprising a continuum of acts ranging from a push to assault with or without a weapon. Within the latter scheme, particular interest and concern are devoted to the more severe actions because of the potential for physical injury to the victim. Straus (1977b), Steinmetz and Straus (1974), and Symonds (1978) distinguish between physical violence and nonphysical, psychological aspects of violence and aggression. Although the psychological concomitants of violence are viewed as important, it is actual physical violence against the person that has received the main focus of attention, based on concern for the physical safety of the victim. Ganley (1981) specifies subtypes of violence along the lines of physical assault, sexual abuse, psychological battery, and damage to property or pets. Whereas the former two subtypes typically involve physical contact with the victim's body, psychological battering and property/pet damage are more symbolic and occur in the context of the pattern of terror that the physical violence elicits.

Flynn (1977) defined violence in terms of any physically aggressive act designed to inflict bodily harm. Thus, intent, in Flynn's definition, appears to be a major defining feature. Whether or not harm is actually inflicted is of less importance. Saunders (1982) has also considered the issue of intent. According to Saunders (1982), violence refers to "the intentional use of physical force or *threatened* use of physical force to harm another" (p. 16; emphasis added). Since battering behavior is *intentional*, it has a specific purpose or *function* for the batterer. Battering is goal-directed behavior. It is through analysis of this *functional* significance of battering behavior that we are able to identify mechanisms of learning and motivation as its proximal causes.

Related to the functional significance of the abusive behavior is its impact upon the victim. This will be elaborated upon in the next section. Recently, however, researchers have begun to measure the impact of battering behaviors. Barnett and Wilshire (1987), for example, include a measure of perceived *impact* of the perpetrator's acts upon the victim. Additional research reported at the Third National Family Violence Research Conference (1987) has followed a similar track. One paper detailed the measurement of emotional abuse (Tolman, 1987), and two papers reported on batterer treatment outcome utilizing measures of psychological or emotional abuse as part of the dependent measure (Shepard, 1987; Tolman,

Beeman, & Mendoza, 1987). Steinmetz and Straus (1974) further distinguish between types of violence along a continuum of purpose (expressive-instrumental) and legitimacy (legitimate-illegitimate) (Gelles & Straus, 1979). Such a classification allows for development of a four-dimensional taxonomy of violent actions. As has been pointed out by Gelles (1980), the legitimacy dimension has been difficult to identify due to cultural and subcultural variability in what actions are considered legitimate. For example, certain types of hitting, such as spanking a child or slapping a spouse, may be considered acceptable in many families as normal disciplinary tools (Gelles, 1980).

Components of Battering

The physical contact and verbal attack of spouse abuse both involve the psychological functions of intent and consequence. The intent of the perpetrator is important because of its impact in altering the physical environment (e.g., kicking down a locked door to get in). It alters the nature of the interpersonal interaction (e.g., stopping an argument), or it alters the behavior of the spouse (e.g., forcing her to do what he wants). Although physical acts have the effect of compromising the health and safety of the victim, they may also result in other rewarding consequences for the perpetrator, as noted above. It can also be assumed that the behavior has been acquired because it has consistent effects and/or because it has been modeled by significant others in the past. Once learned, it may be precipitated and performed because of motivational states such as anger, fear and jealousy.

Nonphysical aspects of abuse, such as threats and disparagement, may also accompany physical violence (Ganley, 1981). Through learning, these nonphysical forms of abuse come to elicit similar types of emotional and physical responses in the victim and thus reduce the necessity of further violence. As a result, threatening words or gestures acquire punitive, controlling, and dominating functions. These functions are acquired through *prior* association of the words, gestures, and so forth, with actual violence and terror, as well as through their prior association with *other* language processes associated with highly negative meaning (i.e., terror and violence).

The ability of language to control the behavior of another human being (in a battering relationship) has direct implications for the health and well-being of the victim. Although the topographic (overt, observational) features of battering have direct impact, the behavior has symbolic functions as well. The overt behaviors, with their direct effects of pain and terror, function as unconditioned stimuli for the victim. The symbolic behaviors acquire conditioned (aversive) stimulus properties and function through their association with actual aggression. We believe that an analysis of both acquired language functions (including covert language) and overt behavior patterns in battering offers a useful model for conceptualizing and intervening into battering behavior.

Cognitive-Behavioral Analysis

The interventions that follow from such an analysis have been called "cognitive-behavioral." They are behavioral in that they are structured and emphasize alteration of *functional* (intentional and consequential) aspects of behavior. They are also cognitive in that they focus upon the verbal-symbolic mediators of the battering behavior. The theory from which such procedures derive is generally known as "social learning" theory, which has a large number of historical and current contributors (Bandura, 1977; Kanfer & Phillips, 1970; Patterson, 1979; Staats, 1963). Although the theory has many proponents, a more integrated and "molecular" model based on principles of learning has been proposed by Staats (1968, 1972, 1975) and has been called "social behaviorism." We will attempt to use the central concepts (and related learning mechanisms) contained in social behaviorism as a means of conceptualizing the cognitive and behavioral processes involved in the acquisition, performance, and maintenance of battering behavior. We will draw on these mechanisms as a means of identifying proximal causes of abuse, by which we mean those features specific to the individual that predispose to and precipitate threat and aggression.

Basic Behavioral Repertoires

Our analysis requires the introduction of the concept of basic behavioral repertoires (Staats, 1975), which includes the emotional-motivational, the verbal-motor, and the language-cognitive repertoires. We will describe the content and organization of these repertoires and will explain their various learning functions. For a more detailed analysis, the reader is referred to Hamberger and Lohr (1984) and Lohr and Hamberger (in press).

Spouse abuse is a subclass of other violent and aggressive behavior. It is a pattern that is familiar to the batterer in both a historical and current sense. The batterer has been witness to such behavior in the past (family of origin), and it is a regular aspect of his current intimate relationship. It is a pattern that has a particular set of features (physical contact, verbal threat/assault), and it is used consistently. As such, we may say that the behavior has the characteristics of a repertoire.

Repertoires are composed of elemental responses that are organized into subroutines, which are further organized into higher-order routines. In the case of battering behavior, there are several sub- and higher-order routines, which include motor components (acts), emotional components (feelings), and cognitive components (expectations and attributions). Basic behavioral repertoires are organized patterns of behavior that are sufficient conditions for the learning of more elaborate skills. For example, in human locomotion, the subrepertoire of crawling is necessary for the acquisition of bipedal locomotion. Bipedal locomotion first involves the development of the constituents of walking before running will occur. In addition, the reinforcing nature of more sophisticated locomotion provides the functional value of the subrepertoire. Thus, basic behavioral repertoires have both *functional* and *structural* or topographic significance.

Language Control of Behavior

Emotional-Motivational Repertoire. The most important vehicle for the interaction between the functional and structural features of behavioral repertoires is that of language. Language, as one element of cognition, is an efficient means by which events that are "not here and not now" can be responded to *as if* they were. As a consequence of this representational function, language processes take on explanatory value. Through language, an individual learns to predict and understand the world. Verbal processes (i.e., language) come to exercise control over the dimensions of behavior. Staats (1968, 1975) has argued that words can come to acquire emotional (positive and negative) properties on the basis of conditioning processes (see Figure 3.1 for an illustration). This "language conditioning" process is one in which the pairing of neutral words or objects with those having strong emotional meaning (positive or negative) results in the transfer of the emotional meaning to the formerly neutral stimuli. A common example is the manner in which ethnic or racial prejudice is acquired by associating a neutral label with pejorative words or concepts. In the context of battering, an example is name calling by the batterer. Referring to one's partner as a "slut" or a "no-good whore" is typically paired with visual and/or *imaginal* representations of the partner. Over time, the batterer emits a negative emotional response to his partner, even in the absence of name calling. He sees her not as a worthwhile human being but as a despicable object.

Moreover, through principles of conditioning and generalization, multiple labels can acquire the same basic emotional/attitudinal meaning. To continue with our example, after several repetitions of verbally labeling his partner's absence as "whoring around" and labeling his partner as a "no-good whore," the batterer has developed associations of "badness" in relation to other aspects of his partner's behavior (actual or otherwise). In a sense, he learns to associate with his partner a wide range of labels that have acquired negative meaning. Hence, not only is his partner a "whore," but she is also "lazy," "inept," "bitchy," and "manipulative." The commonality of these labels is the *negative emotional response* they elicit (see Figure 3.2 for an illustration). The negative emotional response, in turn, is capable of eliciting a wide range of behavioral responses, including, most notably, aggression. Because she (as a physical stimulus) has been associated with labels of a highly negative meaning, the spouse acquires stimulus properties. These properties include atti-

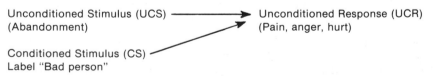

"My wife stayed out too late last night. I felt abandoned. Because she abandoned me, she is a bad person."

Unconditioned Stimulus (UCS) ⟶ Unconditioned Response (UCR)
(Abandonment)   (Pain, anger, hurt)

Conditioned Stimulus (CS)
Label "Bad person"

Figure 3.1 Development of word meaning: the motivational-emotional repertoire in battering.

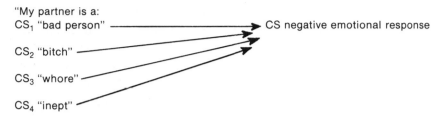

"My partner is a:
CS₁ "bad person" ⟶ CS negative emotional response
CS₂ "bitch"
CS₃ "whore"
CS₄ "inept"

Figure 3.2   Transfer/generalization of word meaning in battering.
Note: Through principles of conditioning, multiple stimuli (i.e., words/labels) can come to elicit the same basic emotional response.

tudinal properties ("She's despicable!"), reinforcing/emotional properties ("bad," "evil"), and discriminative properties ("*She's* the one" or "*Women* are all this way"). Such properties represent the emotional-motivational repertoire.

In this analysis, it is not necessary that an emotional response more specific than "negative" or "positive" be part of the emotional-motivational repertoire. This is because specific verbal labels for various feeling states are also learned according to the same principles as other aspects of language conditioning. Therefore, as pointed out by Gondolf and Russell (1986), it is not necessary to posit anger as the main underlying emotion in battering. The specific label utilized is a result of appraising and responding to internal physiological cues and external environmental cues (Lazarus & Alfert, 1964; Lazarus, Opton, Nomikos, & Rankin, 1965; Schachter & Singer, 1962). Therefore, specific emotions emitted by an individual batterer in a given situation must be determined empirically through individual assessment and cannot be assumed.

One important component of emotional arousal is physiological arousal. A considerable body of literature has evolved demonstrating the physiological basis of negative emotions and the ability of self-relevant emotionally valenced self-statements to elicit autonomic responses in humans. For example, an individual may elicit such autonomic responses by telling himself that his partner is "an awful bitch for daring to challenge my authority by whoring around on me." The statement is *self-relevant* because it involves a threat to him. It is *emotionally valenced* in terms of the meaning of the content; that is, she is "breaking" a taboo (Hamberger & Lohr, 1984, pp. 125–130). The function of the emotional-motivational repertoire is very similar to the concept of *appraisal* proposed by Lazarus and Folkman (1984) in the context of stress. Lazarus and his associates suggest that overt behavioral responses are mediated by cognitive processes. The person initially responds to a situation utilizing appraisal processes by which the situation is construed or labeled as *harm* or *threat*, or as a *challenge*. If the former labels (harm or threat) are used, they serve to mediate *defensive* responses. If the latter label (challenge) is used, it will mediate a problem-solving or other adaptive *coping* response. Lazarus as well as others (i.e., Glass, 1977; Janis & Mann, 1977; Shalit, 1977) suggests that other factors influence behavioral outcome also. Such factors include intensity of emotional arousal, *perceived* ability to respond adequately (as well as actual response availability), and a cost-benefit analysis regarding a particular strategy.

Verbal-Motor Repertoire. The content of a specific emotional-motivational repertoire, such as that regarding attitudes toward women, then, serves as the basis for the development of other basic behavioral repertoires, such as the verbal-motor repertoire. Using our example from above, calling his partner a "bitch" and a "no-good whore" elicits negative emotional responses within the batterer. The negative emotions, in turn, constitute a motivational state within the batterer to act to reduce or eliminate the aversive feelings (emotional and physiological). To extend the example, the batterer may tell himself, "If she doesn't get home by 10:30, she must be whoring around. Therefore, when she gets in the door, I'm going to let her have it." In essence, the batterer creates his own negative emotional arousal (emotional-motivational repertoire) as a function of his labeling processes and selections. He then instructs himself as to what to do (verbal-motor repertoire) about the situation to reduce his negative arousal state (see Figure 3.3 for an illustration). Note, from the example above, that it is not necessary for the primary stimulus (the man's partner) to be physically present for the basic behavioral repertoires to be learned, developed, and utilized. This is because language provides the vehicle for responding to past or anticipated events as if they were present. It is not even necessary for the female partner to have actually committed any type of "bad behavior." All that is required is that the batterer utilize a labeling (emotional-motivational) repertoire that suggests "bad," "evil," "awful" behavior on her part, for him to have a stimulus (albeit self-

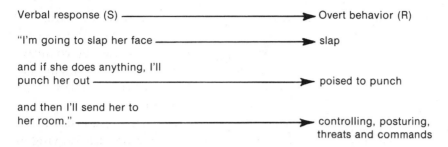

Figure 3.3   Verbal-motor repertoire.

produced) to which he can respond. The labels, through the emotional response, elicit and mediate a particular set of instrumental responses that function to control the environment (i.e., the partner) and reduce negative arousal.

Language-Cognitive Repertoire. It is language that enables a person to communicate, reason, solve problems, plan, interpret information, and so on. The language-cognitive repertoire constitutes the knowledge that the person has. Such a repertoire also allows the person to predict events and to respond by reasoning and problem solving. Three factors are generally involved in such processes. The first is the manner in which things and events are labeled. The second involves the sequencing and organization of the labels employed. Lastly, an overt act is elicited in order to influence events, and it too is represented by verbal processes. The language-cognitive repertoire provides a means of explaining the way in which language processes maintain behavior such as battering.

Labeling repertoires are learned, beginning with concrete objects or classes of objects, proceeding to more complex labeling processes, and giving rise to grammatical classes. One example of complex labeling repertoires is social and self-labeling. Complex combinations of stimuli are labeled as anger, boredom, acting suspicious, or "whoring around." Labeling processes also have important implications for effective reasoning and problem solving. The emotional valence of the labels that are used may affect reasoning. The reasoning process is likely to be adversely affected according to the degree to which such labels are inaccurate and elicit highly negative or positive emotional responses. Adaptive behavior may be interfered with, and/or maladaptive behavior may be elicited.

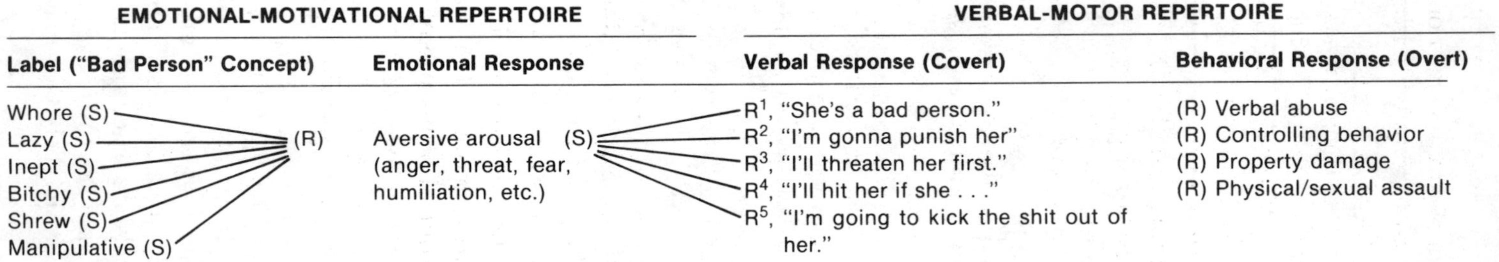

Figure 3.4 Labeling/language control over emotional arousal and behavioral response.

The initial labeling of a stimulus situation often elicits a sequence of additional verbal responses. In this way, labels for one's own behavior function as stimuli for other behavior. The particular word association sequence elicited by a label is idiosyncratic to the person, based on his or her unique learning history. To the degree that the word association sequence is consistent with the observed events, the associated reasoning and problem solving will be facilitated. Further, if overt behavior is the end point of the reasoning, then the behavior may be appropriate or inappropriate, depending on the consistency of the reasoning sequence in relation to the actual events. In the case of battering, we suggest that the reasoning sequence is usually not consistent with respect to actual events. The basis of such faulty reasoning or problem solving can often be found in deficient labeling. For example, in the case of the female spouse coming home late, an objective event ("My spouse is late") is inappropriately labeled as "bad." The word "bad" will, in turn, elicit a negative emotional response, along with an associated verbal reasoning sequence that suggests the following train of thought: "Only loose women are out late by themselves at night" (an inaccurate premise). "My wife is late. Therefore, she must be whoring around" (an inaccurate conclusion). "I'm going to have to punish and control her" (an inappropriate self-produced instruction). The likely consequence of such reasoning, then, is overt violence, verbal assault, and/or physical assault.

Language-cognitive repertoires also account for defense mechanisms observed in male batterers. For example, if the batterer minimizes his violence by labeling a fight with his wife a "slight" or "a little disagreement," he experiences much less of a negative emotional response than if he labeled his violence as "a beating" or "attempted murder." Furthermore, if the batterer considers his behavior to be under the control of his partner's actions (e.g., "If you wouldn't mess around on me, I wouldn't have to hit you"), he may further reduce his anxiety and guilt after severely beating his wife. Such verbal-cognitive constructions can also serve as reasons or justifications (excuses) for engaging in otherwise inappropriate behavior. If the batterer mislabels reality by such defensive statements, he effectively prevents the internalization of appropriate social disapproval and personal aversive consequences that might otherwise modify the problematic behavior. In this manner, the batterer contributes to his own psychological isolation—a common phenomenon observed by those who work with batterers.

Self-Control of Battering Behavior Through Language Mechanisms

One very important implication of the above discussion is that although battering may *appear* to represent a "loss of control" over "impulses," the above analysis would suggest otherwise. Indeed, by using the concept of basic behavioral repertoires, battering behavior can be clearly seen as purposeful, goal-directed, and self-produced patterns of behavior that are under the control of the batterer. Paradoxical as it may appear, the batterer not only is engaging in the control of another human being but also is exercising a form of self-control in terms of the strategies he *decides* to use, as well as the problem-solving processes he engages in to select and execute a particular strategy. This conceptualization is consistent with profeminist theory about the purposeful nature of battering behavior (Gondolf & Russell, 1986; Martin, 1985). Clinically, it is typical to observe a batterer explain a slap or a punch as a result of having "lost control." When challenged to explain why, in his state of discontrol, he did not maim or kill his partner, the batterer may explain that he had no intention (rule or strategy) of hurting her that badly.

It should be noted, in contrast, that there may exist specific deficits in basic behavioral repertoires of the batterer that also increase the probability of continued battering behavior. In studying children, for example, Camp (1977) has described what appears to be a deficiency in aggressive boys to produce nonaggressive verbal mediators or to control aggressive verbal mediators. Such boys were less likely than nonaggressive boys to tell themselves to go slowly when performing certain tasks and hence made more errors. Moreover, experimental evidence suggests that verbal stimuli can acquire the ability to direct and control such behavior (Kanfer, Karoly, & Newman, 1975; Karoly & Dirks, 1977). It could be that batterers exhibit similar deficits—inaccurate labeling tendencies (i.e., they see everything as a threat) and inappropriate problem-solving strategies—in their intimate relationships and more general attitudes toward women.

Moreover, as suggested by Staats (1975, p. 167), the ability to use self-produced verbal processes to solve problems may be related to level of intensity of negative emotional arousal (i.e., how upset one is) in the problematic situation. The more upset one is, the less efficient and appropriate will be one's own behavior. Rosenbaum and O'Leary (1981), for example, have found that batterers are less assertive than nonbatterers. Hence, intense emotional arousal, in combination with threat-oriented labeling, maladaptive problem solving, and nonviolent skills deficits, may culminate in aggressive and assaultive behavior when other behaviors are unavailable. It should be pointed out, however, that it is not necessary to assume that batterers uniformly exhibit skills deficits. Batterers are not constantly violent and in many situations may not be violent at all. As previously noted, one must also evaluate parameters such as cost-benefit analyses and problem-solving skills in the understanding of battering. These concepts suggest the operation of the language-cognitive repertoire.

Applications to the Modification of Battering

At this point, let us summarize the basic tenets of our analysis of the role of language factors in battering. First, language (and imagery) acquire the ability to elicit emotional responses that may have physiologic as well as cognitive bases. Such responses also have stimulus properties that, through learning, are able to both *direct* behavior and *reinforce* behavior. The basic processes involved in such language functions include *labeling* of both internal and external stimuli and the production of self-instructional verbal sequences (i.e., problem solving) that lead to some behavioral outcome. From a cognitive-behavioral viewpoint, wife assault is largely a function of maladaptive labeling and/or verbal self-instructions. The presentation thus far suggests a linear model of labeling → arousal → problem solving → behavior → arousal reduction (positive or negative reinforcement) and subsequent strengthening of various basic behavioral repertoires. Such learning can take place both experientially and vicariously. We suggest that battering behavior is part of a more interactional process between cognitive, physiological, and behavioral response components. Zajonc (1980), for example, has argued that much of human affective responding is not mediated by cognitions. Instead, he proposes a model in which emotional and physiological arousal is *followed* by labeling, interpreting, and verbally directive processes. This observation would be consistent with the anecdotal report of many batterers of initial intense physiological arousal, *followed* by overt behavior (battering) and ending in some type of verbal-cognitive reaction to the over-all situation. Each response component is therefore *capable* of influencing and being influenced by each of the other components. The particular sequence and functional significance of each response component in battering will differ as a function of the unique learning history of different battering males, as will be illustrated below.

Multicomponent Analysis

Battering is a complex, multicomponent phenomenon that is the outcome of the interaction of physiological, cognitive, and behavioral processes. Each of the three response components is considered a gross subclassification having many possible response combinations. Furthermore, the three response components may differ in how each is acquired and in how each functions to culminate in battering (Borkovec, 1976). The individual's learning history may result in each component being different in intensity and/or functional importance. As an example, one batterer may have begun battering as a function of the sequence spelled out above—labeling → arousal → reasoning → behavioral outcome. Across time, however, the affective-arousal component or the reasoning component may cease to have functional significance. That is, the overt behavior pattern continues solely because it has direct reinforcing effects; that is, battering gets for the batterer what he wants, regardless of the initial emotional response. Another batterer, in contrast, may have *initiated* battering on a "purely" behavioral level but *continued* the pattern after labeling it "appropriate" and "justified." Yet another batterer may respond initially with a cognitive response (e.g., a "rule") that leads directly to a behavioral outcome, bypassing emotional reactivity (e.g., "If all she does is yell, fine, but if she touches me, I'll cream her"). Some batterers, then, will be primarily "cognitive" responders, others, "behavioral," and still others, "physiological," with various levels of weaker prepotency of each of the other two response components in both the initiation and maintenance of battering patterns. This analysis suggests the importance of understanding the role of individual differences among batterers in designing assessment and intervention strategies (Hamberger & Hastings, 1986, 1987; Hersen & Barlow, 1976; Saunders, 1987).

Treatment Implications

The therapeutic task is to assess the interaction of the various response components and to determine how they lead to battering for each individual batterer. Such an evaluation involves the identification and differentiation of response-initiating variables from response-maintaining variables, as described in the previous section. It is with such an evaluation that precise targeting of verbal-behavioral and language-cognitive production deficits and of overt behavioral deficits and excesses can be accomplished prior to intervention. Procedural issues for conducting such an evaluation will be provided in Chapter 4 on cognitive-behavioral intervention strategies.

Because battering behavior is a multicomponent phenomenon, it is necessary to expand and modify what was illustrated in Figure 3.4, which emphasized the linear model of language-cognitive processes. It is not necessary to assume that cognitive factors are either the starting point or the most influential factors in any given battering incident. However, knowledge of cognitive components and processes allow us to understand the following aspects of battering behavior. First, battering is self-produced behavior. It is neither necessary nor sufficient to point to an objective, external "triggering stimulus" as a "cause" of battering. As illustrated in Figure 3.5, we can understand battering on the basis of unique, *learned* patterns of self-produced self-talk, overt behavior, and physiological arousal of the individual batterer, even in the absence of external variables. As such, the individual batterer is clearly responsible for his own behavior. Furthermore, he is assessed to be capable of and responsible for learning new, nonviolent behavior patterns. Simply put, nobody "made" him batter, and only he can change his behavior.

An important advantage of the present analysis is that specific direction is provided for assessment and intervention strategies. Moreover, the attention given to the multiple components of battering behavior by a cognitive-behavioral approach facilitates a flexible intervention approach based on the identification of individual abusive patterns. While the goal of all intervention is to eliminate all forms of battering behavior, the specific mechanism of such change may differ between batterers, even within the same structured treatment group.

There are some pitfalls of this approach that warrant discussion. One major disadvantage of a cognitive-behavioral model of

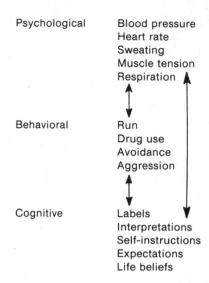

Figure 3.5   Multicomponent, interactional model of battering behavior.

battering involves a temptation to emphasize self-talk to the detri-
ment of attention to battering behavior. This undermines the very
accomplishment that cognitive-behavioral theories have achieved in
facilitating understanding of human behavior, that is, that emotions
and behaviors are affected and mediated by cognitive processes.
There is a tendency to focus on dysfunctional attitudes, irrational
beliefs, and faulty self-statements while spending relatively little
time and effort on modifying battering behavior. Although expend-
ing therapeutic effort on the cognitive components of battering
behavior is important, such targets may not always be the most
salient *unless*, through careful assessment, they are causally linked to
the initiation and/or to the maintenance of battering behaviors (and
the context in which they occur). Moreover, although cognitions are
one part of the cognitive-behavioral formula, attention to the
behavioral components that are functionally related to battering is
also critical. Although batterers may exhibit similar behavioral problems and similar cognitive "deficits," these topographically similar
behaviors may be the end products of different repertoires. Hence, a
cognitive-behavioral therapist requires flexibility in analyzing and
modifying these repertoires in the treatment of batterers.

The second weakness of the cognitive-behavioral model is in viewing battering as solely a problem of anger or stress management. Intervention approaches have been developed to assist with problems such as anxiety (Ellis, 1973), depression (Beck, 1976), stress (Meichenbaum, 1977) and pain (Turk, Meichenbaum, & Genest, 1983), and anger (Novaco, 1975). Cognitive-behavioral approaches to the treatment of batterers have borrowed heavily from these systems and thus run the risk of (1) stereotyping all batterers as anger prone or "under stress" and (2) attempting to focus treatment exclusively on managing anger and/or stress. As noted previously, cognitive-behavioral analysis does not presuppose but allows for the specification of mediation of negative emotional arousal. Hamberger and Hastings (1985, 1986) and Gondolf and Russell (1986) have argued that not all batterers can be characterized as having problems with anger management. Similarly, "stress" has not been found to be differentially characteristic of batterers versus other populations. Anger management or other types of "stress management" may be seen as *components* of batterer treatment programs but should not comprise the entire program format, nor should they be the only goals.

Societal Implications

Although we have focused primarily on proximal, intrapersonal factors that initiate and maintain battering behavior, we believe that a cognitive-behavioral analysis can be applied to a broader (distal) sociopolitical understanding of battering's etiology. Earlier, we used the term "responsibility" in our discussion of the self-control of battering behavior. We do not use the term as a synonym for "blameworthiness." The latter term may have significance for the legal system, but it is irrelevant for the purposes of implementing behavioral change interventions. Instead, we use the term "behavioral responsibility," which implies assuming the consequences of one's inappropriate behavior (fine, imprisonment, social disapprobation) and participation in the psychological change process (treatment) following the invalidation of cultural or personal "excuses" for engaging in abusive behavior. By the same token, the cultural, social, and political practices or factors by which men control, dominate, and oppress women must also be held responsible and made subject to modification. For it is within this active and dynamic matrix that basic behavioral repertoires are acquired. Boys learn to label girls in demeaning ways, and it follows directly that girls are perceived as inferior. Males may also learn that it is acceptable to use violence with a "subordinate" to achieve certain goals. The emotional-motivational, verbal-motor, and language-cognitive repertoires that derive from these experiences are further bolstered by repeated examples witnessed in the media (entertainment and news), as well as by direct daily experiences of unequal opportunities for men and women in our society. Batterers should be viewed within this broader context. Intervention with individuals or groups of batterers is viewed as taking place in the community, and it should be viewed as one component of the broader community intervention response to the problem of battery. Concretely, this involves working to change laws, policies, and procedures to conform with values of equality and to confront the wrongfulness of violence toward women. Such work also involves public and media presentations in which clear, unambiguous, and specific messages are communicated about the wrongfulness of battering behavior, with such messages being aimed at modifying behavioral, affective, and cognitive components of spouse abuse.

References

Adams, D. (1988). Counseling men who batter: A profeminist analysis of five treatment models. In M. Bograd & K. Yllö (Eds.), *Feminist perspectives on wife abuse* (pp. 176–199). Beverly Hills, CA: Sage.

Bandura, A. (1977). *Social learning theory.* New York: Prentice-Hall.

Barnett, O., & Wilshire, T. W. (1987, July). *Forms and frequencies of wife abuse.* Paper presented at the meeting of the Third National Family Violence Research Conference, University of New Hampshire, Durham, NH.

Beck, A. T. (1976). *Cognitive therapy and emotional disorders.* New York: International Universities Press.

Borkovec, T. D. (1976). Physiological and cognitive processes in the regulation of anxiety. In G. E. Schwartz & D. Shapiro (Eds.), *Consciousness and self-regulation* (pp. 261–312). New York: Plenum Press.

Caesar, P. L. (1986). Men who batter: A heterogenous group. In L. K. Hamberger (Chair), *The male batterer: Characteristics of a heterogeneous population.* Symposium presented at the meeting of the American Psychological Association, Washington, DC.

Camp, B. W. (1977). Verbal mediation in young aggressive boys. *Journal of Abnormal Psychology, 86,* 145–153.

Dobash, E. R., & Dobash, R. (1977). *Violence against wives: A case against the patriarchy.* New York: Free Press.

Ellis, A. (1973). *Humanistic psychotherapy.* New York: McGraw-Hill.

Flynn, J. P. (1977). Recent findings related to wife abuse. *Social Casework, 58,* 13–20.

Ganley, A. L. (1981). *Court mandated counseling for men who batter: A three-day workshop for mental health professionals.* (Participants' Manual). Washington, DC: Center for Women's Policy Studies.

Geller, J. A., & Wasserstrom, J. (1984). Conjoint therapy for the treatment of domestic violence. In A. R. Roberts (Ed.), *Battered women and their families: Intervention strategies and treatment programs* (pp. 33–48). New York: Springer.

Gelles, R. J. (1977). No place to go: The social dynamics of marital violence. In M. Roy (Ed.), *Battered women: A psychosociological study of domestic violence* (pp. 46–63). New York: Van Nostrand Reinhold.

Gelles, R. J. (1980). Violence in the family: A review of research in the seventies. *Journal of Marriage and the Family, 42,* 873–885.

Gelles, R. J., & Straus, M. A. (1979). Determinants of violence in the family: Toward a theoretical integration. In W. R. Burr, R. Hill, F. Ivan Nye, & I. L. Reiss (Eds.), *Contemporary theories about the family* (Vol. 1, pp. 549–581). New York: Free Press.

Glass, D. C. (1977). *Behavior patterns, stress and coronary disease.* New York: Lawrence Erlbaum Associates.

Goldberg, W., & Carey, A. L. (1982). Domestic violence victims in the emergency setting. *Topics in Emergency Medicine, 3,* 65–75.

Goldstein, D., & Rosenbaum, A. (1985). An evaluation of the self-esteem of maritally violent men. *Family Relations, 34,* 425–428.

Gondolf, E. W. (1987, July). *Who are those guys? A typology of batterers based on shelter interview.* Paper presented at the meeting of the Third National Family Violence Research Conference, University of New Hampshire, Durham, NH.

Gondolf, E., & Russell, D. (1986). The case against anger control treatment programs for batterers. *Response to the Victimization of Women and Children, 9,* 2–5.

Goodstein, R. K., & Page, A. W. (1981). Battered wife syndrome: Overview of dynamics and treatment. *American Journal of Psychiatry, 138,* 1036–1044.

Hamberger, L. K., & Hastings, J. E. (1985, March). *Personality correlates of men who abuse their partners: Some preliminary data.* Paper presented at the meeting of the Society of Personality Assessment, Berkeley, CA.

Hamberger, L. K., & Hastings, J. E. (1986). Personality correlates of men who abuse their partners: A cross-validation study. *Journal of Family Violence, 1,* 323–341.

Hamberger, L. K., & Hastings, J. E. (1987, April). The male batterer and alcohol abuse: Differential personality characteristics. In O. W. Barnett (Chair), *The male batterer: Alcohol use, jealousy and consequences of abuse.* Symposium presented at the meeting of the Western Psychological Association, Long Beach, CA.

Hamberger, L. K., & Lohr, J. M. (1984). *Stress and stress management: Research and applications.* New York: Springer.

Hastings, J. E., & Hamberger, L. K. (1988). Personality characteristics of spouse abusers: A controlled comparison. *Violence and Victims, 3*(1), 31–48.

Hersen, J., & Barlow, D. (1976). *Single case experimental designs.* New York: Pergamon Press.

Janis, I. L., & Mann, L. (1977). Emergency decision making: A theoretical analysis of responses to disaster warnings. *Journal of Human Stress, 3,* 35–47.

Kanfer, F. H., Karoly, P., & Newman, A. (1975). Reduction of children's fear of the dark by competence-related and situational threat-related verbal cues. *Journal of Consulting and Clinical Psychology, 43,* 251–258.

Kanfer, F. H., & Phillips, J. S. (1970). *Learning foundations of behavioral therapy.* New York: Wiley.

Karoly, P., & Dirks, M. J. (1977). Developing self-control in preschool children through correspondence training. *Behavioral Therapy, 8,* 398–405.

Kiesler, D. J. (1966). Some myths of psychotherapy research and the search for paradigm. *Psychological Bulletin, 65,* 110–136.

Lazarus, R., & Folkman, S. (1984). *Stress, appraisal and coping.* New York: Springer.

Lazarus, R. S., & Alfert, E. (1964). Short-circuiting of threat by experimentally altering cognitive appraisal. *Journal of Abnormal Psychology, 69,* 192–205.

Lazarus, R. S., Opton, E. M., Nomikos, M. S., & Rankin, M. O. (1965). The principle of short-circuiting of threat: Further evidence. *Journal of Personality, 33,* 622–635.

Lohr, J. M., & Hamberger, L. K. (in press). Verbal and emotional repertoires in the regulation of dysfunctional behavior. In I. M. Evans (Ed.), *Paradigmatic behavior therapy: Critical perspectives on applied social behaviors.* New York: Springer.

Martin, D. (1985). Domestic violence: A sociological perspective. In D. J. Sonkin, D. Martin, & L. E. A. Walker (Eds.), *The male batterer: A treatment approach* (pp. 1–32). New York: Springer.

Mederos, F. (1987, July). *Theorizing continuities and discontinuities between normal men and abusive men: Work in progress.* Paper presented at the meeting of the Third National Family Violence Research Conference, University of New Hampshire, Durham, NH.

Meichenbaum, D. (1977). *Cognitive behavior modification.* New York: Plenum Press.

Novaco, R. W. (1975). *Anger control: The development and evaluation of an experimental treatment.* Lexington, MA: Lexington Books.

Parker, B., & Schumacher, D. N. (1977). The battered wife syndrome and violence in the nuclear family origin: A controlled pilot study. *American Journal of Public Health, 67,* 760-761.

Patterson, G. R. (1979). Behavioral techniques based upon social learning. In C. M. Franks (Ed.), *Behavior therapy: Appraisal and status.* New York: McGraw-Hill.

Pence, E., & Paymar, M. (1985). *Criminal justice response to domestic assault cases: A guide for policy development.* Duluth, MN: Minnesota Program Development, Inc.

Roberts, A. R. (1984). Preface. In A. R. Roberts (Ed.), *Battered women and their families: Intervention strategies and treatment programs* (pp. ix-x). New York: Springer.

Rosenbaum, A., & O'Leary, K. D. (1981). Marital violence: Characteristics of abusive couples. *Journal of Consulting and Clinical Psychology, 49,* 63-71.

Rounsaville, B. J. (1978). Theories in marital violence: Evidence from a study of battered women. *Victimology: An International Journal, 3,* 11-31.

Rounsaville, B. J., & Weissman, M. M. (1978). Battered women: A medical problem requiring detection. *International Journal of Psychiatry in Medicine, 8,* 191-202.

Saunders, D. G. (1982). Counseling the violent husband. In P. A. Keller & L. G. Ritt (Eds.), *Innovations in clinical practice: A source book* (Vol. 1, pp. 16-29). Sarasota, FL: Professional Resource Exchange.

Saunders, D. G. (1987, July). *Are there different types of men who batter? An empirical study with possible implications for treatment.* Paper presented at the Third National Family Violence Research Conference, University of New Hampshire, Durham, NH.

Scott, M. E. (1980). The battered spouse syndrome. *Virginia Medical Journal, 107,* 41-43.

Schachter, S., & Singer, J. (1962). Cognitive, social and physiological determinants of emotional state. *Psychological Review, 69,* 379-399.

Shalit, B. (1977). Structural ambiguity and limits to coping. *Journal of Human Stress, 3,* 32-46.

Shepard, M. (1987, July). *Intervention with men who batter: An evaluation of a domestic abuse program.* Paper presented at the meeting of the Third National Family Violence Research Conference, University of New Hampshire, Durham, NH.

Staats, A. W. (1963). *Complex human behavior.* New York: Holt, Rinehart & Winston. (With contributions by C. K. Staats)

Staats, A. W. (1968). *Learning, language and cognition.* New York: Holt, Rinehart & Winston.

Staats, A. W. (1972). Language behavior therapy: A derivative of social behaviorism. *Behavior Therapy, 3,* 165–192.

Staats, A. W. (1975). *Social behaviorism.* Homewood, IL: Dorsey Press.

Stahly, G. B. (1978). A review of select literature of spousal violence. *Victimology: An International Journal, 2,* 591–607.

Stark, E., Flitcraft, A., & Frazier, W. (1979). Medicine and patriarchal violence: The social construction of a "private" event. *International Journal of Health Services, 9,* 461–493.

Steinmetz, S. K., & Straus, M. A. (1974). General introduction: Social myths and social system in study of intra-family violence. In S. K. Steinmetz & M. A. Straus (Eds.), *Violence in the family* (pp. 3–24). New York: Dodd, Mead.

Stewart, M. A., & deBlois, C. S. (1981). Wife abuse among families attending a child psychiatry clinic. *Journal of the American Academy of Child Psychiatry, 20,* 845–862.

Straus, M. A. (1976). Sexual inequality, cultural norms, and wife beating. *Victimology: An International Journal, 1,* 54–76.

Straus, M. A. (1977a). A sociological perspective on the prevention and treatment of wife-beating. In M. Roy (Ed.), *Battered women: A psychosociological study of domestic violence* (pp. 194–239). New York: Van Nostrand Reinhold.

Straus, M. A. (1977b). Wife-beating: How common and why? *Victimology: An International Journal, 2,* 402–418.

Symonds, M. (1978). The psychodynamics of violence-prone marriages. *The American Journal of Psychoanalysis, 38,* 213–222.

Tolman, R. M. (1987, July). *The development and validation of a scale of nonphysical abuse.* Paper presented at the meeting of the Third National Family Violence Research Conference, University of New Hampshire, Durham, NH.

Tolman, R. M., Beeman, S., & Mendoza, C. (1987, July). *The effectiveness of a shelter-sponsored program for men who batter: Preliminary results.* Paper presented at the meeting of the Third National Family Violence Research Conference, University of New Hampshire, Durham, NH.

Turk, D. C., Meichenbaum, D., & Genest, M. (1983). *Pain and behavioral medicine: A cognitive-behavioral perspective.* New York: Guilford Press.

Westra, B., & Martin, H. P. (1981). Children of battered women. *Maternal-Child Nursing Journal, 10,* 41–54.

Zajonc, R. B. (1980). Feelings and thinking: Preferences need no inferences. *American Psychologist, 35,* 151–175.

4
Cognitive and Behavioral Interventions with Men Who Batter: Application and Outcome

Daniel G. Saunders

The preceding chapter by Hamberger and Lohr laid the theoretical foundation for cognitive-behavioral interventions. The authors made clear the advantages of analyzing multiple dimensions of abuse and its multiple causes within the batterer. This chapter will describe the ways in which cognitive and behavioral principles are commonly applied in the treatment of men who batter. It will also describe how the principles can be used to guide large-scale interventions that may not be thought of as treatment per se. The advantages and limitations of the approach will be explained, and a brief review of outcome studies will be presented.

There is no monolithic theory or integrated set of procedures that can be called "cognitive-behavioral." Rather, the term covers a collection of principles and procedures that many practitioners have not attempted to link theoretically. Cognitive and behavioral treatments have their roots in the principles and procedures of operant conditioning and classical conditioning. Bandura's (1969, 1977) social learning theory emphasized the cognitive aspects of these two conditioning principles and demonstrated in addition that much behavior is learned through imitation or modeling, without being externally conditioned. One of Bandura's (1973) first applications of social learning theory was with the problem of aggression. Reviews of empirical studies of behavioral treatment of aggressive disorders have been published (Fehrenbach & Thelan, 1982). Modern social learning theory highlights the reciprocal influence of people and their environment and emphasizes the human capacity for self-directed change. Operant and classical conditioning and modeling usually fall under the rubric of behavior therapy, whereas cognitive therapy has three major forms: rational psychotherapies, coping-skills training, and problem solving (Mahoney & Arnkoff, 1978). O'Leary (1988) applies a social learning model to factors associated with wife abuse and finds that many factors fit the model well, for example, violence in the family of origin, stress, and alcohol abuse.

Cognitive and behavioral approaches, especially assertiveness training and relaxation training, have been quite popular in working with men who batter. National surveys of abuser programs show that the use of these procedures is widespread in all types of settings, including shelter-based and specialized programs, as well as more traditional service agencies (Eddy & Myers, 1984; Feazell, Mayers, & Deschner, 1984). Other methods are also popular and are usually combined with cognitive-behavioral methods. The other commonly used methods include the building of emotional awareness, sex role resocialization, and the development of social support.

Definition of Battering

Battering is defined in this chapter as any attempt to intentionally cause physical hurt or to restrain another person, whether or not injury actually results. In other words, throwing an object with the intention of hurting another would qualify as battery whether or not the object hit the person. This definition is obviously broader than the usual legal one but is consistent with most researchers' definition of physical aggression (Gelles & Straus, 1979). "Battery" in this sense is the same as "physical aggression" and covers the full range of severity from a slap to sexual assault to the use of a knife or gun. "Abuse" is a broader term with political connotations and refers to intended psychological as well as physical hurt. It includes threats, withholding of affection, and sexual coercion. "Aggression" will refer to both physical and verbal behavior.

Application of Cognitive and Behavioral Principles

The description of cognitive and behavioral applications will be presented in the context of general principles that have been developed, tested, and applied to the alleviation of many types of problems. The application of cognitive-behavioral methods in working with men who batter usually consists of a combination of methods, most commonly assertiveness training, relaxation training, and some of the cognitive therapies (Edleson, 1984b; Ganley, 1981; Neidig & Friedman, 1984; Saunders, 1984; Sonkin & Durphy, 1982). As mentioned above, these methods are usually combined with other methods, such as sex role resocialization. They are most often used in either a men's group or couples' group format. Some cognitive-behavioral methods emphasize the consequences for behavior, and these have the potential for more use as the criminal justice system becomes more involved in addressing the problem. Practitioners are also increasingly aware that different types of abusers may respond best to different types of intervention; thus, treatment methods can be tailored to suit the type of abuser.

Contingency Management

The application of operant principles is called *contingency management* because the immediate consequences, or contingencies, of behavior are modified. Aggression, like alcohol abuse, is a difficult behavior to treat because the abuser's discomfort and pain from the behavior are often delayed for a considerable period of time. The rewards, on the other hand, may be immediate, including "having one's way" or a reduced fear of abandonment if the partner threatens to leave and then stays. The analysis of rewards and punishers fits the exchange/social control model described by Gelles (1983). Operant principles include not only punishment and positive reinforcement but also extinction and negative reinforcement. Operant conditioning is most often used for the treatment of aggressive children, adolescents, and institutionalized adults. For example, positive reinforcement of behaviors incompatible with aggression (e.g., empathy) and removal of reinforcement for aggressive behaviors (extinction) are commonly used, and the support for their effectiveness is substantial (see Carr, 1981, for a review).

Men entering abuser programs are often motivated to attend the programs out of a fear of punishment, either the formal punishment of criminal justice sanctions or that of losing their partners. Fear of punishment may also have an impact on the abusive behavior itself. When women tell their partners they will not return to them until they enter or complete treatment, they are applying negative reinforcement—his pain will end when he complies. There is growing evidence that arrest (Langan & Innes, 1986; Sherman & Berk, 1984), fear of arrest (Carmody & Williams, 1987), and warnings of legal action from women (Bowker, 1983) are deterrents of further abuse. There is also evidence, however, that arrest alone is not enough and that arrest plus treatment is much more effective (Dutton, 1986).

In order to make abusers more aware of the potential rewards and costs for aggression, Steinfeld (1986) gives examples of questions that therapists can ask them:

Gain via the aggressive behavior
"What specifically Joe, did you want to happen when you hit Mary?"
Responses might include factors such as
(1) Remove aversive behavior—"She was nagging me"; "I wanted to get away."
(2) Vindictiveness—"I wanted to hurt her back."
(3) Power—"I felt so helpless with her; I wanted to get through to her; to hear me out; I wanted to beat her to a pulp."
(4) Control—"I should tell her what to do"; "I'm the boss."
(5) Ego enhancement—"If I let her do that, what kind of man would I be? I can't let her push me around."

Strength of punishment
"What specifically did you feel might happen if you hit her?" Responses might include:
(1) "Nothing."
(2) "She could hit me back, kill me, she could leave."
(3) "Cops would come—things would blow over."
(4) "I could go to jail."
(5) "I would be fined."

Probability of Payoff
"What is the likelihood that the above (punishment, response costs) would actually occur?"

Another way to make negative consequences more salient is with covert sensitization (Cautela, 1967). Through imagery, the aggressive behavior is paired with aversive thoughts such as sitting in jail or losing one's partner. An image of constructive behavior is used to relieve the aversive scene (see Saunders, 1977, for a case example).

Incarceration is obviously a drastic intervention. It acts to remove the usual positive reinforcement from the abuser and provides a severe form of punishment. Since the operant conditioning literature suggests that the consequences for behavior are most powerful if they are immediate and certain (Carr, 1981), therapists can work with the criminal justice system to create contracts that include jail time. This is most feasible when the men are on probation or parole, because the system can respond quickly yet flexibly under these conditions. These methods are likely to work best for premeditated, instrumental violence, because the offender must be able to weigh the response costs and see the deterrent effects of punishment. The perceptions of offenders who are intensely angry may be too clouded to permit them to assess the costs of their behavior (Steinfeld, 1986).

One component of the behavioral treatment of men who batter that has an element of extinction (the removal of positive reinforcement for the problem behavior) is the time-out technique. With time-out, the abuser recognizes the buildup of anger, tells his partner he is taking a time-out, and then leaves for an hour or more in order to cool off (Sonkin & Durphy, 1982). It is meant to be a time-out from conflict and angry emotions, but it may also operate as an extinction technique, because the abuser does not get his way.

The shame, guilt, and anxiety that some men feel following their aggression, either from external sources or internal ones, is probably a short-lived means of behavior change. Indeed, for the type of man who already feels excessive guilt, more punishment may increase his aggressiveness. Behavior therapists recommend that if punishment is used at all, that it be quickly followed by an offer to teach clients positive behavior. Positive reinforcement is used most commonly in treating men who batter by giving praise for learning skills that are incompatible with aggression. Naturally, this reinforcement will be more powerful if a positive relationship has been formed with the client, which can often occur through an understanding of the client's feelings and acceptance of his humanness. In a group setting, the men can be taught to praise one another by making specific, reinforcing comments both for reports of progress during the week and for acquiring skills during the sessions. This peer support appears to be one of the strongest forms of reinforcement the men can receive, and they report that it is a very useful part of the group experience (Gondolf, 1984). The support is one of the ways the men can decrease the strong dependence for praise and acceptance they often have on their partners. The men's overdependence on others can be lowered even more if they learn to praise themselves, a skill emphasized by some cognitive therapists (to be described later).

Because many of the men have low self-esteem, it may be very difficult for them to accept praise or to think of ways in which they have made progress. One way to overcome this is to begin each group session with each man stating one way in which he applied a skill used in the group. When a man says "nothing" as his response, it may take several prompts to encourage him to relate a success. In later sessions, the men are taught to give specific, positive feedback to one another as they are acquiring skills.

One of the reinforcers that appears to maintain abusive patterns is inadvertently given by women after their partners' coercion or abuse. It is part of the cycle of violence which includes a honeymoon phase after the violence (Deschner, 1984; Walker, 1984). Out of her fear, she may give in to his coercion, placate him after the abuse, or agree to stay after threatening to leave. In a case study, Follingstad (1980) showed how a battered woman systematically changed the contingencies for her partner's obsessive phone calling. The consequences for noncompliance were carefully stated for him, along with positive alternative strategies. Before trying the procedure, the behaviors were carefully role played so that she could carry them out even under stress if necessary. She was able to relabel his attributions about her motives and give him positive alternatives, for example, "If you'll calm down and speak to me quietly, I'll come visit you after I return from my trip." Just as with children whose tempers initially become worse when they are ignored, the client was also warned that her partner's behavior might become worse before it became better. It should be noted that the procedure was part of comprehensive counseling that included advice on legal options. One of the clearest contingencies the couple can agree to as part of couples' treatment is that she will separate temporarily or permanently if there is further abuse (Saunders, 1977; Steinfeld, 1986).

Arousal Reduction

Although anger is neither a necessary nor sufficient condition for woman abuse or other forms of aggression (Hamberger & Lohr, Chapter 3, this volume; Novaco, 1978), it is often associated with it. One of the necessary ingredients of anger and other emotions, however, is physiological arousal. Thus, if arousal can be decreased, anger can be decreased as well. Behavior therapists have long used relaxation training, biofeedback, and similar methods to treat anxiety. These same methods are now being used to reduce the arousal component of anger in men who batter and also the stress reactions that are antecedents of anger. Relaxation as a coping skill for anger reduction in the general population has received empirical support (Deffenbacher, Demm, & Brandon, 1986, Novaco, 1976). Although one study indicated that it had the most powerful effect when combined with stress inoculation (Novaco, 1975), this is not a consistent finding (Hazaleus & Deffenbacher, 1986). The most common way for physiological arousal to be reduced is to teach progressive relaxation (Bernstein & Borkevec, 1973). A large number of muscle groups are used at first, with the therapist instructing the client to alternately tense and relase them. As the client gains experience, fewer muscle groups are used, with the client eventually being able to relax quickly by simply recalling the feelings of relaxation or by repeating a word that has been associated with the relaxed state. Because the training is usually conducted in a prone position with eyes closed, many men may resist practicing the exercises. This resistance may be especially pronounced in a group setting with other aggressive men. Some men feel more comfortable in a sitting position or turned away from the group.

As an adjunct or substitute for progressive relaxation, some men may find other relaxation methods are useful. There are a number of possible substitutes for relaxation that appeal to men, for example, biofeedback (because it is "high-tech") or Tai Chi, the martial art that is a form of exercise, relaxation, and meditation. Aerobic exercise may also be more appealing, and there is some recent evidence for its stress-reducing qualities (Raglin & Morgan, 1985).

Relaxation can be practiced as an active coping skill by having clients imagine an anger-produced situation, becoming aware of internal cues, and then actively relaxing away anger (Deffenbacher & Suinn, 1982). This procedure differs from the passive counterconditioning methods of desensitization developed by Wolpe (1958).

Classical Conditioning

Once relaxation is mastered, it can be combined with a series of anger-producing scenes in a classical conditioning paradigm. Studies of desensitization have been conducted for the treatment of dysfunctional anger, usually in single case designs (e.g., Herrell, 1971) but also in group comparison designs with no-treatment control groups (e.g., Hearn & Evans, 1972). Reviews of these studies show that desensitization is a promising method for treating dysfunctional anger and aggression (Warren & McLellarn, 1982). Studies have yet to be conducted of treatment for men who batter in which desensitization is the sole treatment.

In the application of this method, we do not use the term "desensitization" but rather refer to the method as an "anger ladder." For homework, the client constructs a "ladder" of about five scenes, from the least to the most upsetting. Following relaxation, the therapist alternates a calm scene with an anger-arousing scene several times, until the stress or anger of the anger-arousing scene is lessened or eliminated. It is important to begin with a scene very low in anger, otherwise the method will be ineffective. If a man reports no progress, he may need extra help constructing scenes low on the hierarchy. For example, instead of a scene of his boss yelling at him, he may need a less upsetting one, perhaps of waiting for a train to pass on the way home from work.

Modeling and Rehearsal

The behavioral methods of modeling and rehearsal as means of learning new behaviors have a strong empirical foundation (Bandura, 1977). The methods based on these principles are used to help the men acquire assertive and other social skills that are incompatible with aggression. Support for the methods comes from both nonexperimental (Foy, Eisler, & Pinkston, 1975; Howells, 1976; Rimm, 1977) and experimental (Allen, 1978; Moon & Eisler, 1983) studies in which subjects had general anger problems, not necessarily in the home. In a study comparing cognitive relaxation treatment with social skills training, both methods appeared to be equally effective (subjects reported somewhat more satisfaction with the cognitive relaxation treatment) (Deffenbacher, Story, Stark, Hogg, & Brandon, 1987). Social skills like assertiveness are appropriate for incidents in which anger is justified and the man is typically passive but eventually blows up. They can also be applied if the man is typically dominant and impulsive. Several studies indicate that men who batter are generally nonassertive (Hotaling & Sugarman, 1986; Maiuro, Cahn, & Vitaliano, 1986), but there also appears to be a subtype of men who are generally dominant and aggressive both inside and outside of the home (Fagan, Stewart, & Hansen, 1983; Saunders, 1987).

Assertiveness training is intended to teach the men to cope with criticism, make requests, say "no" assertively, empathize with others' feelings, or express feelings. The emphasis is on responsible assertiveness and egalitarian decision making (Saunders, 1984; Saunders & Hanusa, 1986). The group leader models each skill in a role play and then guides each client through a role play rehearsal using a "canned" situation. The skills can then be applied to real life situations that the men are asked to define specifically. They are helped to define a "critical moment" in which an assertive rather than a passive or aggressive path could have been taken. After a skill is applied in a role play rehearsal, the men receive constructive feedback from the leader and group members. The feedback focuses on nonverbal as well as verbal communication. The client then rehearses the situation again using the feedback. Very often these situations do not involve the partner at all but rather a stressful problem at work, which is a major source of stress for many of the men (Barling & Rosenbaum, 1986). The steps of behavioral rehearsal are described in detail in a number of leader manuals (Lange & Jakubowski, 1976; Rose, Hanusa, Tolman, & Hall, 1982). One of the indirect ways of teaching flexible sex role behavior and egalitarian decision making is to use a male-female therapy team that acts as a model of such behavior.

Cognitive Techniques

Cognitive methods are among the most difficult to apply because the men are required to become introspective and focus on "irrational" or "automatic" thoughts. The methods are important, however, because they clearly place responsibility for anger arousal on the individual, not on the interaction. In contrast to social skills training, they also have the advantage of being applied to situations that are not interpersonal—for example, anger that might result from bad weather, lost keys, or being stuck in a traffic jam.

The most common cognitive methods used with men who batter are those Novaco (1975, 1978) adapted from the stress inoculation work of Meichenbaum (1977). This cognitive model explains aggression in several steps. First, one has certain unmet expectations or faulty appraisals of aversive events. The subsequent arousal is labeled as anger, which then often leads to aggression. Along with Novaco's original test of the treatment, there is some controlled research showing its effectiveness with forensic patients (Stermac, 1987). First, clients are given the rationale that anger is often related to self-doubt or feelings of threat. They are taught to distinguish between self-defeating statements and self-enhancing statements that will help them to cope. If these are difficult to uncover, the men can be placed in a role play situation until anger is aroused and then can be asked to "talk aloud" their anger-producing self-talk. They are then taught to use self-statements at various stages of a situation that typically arouses anger. The situations are made more manageable by breaking them into stages: preparation, entering the situation, coping with arousal, and reflection after the situation. Novaco gives examples of each stage: "Remember, stick to the issue and don't take it personally" (preparation); "You don't need to prove yourself. Don't make more out of this than you have to" (confronting the situation); "Muscles are getting tight. Relax and slow things down" (arousal); "I handled that one pretty well. That's doing a good job" (conflict resolved); "Try to shake it off. Don't let it interfere with your job" (conflict unresolved). Such coping statements can be given to the men to use, but it will probably be more effective if the men shape their own statements. Often the statements are not very "believable" at first. Relaxation combined with the statements may help them to "sink in" and feel more real. The men may also need help reshaping some of the statements, trying out ones suggested by the therapist until one is at least somewhat believable.

Other cognitive methods have also been applied. For example, Edleson (1984b) applied Ellis's (1977) Rational Emotive Therapy (RET) in a group for men who batter. RET helps clients confront their irrational beliefs that lead to unrealistic expectations of themselves and others. The premise is that anger is likely to result if men believe they *must* always have the love and approval of those close to them. Anger may also be aroused if they believe that they must be thoroughly competent in all they do, or if they view life as catastrophic when things do not go the way that they want. Ellis gives numerous examples of ways to understand and dispute self-angering philosophies. He divides the analysis of self-statements into four categories. For instance, in response to a broken agreement a rational belief would be "What a bad action!" An irrational belief would be "How *awful*; I just can't stand her treating me in that manner. She *should not, must not* behave in that way toward me, and I think that she is a *horrible person* for doing so and that she *should be punished!*" An appropriate consequence to a broken agreement would be disappointment and feelings of rejection; an inappropriate consequence would be feelings of hostility and the desire for revenge or punishment. Meichenbaum (1977) makes the point that the presence of irrational beliefs may not be the problem as much as a lack of coping techniques; thus, cognitive and behavioral coping skills may be essential. Ellis also emphasizes the need to practice new behaviors outside of therapy.

Closely related to RET is Beck's analysis of dysfunctional cognitive styles. These styles include the tendency to make arbitrary inferences, to magnify the meaning of an event, to use rigid, "black and white" thinking, and to overgeneralize (e.g., taking a single mistake as a sign of incompetence). Bedrosian (1982) shows how he helped a husband detect his automatic thoughts that revealed his cognitive styles:

THERAPIST: What were you thinking when your wife came home?

HUSBAND: I don't remember. It was just bullshit.

THERAPIST: Okay. Can you remember where you were and what you were thinking when you first realized she was late?

HUSBAND: Well, I was sitting downstairs on the couch. The first thing I thought was, what if she had an accident?

THERAPIST: How did you feel then?

HUSBAND: Scared. I remembered her accident from last month.

THERAPIST: So then what did you think when she came home?

HUSBAND: First I was relieved. Then I thought, she's always doing this to me, she doesn't give a shit about me, all I do is work my tail off for this family, and this is the thanks I get.

THERAPIST: And then you hit the ceiling. (p. 128)

Bedrosian explains how the husband would experience fear when he thought about threats to his wife's safety and then disappointment when she did not call him. These feelings quickly turned into anger, however, because he interpreted her actions as personally directed at him.

Another cognitive therapy, called problem-solving treatment, (D'Zurilla & Goldfried, 1971), has not been used directly with abusers. However, the mutual problem solving and support that occurs in many Batterers Anonymous self-help groups uses many of the steps of systematic problem solving. Thought stopping is another seldom used cognitive method that seems to work well with some clients. It pairs an aversive event (like a loud noise) with the client's irrational ruminations. It works best for obsessive thoughts, like those surrounding irrational jealousy, that the client knows are false but cannot seem to shake.

Cognitive methods are especially compatible with feminist approaches. They can be used to change the feelings of threat that the men may feel from women's independence and competence. Cognitive restructuring can help turn typical male "scripts" of possessiveness, competition, and achievement striving into more flexible behavior. For example, the self-statement "I must win every argument" can be transformed into the self-statement "If I win, our relationship loses."

By the end of treatment, it should be possible to integrate most of the cognitive-behavioral skills that have been described above. For example, in preparing for a situation, a client should be able to assess the costs and rewards of keeping aggressive behavior, identify and restructure cognitive distortions, relax away tension, and communicate assertively. The building blocks of skills that were constructed throughout treatment can hopefully be combined quickly into a new way of feeling, thinking, and relating.

Advantages and Disadvantages

There are a number of advantages to the use of the methods just described. First, they are based on empirically derived principles that have been used with other aggressive populations, and they can be evaluated more easily than most. For example, role play assessments can be conducted inside or outside of a group setting, with ratings of skill acquisition made by leaders and/or members. Changes in cognitions, of course, are more difficult to measure. However, self-report measures are available for irrational beliefs (Jones, 1969), general expectations of others (Eisler, Frederiksen, & Peterson, 1978), attitudes toward women (Spence & Helmreich, 1978), and attitudes about woman abuse (Saunders, Lynch, Grayson, & Linz, 1987). Second, because the methods are concrete and skill-based, clients often greet them with less resistance, they can be learned relatively quickly, and the methods can be transferred between programs. Third, the methods are quite compatible with feminist approaches and with the goals of the criminal justice system. The methods do not presume that the violence is the symptom of an underlying mental disorder or relationship problem. Rather, the anger and violence are usually addressed directly. Finally, because the methods are based on the assumption that aggression is learned behavior over which self-control is possible, clients and practitioners may have more hope for change than when faced with instinctual or genetic theories of aggression. The methods also show promise for treating the risk factors associated with woman abuse, such as jealousy (Cobb & Marks, 1979; Teismann, 1979), alcoholism (Miller & Munoz, 1976), and child abuse (Wolfe, Kaufman, Aragona, & Sandler, 1981).

Among the disadvantages, there is the risk that the methods will not be able to overcome the social reinforcement for woman abuse in patriarchal society unless they are integrated with a profeminist approach (Gondolf & Russell, 1986) As with some other approaches, cognitive-behavioral methods may seem like a "quick fix" to the men, their partners, and therapists, and false hopes may develop after short-term gains are made. However, the methods seem to offer the best hope for stopping the abuse quickly so that other methods can be used (Tolman & Saunders, 1988). Another disadvantage, if the partners are not well informed about the training, is that the men's first attempts to communicate in new ways may bring negative comments from their partners, who see the behavior as phony. Finally, it has become clear that most of the men were traumatized as children, either by being abused or by witnessing their mothers being abused (Hotaling & Sugarman, 1986). If violence in the nuclear family is due to displaced aggression or unresolved anger from childhood, then cognitive-behavioral methods may be less effective for long-term change than methods that attempt to directly resolve early trauma (e.g., Jennings, 1987).

Evaluations of Outcome

Several early case studies indicated that cognitive-behavioral methods held some promise for treating abusers. The techniques used in the studies included thought stopping (Bass, 1973), assertiveness training (Foy et al., 1975), behavioral contracting, communication training and problem solving (Margolin, 1979; Saunders, 1977), and a combination of assertiveness training, relaxation training, and RET (Edleson, Miller, Stone, & Chapman, 1985).

More recently, large-scale outcome studies have been conducted. Most of these studies evaluated "packages" of cognitive-behavioral methods (cognitive restructuring, relaxation training, and assertiveness training) combined with sex role resocialization. A couple of studies relied on the abusers' reports of recidivism. DeMaris and Jackson (1987), for example, asked former clients to return mailed questionnaires. For couples living together, about 40% of the men reported a recurrence of abuse. However, only 17% of the clients responded to the questionnaire, and these were the ones least likely to have problems initially. The use of time-outs and awareness of the physical signs of anger were related to reports of decreased violence.

Kelso and Personette (1985) contacted men over the course of 6 months of treatment. Of the men contacted (about half of the sample), the recidivism rate ranged from 4% to 22% for any particular month. Mental abuse was more likely to recur (35% to 61%). One of the factors that deflated the reports of recidivism was that the data included reports from separated couples. Those who completed treatment reported less violence than those who left treatment.

Saunders and Hanusa (1986) used a pre-post design with a sample of men who had completed group treatment. There were significant decreases in the men's reports of depression, anger toward partners, anger over work or friend situations, and jealousy. The men reported more liberal attitudes about sex roles after treatment. All of the changes were maintained after statistically controlling for social desirability response bias. For a subsample, the decreases in anger corresponded to decreases in violence reported by the women.

Maiuro and his associates (Maiuro et al., 1987) compared men on a waiting list who received minimal treatment with men who completed treatment. The treated men reported decreases in levels of anger, depression, and maladaptive coping and increases in problem-focused coping. The waiting list group reported positive change on only 1 of the 12 scales used. A subsample of the treated group showed the persistence of change, when contacted a year after treatment.

Three studies report on the use of a couples' group format. In a study by Deschner (Deschner, 1984; Deschner & McNeil, 1986), after treatment the men reported being less nervous, depressed, inhibited, and submissive on the Taylor-Johnson Temperament Analysis. Scores on "hostility" and five other subscales did not change significantly. Over the course of treatment, the rate of violence decreased by 50%. At 8 months follow-up, 15% of those who could be reached (about half the sample) said that violence had not recurred. However, some of these couples were separated at the time of follow-up.

Myers (1984) evaluated a combination of 6 months of psychotherapy and skills training. The abusers showed significant improvement in affective and problem-solving communication and decreases in depression and psychopathy on the Minnesota Multiphasic Personality Inventory (MMPI). They also improved significantly on a measure of child abuse potential.

Neidig's (1986) evaluation of a couples' treatment program relied on the Dyadic Adjustment Scale and a measure of locus of control. Of the 40 men who completed treatment, there were significant improvements in consensus, satisfaction, and cohesion in the relationship and a greater internal locus of control.

A controversy continues over the use of a couples' format. Some clinicians who favor it claim that it lessens the stigma on the abuser and emphasizes the "systems" aspects of the abuse (Neidig, 1984). Those who oppose it claim that the victim is placed at risk for further abuse if she talks about the abuse with the abuser present or discloses her plans to leave him. There is also the risk that joint sessions will equalize the responsibility for the abuse (Edleson, 1984a).

Because reports on violence from women are likely to be more reliable than reports from men, a number of studies of men's groups rely on women's reports. Edleson and Grusznski (1989) report on three studies from the Minnneapolis Domestic Abuse Project that used reports of violence from the men's partners. The first study assessed a combination of cognitive-behavioral and self-help treatment (also reported by Lund et al., 1982). Of the partners who could be contacted an average of 6 months after treatment (66% of the sample), 23% of the women whose partners completed treatment reported recurrence of violence, compared with 46% of the women whose partners dropped from treatment. The level of threats, however, did not differ between the two groups. The men reported that they became less traditional in their views of women's roles and improved their levels of affective communication.

A second study assessed cognitive-behavioral treatment that was followed by traditional group psychotherapy. At an average of 9 months after treatment, 32% of the women reported that violence recurred. About three-fourths of the men, however, continued to make threats.

In a third study, the cognitive-behavioral and psychotherapy combination was again evaluated. During about 6 months following treatment, 15% of the completers and 22% of the noncompleters were reported to be severely violent. However, for all forms of violence, the difference between groups was not significant; 41% of the completers and 48% of the noncompleters repeated the violence. In this last study, the results may have been poorer because more of the men had mental health and substance abuse problems; also, many of the noncompleters received a substantial amount of treatment.

Several other studies have compared treated groups with noncompleters or untreated subjects. Dutton (1986) compared treated men with a matched group of untreated men who were matched for prior violence and criminal justice contact. The rearrest rate for the untreated group was much higher than for the treated group (40% vs. 4%). Sixteen percent of the wives of treated partners reported "severe" violence during the follow-up; however, 21% reported an increase in verbal aggression.

A study by Douglas and Perrin (1987) showed a higher arrest rate for noncompleters (29% vs. 15%) and positive changes for the treated group on measures of assertiveness and alcohol abuse. Completers did not change on measures of depression and attitudes toward women.

Hamberger and Hastings (1986) also compared completers and noncompleters and used either abuser or partner self-report. Twenty-eight percent of the completers and 47% of the noncompleters were reported as being violent during follow-up. Completers showed significant decreases in violence, anger, and depression over the course of treatment.

Shepard (1987) compared men from the beginning, middle, and last phases of treatment. Cognitive-behavioral treatment was followed by educational groups that tried to decrease abusers' need to control. Reports from victims revealed a 39% recidivism rate during the first phase and 31% during the second phase and follow-up. Psychological abuse did not differ between the treatment groups but was lower for the follow-up group.

A couple of multiprogram studies have been completed, but they suffer from serious methodological flaws, including combining data from diverse programs and having no base line data (Pirog-Good & Stets-Kealey, 1986; Stacey & Shupe, 1984; see Saunders & Azar, 1989, for discussion).

The studies reported above indicate some promise for using cognitive-behavioral approaches for stopping or reducing assaults, as well as reducing levels of anger, depression, and rigid sex role beliefs. The evidence is less encouraging for the reduction of psychological abuse. No firm conclusions can be made at this time about the efficacy of a cognitive-behavioral approach because of the many flaws in the studies' designs. First, noncognitive-behavioral methods were often included. Second, noncompleters do not provide a good comparison group because their motivation, educational levels, and severity of violence are likely to differ from completers. Third, self-reports by abusers were usually not adjusted for response bias. Fourth, only one study used a waiting list (minimal treatment) control group and none experimentally compared two or more forms of treatment. Most studies also did not try to control for factors such as separation of the couple or arrest of the abuser, which are likely to have a strong impact on the men's behavior. Both abusers and nonabusers see arrest, divorce, and social condemnation as severe consequences for woman abuse (Carmody & Williams, 1987). These are only a few of the problems with the studies. More thorough reviews of the outcome studies are provided elsewhere (Gondolf, 1987b; Saunders, 1988; Saunders & Azar, 1989).

Conclusion

This chapter reviewed some ways in which the many principles and procedures of cognitive and behavioral therapy are being applied to treat woman abuse. The procedures have the advantages of being concrete and empirically based. The evaluation of their application to the treatment of men who batter, however, is in its infancy. Hopefully, practitioners and researchers will continue to work together to find the best methods for alleviating the suffering caused by woman abuse.

References

Allen, R. D. (1978). An analysis of the impact of two forms of short-term assertive training on aggressive behavior. *Dissertation Abstracts International, 39,* 2058A.

Bandura, A. (1969). *Principles of behavior modification.* New York: Holt, Rinehart & Winston.

Bandura, A. (1973). *Aggression: A social learning analysis.* Englewood Cliffs, NJ: Prentice-Hall.

Bandura, A. (1977). *Social learning theory.* Englewood Cliffs, NJ: Prentice-Hall.

Barling, J., & Rosenbaum, A. (1986). Work stressors and wife abuse. *Journal of Applied Psychology, 71,* 346-348.

Bass, B. (1973). An unusual behavioral technique for treating obsessive ruminations. *Psychotherapy: Theory, Research, and Practice, 10,* 191-192.

Bedrosian, R. C. (1982). Using cognitive and systems intervention in the treatment of marital violence. In L. R. Barnhill (Ed.), *Clinical approaches to family violence* (pp. 117-138). Rockville, MD: Aspen Systems.

Bernstein, D. A., & Borkevec, T. D. (1973). *Progressive relaxation training.* Champaign, IL: Research Press.

Bowker, L. H. (1983). *Beating wife-beating.* Lexington, MA: D. C. Heath.

Carmody, D. C., & Williams, K. R. (1987). Wife assault and perceptions of sanctions. *Violence and Victims, 2,* 25-38.

Carr, E. G. (1981). Contingency management. In A. P. Goldstein, E. G. Carr, W. S. Davidson II, & P. Wehr (Eds.), *In response to aggression* (pp. 1-65). New York: Pergamon Press.

Cautela, J. (1967). Covert sensitization. *Psychological Reports, 20,* 459-468.

Cobb, J. P., & Marks, I. (1979). Morbid jealousy featuring as obsessive-compulsive neurosis: Treatment by behavioral psychotherapy. *British Journal of Psychotherapy, 134,* 301–305.

Deffenbacher, J. L., Demm, P. M., & Brandon, A. D. (1986). High general anger: Correlates and treatment. *Behavior Research and Therapy, 24,* 481–489.

Deffenbacher, J. L., Story, D. A., Stark, R. S., Hogg, J. A., & Brandon, A. D. (1987). *Journal of Counseling Psychology, 34,* 171–176.

Deffenbacher, J. L., & Suinn, R. M. (1982). The self-control of anxiety. In P. Karoly & F. H. Kanfer (Eds.), *Self-management and behavior change* (pp. 393–442). New York: Pergamon Press.

DeMaris, A., & Jackson, J. (1987). Batterers' reports of recidivism after counseling. *Social Casework, 68,* 458–465.

Deschner, J. P. (1984). *The results of anger control for violent couples.* Paper presented at the Second National Conference for Family Violence Researchers, University of New Hampshire, Durham, NH.

Deschner, J. P., & McNeil, J. S. (1986). Results of anger control training for battering couples. *Journal of Family Violence, 1*(2), 111–120.

Douglas, M. A., & Perrin, S. (1987, July). *Recidivism and accuracy of self-reported violence and arrest in court-ordered to treatment batterers.* Paper presented at the Third National Family Violence Research Conference, University of New Hampshire, Durham, NH.

Dutton, D. (1986). The outcome of court-mandated treatment for wife assault: A quasi-experimental evaluation. *Violence and Victims, 1,* 163–176.

D'Zurrila, T., & Goldfried, M. (1971). Problem solving and behavior modification. *Journal of Abnormal Psychology, 78,* 107–126.

Eddy, M. J., & Myers, T. (1984). *Helping men who batter: A profile of programs in the U.S.* Austin, TX: Texas Department of Human Resources.

Edleson, J. L. (1984a). Violence is the issue: A critique of Neidig's assumptions. *Victimology: An International Journal, 9,* 483–489.

Edleson, J. L. (1984b). Working with men who batter. *Social Work, 29,* 237–242.

Edleson, J. L., & Grusznski, R. J. (1989). Treating men who batter: Four years of outcome data from the domestic abuse project. *Journal of Social Service Research, 12,* 3–22.

Edleson, J. F., Miller, D. M., Stone, G. W., & Chapman, D. G. (1985). Group treatment for men who batter. *Social Work Research and Abstracts, 21,* 18–21.

Eisler, R. M., Frederiksen, L. W., & Peterson, G. L. (1978). The relationship of cognitive variables to the expression of assertiveness. *Behavior Therapy, 9,* 419–427.

Ellis, A. (1977). *How to live with—and without—anger*. New York: Reader's Digest Press.

Fagan, J. A., Stewart, D. K., & Hansen, K. V. (1983). Violent men or violent husbands? Background factors and situational correlates. In D. Finkelhor, R. J. Gelles, G. T. Hotaling, & M. A. Straus (Eds.), *The dark side of families: Current family violence research* (pp. 49-68). Beverly Hills, CA: Sage.

Feazell, C. S., Mayers, R. S., & Deschner, J. (1984). Services of men who batter: Implications for programs and policies. *Family Relations, 33*, 217-223.

Fehrenbach, P. A., & Thelan, M. H. Behavioral approaches to the treatment of aggressive disorders. *Behavior Modification, 6*, 465-497.

Follingstad, D. R. (1980). A reconceptualization of issues in the treatment of abused women: A case study. *Psychotherapy: Theory, Research and Practice, 17*, 294-303.

Foy, D. W., Eisler, R. M., & Pinkston, S. (1975). Modeled assertion in a case of explosive rage. *Journal of Behavior Therapy and Experimental Psychiatry, 6*, 135-137.

Ganley, A. (1981). *Court-mandated counseling for men who batter: A three-day workshop*. Washington, DC: Center for Women's Policy Studies.

Gelles, R. J. (1983). An exchange/social control theory. In D. Finkelhor, R. J. Gelles, G. T. Hotaling, & M. A. Straus (Eds.), *The dark side of families: Current family violence research* (pp. 151-165). Beverly Hills, CA: Sage.

Gelles, R. J., & Straus, M. A. (1979). Determinants of violence in the family: Toward a theoretical integration. In W. R. Burr, R. Hill, F. I. Nye, & I. L. Reiss (Eds.), *Contemporary theories about the family* (pp. 151-165). New York: Free Press.

Goffman, J. M. (1980). *Batterers Anonymous: Mutual support counseling for woman-batterers*. Redlands, CA: Coalition for the Prevention of Abuse of Women and Children.

Goffman, J. M. (1984). *Batterers Anonymous: Self-help counseling for men who batter women*. San Bernardino, CA: B. A. Press.

Gondolf, E. (1988). How some men stop their abuse: An Exploratory Program Evaluation. In G. T. Hotaling, D. Finkelhor, J. T. Kirkpatrick, & M. A. Straus. (Eds.) *Coping with family violence*. Newbury Park, CA: Sage.

Gondolf, E. (1987a). The gender warrior: Reformed batterers on abuse, treatment, and change. *Journal of Family Violence, 2*(2), 177-191.

Gondolf, E. W. (1987b). A guide to batterer program evaluations: Seeing through the smoke and mirrors. *Response to the Victimization of Women and Children, 10*(3), 16-19.

Gondolf, E. W., & Russell, D. (1986). The case against anger control treatment programs for batterers. *Response to the Victimization of Women and Children, 9*(3), 2-5.

Hamberger, L. K., & Hastings, J. H. (1988). Skills training for treatment of spouse abusers: An outcome study. *Journal of Family Violence, 3*(2) 121–130.

Hazaleus, S. L., & Deffenbacher, J. L. (1986). Relaxation and cognitive treatments of anger. *Journal of Consulting and Clinical Psychology, 54,* 222–226.

Hearn, M. T., & Evans, D. R. (1972). Anger and reciprocal inhibition therapy. *Psychological Reports, 30,* 943–948.

Herrell, J. M. (1971). Use of systematic desensitization to eliminate inappropriate anger. *Proceedings of the Seventy-Ninth Annual Convention of the American Psychological Association, 6,* 431–432.

Hotaling, G. T., & Sugarman, D. B. (1986). An analysis of risk markers in husband to wife violence: The current state of knowledge. *Violence and Victims, 1,* 101–124.

Howells, K. (1976). Interpersonal aggression. *International Journal of Criminology and Penology, 4,* 319–330.

Jennings, J. L. (1987). History and issues in treatment of battering men: A case for unstructured group therapy. *Journal of Family Violence, 2,* 193–213.

Jones, R. G. (1969). *The irrational beliefs test.* Wichita, KS: Test Systems.

Kelso, D., & Personette, L. (1985). *Domestic violence and treatment services for victims and abusers.* Anchorage, AK: Altam Associates.

Langan, P. A., & Innes, C. A. (1986). *Preventing domestic violence against women* (Special report, Bureau of Justice Statistics, NIJ-102037). Washington, DC: U.S. Department of Justice.

Lange, A. J., & Jakubowski, P. (1976). *Responsible assertive behavior: Cognitive-behavioral procedures for trainers.* Champaign, IL: Research Press.

Lund, S. H., Larsen, N. E., & Schultz, S. K. (1982). *Exploratory evaluation of the Domestic Abuse Project.* Unpublished manuscript, Program Evaluation Resource Center, Minneapolis, MN.

Mahoney, M. J., & Arnkoff, D. (1978). Cognitive self-control therapies. In S. L. Garfield & A. E. Bergin (Eds.), *Handbook of psychotherapy and behavior change* (2nd ed.). New York: Wiley.

Maiuro, R. D., Cahn, T. S., & Vitaliano, P. P. (1986). Assertiveness deficits and hostility in domestically violent men. *Violence and Victims, 1,* 279–290.

Maiuro, R. D., Cahn, T. S., Vitaliano, P. P., & Zegree, J. B. (1987, August). *Treatment for domestically violent men: Outcome and follow-up data.* Paper presented at the 95th annual convention of the American Psychological Association, New York.

Margolin, G. (1979). Conjoint marital therapy to enhance anger management and reduce spouse abuse. *American Journal of Family Therapy, 7,* 13–23.

Meichenbaum, D. (1977). *Cognitive-behavior modification: An integrative approach*. New York: Plenum Press.

Miller, W. R., & Munoz, R. F. (1976). *How to control your drinking*. Englewood Cliffs, NJ: Prentice-Hall.

Moon, J. R., & Eisler, R. M. (1983). Anger control: An experimental comparison of three behavioral treatments. *Behavioral Therapy*, *14*, 493-505.

Myers, C. (1984, August). *The Family Violence Project: Some preliminary data on a treatment program for spouse abuse*. Paper presented at the Second National Conference for Family Violence Researchers, University of New Hampshire, Durham, NH.

Neidig, P. H. (1984). Women's shelters, men's collectives, and other factors in the field of spouse abuse. *Victimology: An International Journal*, *9*, 464-476.

Neidig, P. H. (1986). The development and evaluation of a spouse abuse treatment program in a military setting. *Evaluation and Program Planning*, *9*, 275-280.

Neidig, P. H., & Friedman, D. H. (1984). *Spouse abuse: A treatment program for couples*. Champaign, IL: Research Press.

Novaco, R. W. (1975). *Anger control: The development and evaluation of an experimental treatment*. Lexington, MA: Lexington Books.

Novaco, R. W. (1978). Anger and coping with stress: Cognitive behavioral interventions. In J. P. Foreyt & D. P. Rathjen (Eds.), *Cognitive behavior therapy: Research and applications* (pp. 135-174). New York: Plenum Press.

O'Leary, K. D. (1988). Physical aggression between spouses: A social learning perspective. In V. B. Van Hasselt, R. L. Morrison, A. S. Bellack, & M. Hersen (Eds.), *Handbook of family violence* (pp. 31-56). New York: Plenum Press.

Pirog-Good, M. A., & Stets-Kealey, J. (in press). Recidivism in programs for abusers. *Victimology: An International Journal*.

Raglin, J. S., & Morgan, W. P. (1985). Influence of vigorous exercise on mood state. *Behavior Therapist*, *8*, 179-189.

Rimm, D. C. (1977). Assertiveness training and the expression of anger. In Alberti, R. E. *Assertiveness: Innovations, applications, and issues*. San Luis Obispo, CA: Impact.

Rose, S. D., Hanusa, D., Tolman, R. M., & Hall, J. A. (1982). *A group leader's guide to assertiveness training*. Unpublished manual, School of Social Work, University of Wisconsin-Madison, Madison, WI.

Saunders, D. G. (1977). Marital violence: Dimensions of the problem and modes of intervention. *Journal of Marriage and Family Counseling*, *3*, 43-52.

Saunders, D. G. (1984). Helping husbands who batter. *Social Casework*, *65*, 347-356.

Saunders, D. G. (1987, August). *Are there different types of men who batter? An empirical study with possible implications for treatment.* Paper presented at the Third National Family Violence Research Conference, University of New Hampshire, Durham, NH.

Saunders, D. G. (1988). Issues in conducting treatment research with men who batter. In G. T. Hotaling, D. Finkelhor, J. T. Kirkpatrick, & M. A. Straus (Eds.), *Coping with family violence: Research and policy perspectives* (pp. 145–157). Newbury Park, CA: Sage.

Saunders, D. G., & Azar, S. (1989). Family violence treatment programs: Description and evaluation. In L. Ohlin & M. Tonry (Eds.), *Family Violence: Crime and Justice, A Review of Research (Vol. II)* (pp. 481–546). Chicago, IL: University of Chicago Press.

Saunders, D. G., & Hanusa, D. (1986). Cognitive-behavioral treatment for men who batter: The short-term effects of group therapy. *Journal of Family Violence, 1,* 357–372.

Saunders, D. G., Lynch, A. B., Grayson, M., & Linz, D. (1987). The inventory of beliefs about wife beating: The construction and initial validation of a measure of beliefs and attitudes. *Violence and Victims, 2,* 39–58.

Shepard, M. (1987, July). *Intervention with men who batter: An evaluation of a domestic abuse program.* Paper presented at the Third National Family Violence Research Conference, University of New Hampshire, Durham, NH.

Sherman, L., & Berk, R. A. (1984). The specific deterrent effects of arrest for domestic assault. *American Sociological Review, 49,* 261–272.

Sonkin, D. J., & Durphy, M. (1982). *Learning to live without violence.* San Francisco: Volcano Press.

Spence, J. T., & Helmreich, R. L. (1978). *Masculinity and femininity: Their psychological dimensions, correlates and antecedents.* Austin, TX: University of Texas.

Stacey, W. A., & Shupe, A. (1984). *An evaluation of three programs for abusive men in Texas.* Report to the Protective Services Families and Children Branch, Texas Department of Human Resources.

Steinfeld, G. J. (1986). Spouse abuse: Clinical implications of research on the control of aggression. *Journal of Family Violence, 1,* 197–208.

Stermac, L. E. (1987). Anger control treatment for forensic patients. *Journal of Interpersonal Violence, 1*(4), 446–457.

Teismann, M. S. (1979). Jealousy: Systematic problem-solving therapy with couples. *Family Process, 18,* 151.

Tolman, R. M., & Saunders, D. G. (1988). The case for the cautious use of anger control with men who batter. *Response to the Victimization of Women and Children, 11*(2), 15–20.

Walker, L. (1984). *The battered woman syndrome.* New York: Springer.

Warren, R., & McLellarn, R. W. (1982). Systematic desensitization as a treatment for maladaptive anger and aggression: A review. *Psychological Reports, 50*, 1095-1102.

Wolfe, D., Kaufman, K., Aragona, J., & Sandler, J. (1981). *Child management program for abusive parents*. Winter Park, FL: Anna Publishing.

Wolpe, J. (1958). *Psychotherapy by reciprocal inhibition*. Stanford: Stanford University Press.

III

Family Systems Approaches

5

A Psychoeducational, Conjoint Therapy Approach to Reducing Family Violence

Robert Geffner
Carol Mantooth
Dawn Franks
Loretta Rao

Recent statistics suggest that violence in the family is so prevalent that it may be considered commonplace in our society (Straus & Gelles, 1986). As a result, more researchers and practitioners have become involved in trying to reduce violence within the family. Although more shelters for battered women and their children have been established and a variety of batterer treatment programs have been developed, many traditional mental health practitioners are not adequately trained to treat the problem of violence in the family.

Furthermore, research concerning the effectiveness of various treatment approaches has not kept up with the proliferation of such programs (Geffner, Rosenbaum, & Hughes, 1988). In addition to the lack of adequate research, the topic of family violence has become an important political issue, and significant controversy has been generated about the most appropriate conceptualization of the problem and its amelioration. Debates concerning the different types of this

103

abuse or possible approaches to reducing it have often been heated and emotionally charged.

The purpose of this chapter is to present a psychoeducational conjoint therapy approach for reducing spouse abuse. The underlying theory will be presented first, followed by a description of the manner in which these ideas have been modified for use in therapy. Our method utilizes basic ideas from cognitive and family systems theories but also includes other techniques to yield an eclectic approach. A detailed explanation of family systems theory and family therapy are available elsewhere (Goldenberg & Goldenberg, 1985; L'Abate, Ganahl, & Hansen, 1986). However, basic ideas will be presented to provide the reader with sufficient information to understand the framework that has led to our approach.

Definition of the Problem

Terminology

The terminology used to define the problem of violence is important because it indicates the assumptions being made by the clinician. There is controversy about what label to use in describing abuse between husband and wife or cohabiting couples. The term "family violence" suggests that the violence is occurring within the family unit, with one or more members directing the abuse toward others. Terms such as "spouse abuse," "wife abuse," "partner abuse," and "marital violence" have also been used.

Feminists in the shelter movement have strongly advocated the use of the term "wife abuse" since the woman is often the person physically assaulted. They are concerned that ambiguous terms imply that both men and women are equally abusive, allow for more blaming of the victim, and downplay the effect on women (Bograd, 1984). Even though recent studies have suggested that there may be more mutual abuse than was previously thought (Straus & Gelles, 1986), it is usually the woman who is physically hurt. Clinicians' choice of terminology always reflects their value systems and underlying assumptions, and we understand the concern that ambiguous terms may obscure the fact that more women than men are beaten. Our approach, however, does not blame the wife for her own abuse nor hold her responsible for injuries inflicted upon her. It does imply that she is trapped in the negative relationship and that her behavior and attitudes influence her husband and vice versa.

We prefer the term "family violence" because it more clearly indicates the importance of patterns of behavior of wife beating that occur in the context of the present family situation and that probably existed, to some degree, in the family of origin of both the batterer and the battered woman. In addition, we use this term to indicate the effect on and importance of the abuse to all family members. Research indicates that one of the strongest risk factors in family violence is having been abused as a child or having witnessed such violence in the home (Hotaling & Sugarman, 1986). This suggests that the violence perpetuates itself because the effect on the child witnesses persists such that the cycle often is repeated when they enter adult relationships (Hershorn & Rosenbaum, 1985; Hughes, Rau, Hampton, & Sablatura, 1985).

Definition of Abuse

It is important to define the types of behaviors that are considered abusive. Ganley (1981) has described the components of abusive relationships that must be considered in any treatment approach. These include actual physical abuse (punching as well as shoving), sexual abuse (forced sexual behavior, including marital rape), property damage (breaking objects or throwing things), and psychological abuse (intimidation, control, and threats). For any program to be successful, all of these behaviors must be addressed as part of the pattern of battering. It may not be sufficient for the physical and sexual abuse to be eliminated if the intimidation and control are maintained, because the relationship is still emotionally abusive.

Broad Theoretical Model

The eclectic counseling program to be discussed later in this chapter is based upon aspects of cognitive, social learning, and family systems theories. Within a social learning framework, family violence seems to occur in the context of psychological abuse and exploitation that has been learned. In some ways, this psychological abuse is similar to a brainwashing process (Ganley, 1981). The victims of family violence are manipulated, their perceptions are controlled, and their view of reality is affected. Families are the primary group in which individuals function and learn, and because social isolation is inherent in violent families, victims often have no countervailing perceptions of themselves and of reality. According to a cognitive framework, one result of this process is the tendency for victims to blame themselves. They identify with the rationalizations that the offenders give to explain the violence. Another aspect of this brainwashing process has to do with the strong allegiance that victims of family violence have to their abusers. This allows a cycle of abuse to be repeated; this cycle can also be described within a family systems framework.

Cycle of Violence

A cycle of violence within the family has been described in detail by Walker (1979, 1984) from a social learning/behavioral perspective. She discusses three stages that occur in abusive relationships: the tension phase, the violent episode, and the reconcilation period. This cycle can be short when violence is frequent or can occur over a long time period in some relationships as the tension gradually builds. This cycle maintains the relationship and allows the abuse to be perpetuated. It appears that both partners may have learned this behavior from their families of origin and may believe that it is the normal or usual way couples react, or they may feel trapped in a "hopeless" situation without knowing how to break the cycle.

From a family systems perspective, Jackson (1965) described such a family as a closed information system; both the abuser and the abused seem to be locked into this system. In one example, the women may act helpless and give out signals of vulnerability. The man, in turn, takes out his frustrations on her with abuse or intimidation. Neither sees how he or she may be influencing the other, and the behavior continues. In viewing a family as such a system, the violent behavior acts to maintain equilibrium or homeostasis. Internal or external stressors unbalance the family system, which leads to instability in the relationship, and this leads to the violence that then stabilizes the system (Goldenberg & Goldenberg, 1985). However, for Dell and Goolishian (1981) and Keeney (1983), homeostasis and stability are not adequate concepts for describing living and changing systems. The family is a system of continuous interlocking relationships that are organized such that the behavior of one family member influences and is influenced by the behavior of other family members. In this case, the violence can become "runaway" instead of "self-corrective." In either case, the violence is perpetuated.

Family systems theory provides a framework for examining how both parties are caught in a negative cycle of violence. The wife is not blamed for being the "victim" nor is the husband accused of being the "victimizer," since neither partner may know alternative behaviors. Since the abusers often have been physically or sexually abused as children (Gelles & Cornell, 1985), they are also "victims" of the intergenerational transmission of violence. Thus, in the recursive cycle of violence, victim becomes victimizer who is again victimized.

The importance of the cycle and the mutual interaction of abuse, over and above individual characteristics or personality, is supported by recent research. Studies of batterers (Geffner, Jordan, Hicks, & Cook, 1985; Hamberger & Hastings, 1986; Rosenbaum & O'Leary, 1981) and research on battered women (Douglas & Colantuano, 1987; Geffner et al., 1985; Pagelow, 1984) seem to indicate that these men and women have certain characteristics in common. These are low self-esteem, stereotyped views of sex roles (patriarchal family structure, male power), lack of emotional expressiveness, lack of assertiveness, impulsiveness, social isolation, employment problems, moodiness, alcohol use, hostility, and abuse in the family of origin. Therefore, our treatment attempts to change the relationship and the patterns of interacting, in addition to the various behaviors and attitudes of those involved.

Power and Control Issues

Traditional therapy approaches focus on power and control in dealing with the problem of abuse, based upon a victim/victimizer dichotomy. The major emphasis is on separation of the couple, usually with the woman being encouraged to go to a battered women's shelter or women's groups. The men are either left alone, or in some cases, are mandated by a court system to attend a group composed of other "victimizers." From a family systems framework, this process perpetuates the symmetrical, adversarial context between men and women.

Family systems theories focus on describing family violence as a pattern in the relationship in which there is unilateral control with little room for negotiation (Cook & Frantz-Cook, 1984). When a couple is locked into a rigid system and the man has learned to be violent in response to stress, battering is likely. In this view, violence erupts as the couple struggle over the functional rules of power and control in the relationship, rather than over the specific problem. It can also occur as an expression of power by the batterer in order to maintain some level of self-esteem. It appears that power and self-esteem issues are important in the relationship, and we include these in our treatment.

Communication in the Family

Another factor that seems to be important in abusive families is communication. Communication in abusive families is often unclear, inconsistent, high on "shoulds" and "oughts," and highly critical of other family members and transmits little information. Thus, treatment programs must address these areas to be successful. The more someone communicates fear, guilt, weakness, helplessness, the worse the situation becomes. The solution to violence with spouses, therefore, is discovered by examining the partners' assumptions about their communication rules, not just the content of the rules. Both the man and the woman must learn to express their feelings, and both need to understand that the free expression of feelings is an important element in raising their self-esteem.

It is necessary to obtain from the clients a description of the violent incident(s), including the events immediately preceding the abuse. Descriptions of when, where, and how often similar episodes occurred are needed, with the role of each participant documented. Verbal and emotional responses of family members to the violent incident should be explored. This is done individually as well as conjointly, since the research is clear that perceptions of violence differ between the abuser and the abused (Geffner et al., 1988; Rosenbaum & O'Leary, 1981). In addition, possible or potential intimidation by the abuser must be carefully monitored.

When assisting clients to express themselves, therapists also should be aware of the "what" and "how" of the communication. Who in the family does the talking, and to whom? Because of the disorganized and volatile communication patterns of violent families, intervention includes helping family members to clarify events and analyze a problem, rather than to blame one another. This occurs while providing the support necessary for dialogue to occur. By developing an understanding of both the life situation (environmental, intrapersonal, and interpersonal) and the family members' goals, the couple can identify a range of behavioral alternatives to the abuse.

Change in Behavior and System Change

Relationships can change, and people can change. It appears that both of these must occur for physical and emotional abuse to be eliminated in a relationship. In the beginning, behavior within the system is changed, but the system remains intact; this is often referred to as first-order change in family systems theory. It involves increments of mastery and adaptation, a need to do something different. This focus is on content and problems. Behavioral techniques such as anger management therapy can be used to bring about this change. Often the spouses cannot think of alternative nonviolent ways of behaving when they are angry because they have not learned how to deal constructively with anger. They need to learn better ways of handling aggressive feelings before their interaction patterns can change. If an individual is in therapy without his or her spouse, changes being made by the individual can be misinterpreted. If just the man is being treated, then the woman may still be angry and sabotage the anger control techniques. Thus, long-term relationship changes may not occur, and the basic assumptions concerning power and gender roles may remain the same. Physical abuse may be reduced or eliminated in the short-term, but intimidation or psychological abuse may still occur.

First-order change occurs within a system that itself remains unchanged. Contemporary family theorists also define change as that which alters the system itself (Watzlawick, Weakland, & Fisch, 1974). Both spouses learn to be something new as a result of the interaction between husband, wife, and therapist. New ideas can be brought forth while the family system changes. Often this entails the husband's learning to be more expressive emotionally and the wife's learning to be more goal oriented (the wife loses her need to be taken care of financially, and the husband lessens his demands to be taken care of emotionally). With second-order changes comes a shift in the balance of control in the relationship. Within the context of the relationship between the couple and the therapist, second-order change addresses new assumptions about power, control, and communication within the family.

Political Philosophy

The cultural acceptance of violence in our society as a means of coping or "solving" problems has been noted by social psychologists (Bandura, 1973), sociologists (Straus, 1980), and family psychologists (Steinfeld, 1986). It is not surprising, then, that many women who are beaten and men who batter were abused themselves as children, or observed parental violence. The attitude that violence is an acceptable response to stress seems to develop in these families to the exclusion of more constructive ways of coping with or reducing stress (Barling & Rosenbaum, 1986). Therefore, our approach focuses on changing the attitudes toward violence, as well as the communication patterns in the family.

There has been controversy regarding programs that counsel couples conjointly (Bograd, 1984). Generally, there is concern that such programs will not only shift the responsibility of the violence from the batterer to the victim but also may escalate the level of violence. Contrary to these concerns, we found that violence was a continuation of previous patterns and did not escalate as a result of counseling. In fact, the essential ingredients of our program include holding the abusers personally responsible for their violent actions and emphasizing that they are not powerless to stop it; trying to obtain objective, independent information about the violent persons and monitoring their behavior during the time they are in counseling; and creating an atmosphere in counseling sessions that physical violence and emotional abuse are neither appropriate nor excused.

Safety issues are quite significant in abusive families, and this must be emphasized in the beginning of treatment. This is an important part of our approach. The focus on power or gender issues involved in abusive relationships is also important, and we address this work in a later phase of therapy. The physical harm and threats to battered women assume priority, and they must be dealt with directly and openly in therapy. It must also be clear that each person is responsible for his or her own behavior, and our approach emphasizes that no one has the right to hit another person in a relationship. Hitting invites both partners, in their own ways, to escalate destructive behavior. This is one of the few "moral" stands advocated in our approach.

Therapists must recognize their own personal value systems as they relate to families and violence. If the therapist cannot see two "victims" in the case of spouse abuse, then the therapist probably will not be able to help both partners. By defining the family network rather than the individual as the focus of attention, therapists are able to appreciate the contextual significance of behavior. Violence can be seen as a social phenomenon rather than as biologically or psychologically motivated.

Counselors should be aware of any unresolved conflicts within themselves regarding domestic violence in general. The issues surrounding the battering of women are likely to stimulate a wide range of emotions within the counselor, depending upon his or her background and personal experience with family violence. An ongoing dialogue with a supportive cotherapist seems an appropriate means to monitor and assist with any difficulties that may arise.

In general, if therapists focus on helping the couple develop new ways of behaving and thinking, instead of focusing on right and wrong behavior, the couple will probably be more cooperative. It is not useful for the therapist to adopt judgmental views if the goal is long-term change by both partners in the relationship. An attitude of neutrality is important, in which multiple sides and views can be taken. This position is viewed by us as more helpful than a "victim/victimizer" stance (Gondolf & Russell, 1986). We do not think it benefits the woman to see herself as helpless, childlike, and victimized. The goals of empowerment and of taking individual responsibility for the course of one's life are more useful.

We should be aware that not all couples now define nor wish to define abuse in the same way as do therapists. As clinicians, we define abuse as any manifestation of intimidation, even at the level of a "minor push or slap." However, some of those in abusive relationships actually do not think that an occasional shove is a problem. We therefore need to be aware of their framework and to determine whether it is useful to try to impose our definition at the beginning of therapy. If it diminishes rapport between therapist and client, it is probably self-defeating for therapists to try to impose their own views of what kind of behavior the clients must adopt in order for them to be "acceptable" as clients. We hope that their framework and awareness of intimidation at all levels will change with therapy.

Advantages and Limitations

There are several advantages to a conjoint approach in treating abusive relationships. The couple are involved, and therefore structural changes can occur that can have long-term consequences that will filter down to the rest of the family. This approach not only empowers the woman but also focuses on changing the man. Not only can the couple's relationship be preserved, but the effect on the children of the parents' portrayal of new role models may also help to end the intergenerational transmission of family violence.

The goal of our approach is not to preserve a dysfunctional family. Instead, the preservation of a functional family (for both the man and the woman) is merely a by-product of successful intervention, when the couple desire this. It appears that more abusive couples would utilize this treatment if it were more widely available, since conjoint therapy is often requested by abusive husbands and battered women (Geller & Wasserstrom, 1984).

The positive results of conjoint therapy will, one hopes, generalize to other situations as well. If the wife merely leaves the relationship, then she may be empowered and become self-reliant and confident as a single person. However, the husband may then find another woman to abuse, and the wife may not have sufficient skills to create a functional relationship should she remarry. In addition, the effects on the children may persist even if the woman changes her behavior and attitudes, so that the perpetuation of violence continues (Sedlak, 1988). Since violence is not the only problem in abusive relationships, treatment of the man only will not alter the communication nor change other aspects of the relationship that are dysfunctional (Geffner, Franks, Patrick, & Mantooth, 1986).

Counseling with couples is effective because both spouses are being taught the same educational materials simultaneously. They also have the opportunity to express their feelings toward and describe their perceptions of the relationship. By agreeing on the problem areas, it is much easier to work toward solutions and compromises. The clients also have the opportunity to talk with their spouses in a safe environment without fear of the situation's getting out of control. The counselors are there to help keep the anxiety and emotional level under control. The therapists can also get both spouses to agree to only deal with the emotional issues during the counseling sessions, until they have learned more effective communication and anger management skills.

Another advantage of working with couples is that the counselors get a more complete view of what is actually happening in the relationship. Working with the couple together also eliminates some of the mistrust that is usually present if the couple go for counseling separately. In conjoint therapy, neither spouse has to wonder what the other has said to the therapist about him or her.

There are disadvantages or limitations to this approach. The cooperation of both individuals must occur; sometimes this may be through court-ordered or "partner-mandated" referrals (Tolman, Beeman, & Mendoza, 1987). Eventually both must interact in the therapy. Both the man and the woman must desire conjoint treatment and be willing to change the abusive relationship, or at least to cooperate in the treatment. If only one partner is emotionally involved in improving the relationship and stopping the violence, the chances are much greater that the noninvolved spouse will drift farther away in his or her ability to understand the partner.

A conjoint therapy approach may not be helpful for those cases in which the batterer beats his wife when no interaction has occurred (e.g., in the middle of the night while she is sleeping, or as soon as he enters the door after work). In these cases, the man may be violent in general, not just in the family. A flow chart for determining the appropriateness of using a conjoint approach or other methods has been suggested by Rosenbaum and O'Leary (1986). Such guidelines, in conjunction with our assessment and interviews, determine whether a couple would seem to be appropriate for our program.

Applications of Psychoeducational Conjoint Therapy

In the fall of 1981, the East Texas Crisis Center in Tyler, Texas, in conjunction with the senior author, embarked on a project with an idealistic, ambitious goal of ending violence in families. The Crisis Center operated a shelter for battered women and their children. The staff noted that a large percentage of the battered women who left the shelter often returned home to the abuser. Frequently these women rejoined the abusers for financial reasons, but shelter and counseling staff also recognized that many times a woman chose to go home because she loved her mate. Thus, couples who chose to remain together needed some help to end the violence. When a woman came to the shelter, the staff would often hear from her mate within a few days. As staff listened to his side of the story, and to hers, they began to get a glimpse of what binds a man and a woman in a violent relationship. Clearly, the world was not full of violent men getting their kicks hurting the women they loved. Nor were women asking to be beaten. In addition, some of these men wanted help to change their behavior; they did not know how to stop on their own. Many of these women did not want to leave their husbands, but they did want the violence to stop.

Background and Early Development

A psychoeducational conjoint counseling approach was developed, which combined a male-female counseling team and a female-male family consulting team. In the early development of our program, a violent couple would come to the office for weekly counseling sessions with the counseling team, and the family consulting team would make weekly visits to the family's home. Therapy, education, and home interventions were combined in order to reduce violence and improve the family relationship. In the early years of the project, the male-female cotherapy team worked with individual couples. These teams provided role models to the couple, and this was helpful in counseling. This approach prevented clients from feeling "ganged up on" by providing two members of the opposite sex. Counseling issues were based on the needs of the couple, which were determined by the completion of extensive social histories, interviews, several tests, and questionnaires.

Originally the family consultants, also a female-male team, were introduced for two reasons. The first goal was to educate the couple in their home about various issues, including family violence, communication, and parenting skills. The home education component was designed to complement the counseling that took place each week in the office. The second goal was to allow the teams a glimpse into the family's personal world, since it was believed that violent family members may exhibit different behaviors in their own home, compared to meeting in a public place or office. Family education and counseling plans were jointly developed by the counseling team and family consultants. During the period that family consultants made home visits, no violent incidents occurred. This may have been due to the positive effects of being in a new treatment (a "flight into health"), the monitoring by the consultants, or a combination of factors.

Throughout the life of the Family Preservation Project (named in part by the couples themselves), participating families were often self-referred. The rate of self-referrals increased as the public became aware of the program. It was common for one spouse to make initial contact, later bringing the other one into the counseling. Both men and women exhibited initiative in seeking help to end the violence. Often the first visit to the center was by both partners together, but this was not required. Since the East Texas Crisis Center operated a shelter for battered women and children, it was assumed that many women choosing to return home would arrange to participate in the program. However, although many shelter women tried to get their husbands to come to the Family Preservation Program, it is estimated that fewer than 25% of these couples actually did complete the program. Most who did were self-referred or from other agencies.

Program Philosophy

During our work with couples, we have made extensive use of the general principles and techniques of Rational Emotive Therapy (RET) (Ellis & Harper, 1975). We speculated that the general RET approach would be particularly effective with domestic violence, especially in the early stages of counseling, because it allowed the counselors to make rapid and effective interventions in spite of the very high levels of emotionality often present during the first few counseling sessions. The counselors do not discourage couples from expressing their feelings or from being emotional. In fact, clinicians consider this expression to be vital. However, we have found that the unchecked ventilation of emotion through several counseling sessions is generally ineffective in achieving the long-term goal of helping the couple change. In order to believe that counseling is effective, the couple must see that change is occurring, that skills are being learned, and that the relationship is improving. In general, we have found that the couples seem to be better able to tolerate high levels of emotional expression later in counseling, after they have learned certain communication techniques, RET, and other cognitive intervention principles. Finally, RET approaches seem to fit easily into the psychoeducational approach, since it is somewhat didactic in nature.

During the initial phase of counseling, there is sometimes an increase in the anxiety level due to problems coming to the surface. The possibility of a violent incident after the counseling session is decreased by directly addressing the issue. Another method of decreasing the probability of a violent incident is the nonviolence contract. Excellent descriptions of such contracts have been presented by Rosenbaum and O'Leary (1986) and Steinfeld (1987). This contract states that a man will not harm his spouse in any way and that if he feels that he is going to be violent, he will immediately use alternative techniques or call the counselor or other agency. A verbal commitment to nonviolence is often a deterrent. The therapist can also decrease the risk of a violent incident by briefly teaching some specific time-out techniques that the batterer can use if he starts getting angry (Gondolf & Russell, 1987).

Counselor availability is also a deterrent to violence. The batterer has someone to whom he can turn; also, just the idea of his behavior's being monitored decreases the risk. The woman also has the support of and access to the counselors but is always encouraged to deal with relationship issues during the regular counseling sessions with her spouse present. She is given information about a shelter in case a violent incident or the threat of one should occur. Safety issues are confronted openly, directly, and in the initial sessions so that the consequences are clearly explained to both the man and the woman. Legal alternatives, agency help, and the immediate separation of the woman from the man are described in detail. We have not had any dangerous incidents as a result of our techniques during the 7 years of operating our counseling program.

Our program is structured to initially diffuse the emotional reactivity by using cognitive-behavioral interventions and psychoeducational techniques. Therapy includes the use of anger control and stress-management techniques and deals with relationship factors that lead to the initiation and escalation of violence. Counseling also provides direct information necessary to increase clients' self-control and improve their interpersonal skills. Indirect instruction, such as the role models presented by therapists, is also an important component of therapy. As the couple use these methods and the anger and violence subside, the program shifts to an exploration of personal, relationship, and family-of-origin issues. The focus is then upon the communication patterns in the relationship and underlying assumptions about communication rules.

In counseling violent couples, there is a need for a certain amount of structure, since many such couples have little structure in their lives. Such structure helps the couples regain control of their lives and relationships. The amount of structure required varies with each couple according to their needs and situation. It is possible that the therapists may be used initially as external controls for the client who may have little internal control or who may feel that his or her life is out of control. Over time, as the couple develop better understanding and internal control, external structure is reduced. Clients also would be initially asked not to discuss issues outside of counseling that could lead to a violent incident. After they have learned ways of dealing with emotional situations, they will be encouraged to talk about a specific problem area at home at a particular time.

When formulating treatment goals, we found that therapist and client expectations were sometimes different. Our value system dictated that we wanted to eliminate all violence, including pushing and slapping. However, many women were shoved or occasionally slapped, yet these events were not registered by them as violence, even though we viewed such acts as violent. Sometimes the men would say, "I only hit her with an open hand; I didn't use my fist." During the reeducation process, the counselors discovered that it was possible to help a woman and man to negotiate the level of violence that was acceptable to each individual, and the therapists also became educated. This process is recursive in that both clients and therapists are cocreating a working definition of violence that is acceptable to all. Eventually this became a useful tool in helping the couple communicate and increase respect for each other's needs. In the long run, this process would often lead to the elimination of the violence.

Counselors try to remain as objective as possible. This is often most difficult in the early stages of intervention. Couples will often relate very shocking and disturbing events involving violence and abuse. It is important that therapists achieve a balance between listening, being concerned, and showing respect for the seriousness of the events related, while not allowing themselves to become overly emotional and overreact. Obviously, a certain amount of therapist control of both verbal and nonverbal communication is necessary. Experience has taught us that if too much emotion is shown, the couple are likely to retreat and be reluctant to reveal further "secrets." As the counseling relationship progresses, it may be possible, and often is appropriate, to be more open in this manner.

The clinicians are usually very supportive of the couple. They openly express their appreciation for the clients' efforts in counseling and commend them for taking the risk of being involved in therapy, no matter how they came to be in the program. The therapists encourage and reinforce the couple's progress. The counselors attempt to be warm and friendly, and most couples seem to respond to this. Therapists try to convey a sense of hope, attempting to be enthusiastic, cheerful, and positive. As such, Rogerian concepts of unconditional positive regard enter into the counseling.

A major emphasis through the counseling sessions is to encourage the spouses to be supportive and to help each other implement what they learn. It is important for the couple to learn to listen to each other and safely talk about a wide range of emotions. This increases the probability of the couple's dealing with problems as they arise, instead of internalizing them until an abusive blow-up occurs. Thus, the emphasis is on listening to each other, giving feedback, and informing each other when an unwanted behavior or nonverbal cue is occurring that the couple had previously agreed to change (Satir, 1972). This helps the emotionally reactive couple to gain some distance from their emotions before they act.

No Blame. Our counseling style is a "no blame" approach. The clinicians actively work to have both partners accept responsibility for their own behavior. RET techniques as well as cognitive therapy approaches have been effectively utilized to promote accountability. The counselors have used "no blame" to build an alliance and trust in the counseling environment. Couples often accuse and blame each other during the initial counseling sessions. The husband blames the wife, stating that it is her fault that he hit her. The wife then blames him for provoking her to say or do something. They both fault the other for the state of the relationship. The therapists have found that couples can and do engage in this seemingly endless cycle of blaming and fault finding. We take an active role in confronting this unproductive behavior.

Before intervening, we usually allow the fault-finding interaction to occur for a while. The counselors then explain to the couple the futility of this behavior and the almost impossible and time-consuming task that the therapist faces in trying to determine who is to blame. They further point out their reluctance to help by being "lawyers" and "judges," since they have no training in this area.

The "no blame" approach further suggests that counselors are nonpunitive and do not seek to punish the violent man. We are adamant in our belief that counselors should not become punishing agents. Assigning blame usually breaks down the rapport between client and therapist and reinforces the low self-esteem that is already a major factor in the violent relationship (Clarke, 1978; Geffner et al., 1985). Many of our male clients have told the counselors of their anxiety and reluctance to enter into counseling, out of fear that the therapists would verbally attack them or "put them down." They usually tell the counselors this as a prelude to reporting how relieved they were to find their preconceptions unfounded. The clinicians have found that this "no blame" approach reduces resistance and promotes cooperation in the men and women. Thus, when each is held accountable in a nonblaming manner by the counselors and their partners, the bonding and trust tends to increase, and the therapy process is enhanced.

Responsibility for Behavior. Responsibility for behavior can be more easily discussed after the couple have been introduced to RET (Ellis & Harper, 1975) and cognitive concepts (Beck, 1979), learned basic communication skills (Satir, 1967), begun to identify their feelings, and learned more about their identities (McKay, Davis, & Fanning, 1983). Each spouse is then directed toward accepting responsibility for his or her feelings, emotions, and behavior. When the man is violent, he is held accountable for his behaviors. The woman is also held accountable for her reactions or behaviors in the situation. Violence, however, is never an acceptable option.

A positive way of encouraging accountability for actions is to let the client talk about what happened and how things got out of control. If the abuser tries to blame the spouse, the counselors could provide some brief education about "ownership" of emotions and behaviors. Counselors also work hard at not taking sides unconsciously or covertly. The unconscious alliance with the male or female partner is difficult to control but is greatly reduced with the use of a female-male cotherapy team. The clinicians can monitor each other and discuss the counseling process regularly, becoming, one hopes, aware of any unconscious alliance and minimizing it.

Occasionally counselors do openly take sides. For example, one counselor may take the position of one spouse to help him or her articulate something; this may also occur during a role play. In any case, the clients are informed of the therapist's intention.

Program Evolution

In the early years of our program, we envisioned ending violence during the course of a 10- to 12-week counseling program. However, experience has taught us that the dynamics of couple violence are complex and that the wounds are mutual as well as deep. A commitment to work with a couple through different stages over a longer period of time has been more productive, and as a result, our programs have undergone changes. A manual has recently been published that describes our current program in depth (Mantooth et al., 1987).

The family consultants and the home visits have been eliminated, leaving the counselors to provide both the therapy and the education in the office. The primary reason for this change was budgetary, not therapeutic. Education and therapy are now combined into single sessions, with one building upon the other. This adaptation has been very successful. The current program has also been expanded to 19 weeks. The initial sessions include intake, screening, assessment, and program explanation. Then there are 16 weeks of structured counseling, which includes anger management, communication skills, self-esteem enhancement, assertiveness training, problem solving, and intimacy issues/sex therapy. At the conclusion of the program, the assessment is then repeated.

In a number of cases, couples returned either after completing the 19-week program or perhaps after dropping out, with the need to again work on various problem areas. Offering relationship enhancement courses/groups as a follow-up to the initial program has evolved from the realization that ending violence in a couple's relationship may be achieved in incremental stages. It appears that an open-door policy, with encouragement to return when they feel the need, enables a couple to continue to reduce violence completely over a period of time.

Currently, the model can also be used in a couples' group format as well as with individual couples. The same program is followed, but the cotherapy team can work with five couples in a group setting.

The initial intake and assessment sessions are still conducted with the couples individually, and then the clients are introduced into the group. We concurrently conduct a beginners' group for couples who are just starting and an advanced group for those who have completed the initial program. The couples' group format has provided peer support to the participating couples, as well as allowing more couples to be admitted to the program.

Working with individual couples has some advantages over couples' group counseling. One advantage is that the counselors have more time to deal with individual couple issues. This also appears to be less threatening, especially to the men. However, an advantage of couples' group counseling is that couples have the opportunity to see and interact with others who have similar problems. Also, the couples can share information about what has been helpful to them in dealing with similar issues. Another asset of couples' group counseling is that the couples learn to communicate and bond with other couples. This is important because often violent couples are isolated and do not have many friends. If they grow comfortable with establishing friendships during the counseling process, it is possible that they can carry this with them outside of therapy.

Assessment

Psychological assessment is used as a method of aiding the counseling and also in determining whether a particular couple would be appropriate for services. Our program, for example, is not as effective for spouses who do not desire treatment, have significant personality disorders (especially strong sociopathy), or exhibit psychotic behavior. The assessment also helps the clinicians to identify problem areas for the couple, and feedback is provided to the partners in joint sessions, which often increases their understanding of each other. Diagnostic assessment provides information concerning the dynamics of the personalities, attitudes, and behaviors of the couple. The assessment includes personality, self-esteem, assertiveness, attitudinal, communication, and relationship measures (Geffner et al., 1985).

Part of the assessment includes a modified version of the Conflict Tactics Scales (Straus, 1979). This is used throughout counseling to measure abusive incidents. A weekly aggressive behavior inventory (Mantooth, Geffner, Franks, & Patrick, 1987) is completed by the couple individually and separately at the beginning of every session. This provides immediate information about ongoing violence. It also facilitates discussion about problem areas and provides an opportunity for the counselors to reinforce positive behaviors and to deal directly with continued abuse. It serves as a monitoring device and may aid in decreasing violent incidents because they will be noted or dealt with weekly. This instrument is also very useful in observing the change in behavior patterns during the program.

The assessment process is client centered, and we encourage the couple to participate fully in the formulation of a treatment regimen. The counselors discuss with the couple the social histories of both spouses. Many couples know very little about each other's background. Sometimes this information can give them a better understanding of their mate and the reasons behind certain relationship difficulties. Information gathered in the social histories can be very valuable in later sessions when problems come up in the relationship that deal directly with the effects of a childhood or previous trauma in the person's life.

Specific Techniques

After the counselors and couples have obtained insight into the dynamics of the relationship, evaluated the extent of the breakdown in communication, determined the specific problem areas, and assessed the level of violence, specific techniques can be utilized. These strategies and techniques fit an eclectic approach. Cognitive and behavioral approaches are used in the beginning of therapy. Many of Albert Ellis's RET techniques (Ellis & Harper, 1975) are used to modify distorted and irrational thinking patterns. Behavior modification techniques are also effective in changing specific behavior patterns.

In the initial sessions, psychoeducational methods are used by structuring the material using clearly defined goals and small, sequentially ordered steps. Clients learn more easily when they understand the rationale for each topic included in therapy. Motivation and the ability to generalize the content to new situations is increased. Each session consists of counseling, education, and homework assignments.

During the counseling segment of the session, the counselor can deal with specific relationship problems and communication issues.

The education segment can be used to teach the clients specific skills in communication, assertiveness, anger management, self-esteem, and stress management. What is learned during the education segment can be applied during the counseling segment. The use of education can help restructure some of the couples' beliefs about sex roles, violence, and marriage in general.

The timing of intervention and the confrontation of denial should be considered in relation to the length of time a couple have been in counseling. For example, it is usually not a good idea to encourage a couple to give unbridled vent to their emotions early in therapy. Our experience is that emotional catharsis is easier to handle after the couple have learned communication techniques or some method of constructively dealing with their emotions. Moreover, confrontation is best postponed until sufficient rapport has been established. Therefore, the counselors need to be adaptable and flexible, as well as sensitive to what the couple can tolerate at any given session. There are times when women may feel more comfortable talking to the male counselor. Some men feel safer expressing some feelings to a female therapist. Men may feel that talking about feelings to another man may make them look less masculine or weak.

Role Playing. There can be a number of different role play combinations in the counseling process. The couple may role play an interaction, practice a communication technique, or act out a particular disagreement. The counselors may role play with each other or may pair up with one of the client partners to role play while the remaining counselor and partner observe. These various pairings can contribute greatly to the effectiveness of the role play, the learning of the educational materials, and the development of insight.

Two examples of role-playing exercises are the reenactment of a misunderstanding and practicing an alternative action when anger begins to increase. One counselor can role play one exercise with one spouse while the other therapist and spouse role play the other exercise. In the first exercise, good communication skills (active listening and "I" messages to express feelings) can be demonstrated by the therapist as a way to resolve the conflict. In the second example, time-out procedures can be demonstrated by the therapist as a way to avoid losing control as anger builds during an argument.

Homework Assignments. Homework assignments are given to reinforce what is taught during the education segment of the session. They are also intended as a way of encouraging clients to practice what they have learned. An example of a homework assignment would be to ask a client to read information concerning relaxation exercises and to practice this method of stress management twice each day until the next session. Homework can strengthen newly learned behaviors for retrieval when problems arise. If a client is not completing homework assignments, the counselors explore this in a matter-of-fact manner to assess special issues and the level of commitment to therapy.

Awareness of Body Cues and Feelings. Couples are taught to become aware of their body cues and physiological responses when they are getting upset. If they can identify the cues, they can respond to situations more appropriately. For example, one man stated that when he got angry, his heart started pounding, he became tense, and his face turned red. If he became aware of these signals, he could stop and reevaluate the situation so that he could find other means of dealing with the anger instead of hitting his wife. Relaxation training helps clients become aware of their physical cues. They are encouraged to be aware of a rapid heartbeat, rapid speech, a rise in the pitch of their voices, sensations from the stomach, or other physiological cues. We often point out these observable physical cues and ask the client about others that may not be visible when the client becomes angry outside of counseling.

In order to heighten awareness, clients are also encouraged to comment spontaneously about what they are feeling. For example, one client stated, "I noticed that when you said you would really rather avoid my mother this weekend that my stomach seemed to tighten." Couples are encouraged to analyze smaller, more manageable segments of behavior. For example, a couple report that they had a "fight." The counselors assist them in breaking down the "fight" into specific behaviors and feelings. Perhaps one of the partners reports that the other is "stubborn" or "irrational." We help them describe "stubborn" and "irrational" in behavioral terms. This not only improves our understanding of what is occurring but is a necessary process in changing the couple's perceptions and behavior.

Fair Fighting. "Fair fight" rules are often emphasized, such as asking for an appointment and taking a time-out if there is a potential for the situation to get out of hand (Bach & Wyden, 1970). Methods of fight analysis are utilized, such as an analysis of a prior fight. The counselor can get the couple to talk about some of the major problem areas in the relationship. They can narrow it down to one specific incident and how each dealt with that incident, the feelings and perceptions of each, and alternative ways of resolving the conflict.

The clients are now ready for "fight training." This consists of teaching the couple how to get their needs met, express themselves, and have a good relationship without resorting to verbal, emotional, or physical violence. The fight training is always done in the office, where the battered spouse can feel safe. Also, the counselors will have the opportunity to observe and give instant feedback. The counselors may move to the role of referees during some of this training. This may be necessary because the therapist may touch on issues in setting up a situation for the fight training that stimulate emotions for the couple. As emotions build and the old patterns of reacting emerge, the counselors give feedback concerning their observations. The couple and the counselors can then discuss other more effective and less harmful ways of handling these or similar situations.

The clients are also taught "dirty fighting techniques" (Mantooth et al., 1987). This is presented in a humorous way to help clients become aware of how they are relating. Much of the dirty fighting is not in a couple's awareness but is a repetitive style of communicating that is guaranteed to destroy a relationship. As counselors present the dirty fighting techniques, couples usually recognize the way in which they have used them. Since our approach is nonblaming and nonthreatening, couples usually are open to talking about which techniques apply to their relationships or communication styles.

Reducing Ritualistic Behaviors. Another issue that counselors address is ritualistic behavior. When discussing with couples the way in which they deal with certain problem areas, it is evident that the precipitating stimuli and subsequent responses are similar much of the time. An example might be that a wife knows her husband will be angry if she is late for their luncheon date. She doesn't call to let him know she will be late; she just shows up late. He may know that she is probably late because she couldn't get out of the office when she planned to, but he responds angrily anyway. The counselors help the couple see the rituals and cues involved and assist with ways to break the pattern. Usually just bringing such a pattern to the couple's attention can make a difference.

Use of Metaphors and Analogies. The use of metaphors, stories, tales, and analogies can be helpful in counseling because the clients get a different view of situations similar to their own. It also keeps them from becoming defensive, because the counselor is not directly dealing with their situation. The story would at some point be brought back and applied to their relationship. These methods also help the clients analyze their own situation and problem-solving techniques. For example, in order to clarify an issue of mind reading for one couple, we used a story about one relationship in which the husband expected the wife to know when she was to come after him when he went outside during an argument. He believed very strongly that she should know by how hard he slammed the door whether to come after him and comfort him or leave him alone. Of course, whether she went after him or left him alone, he would hit her anyway because, according to him, she had not done the right thing. She couldn't tell what the slamming of the door meant; therefore, she would lose either way.

An example of an analogy that has been useful in getting couples to spend more time together involves explaining that relationships are like plants; if they are nurtured, they grow and are beautiful, but if left unattended, they wither and die. An unpleasant analogy labeled "watching snakes" has been effective in reinforcing the need for the couple to attend to each other when they are communicating. The couple are asked to imagine that there is a large snake in the room. They are asked whether they would be looking at the snake. Would they know what it was doing? Would they know its whereabouts? Would they be easily distracted from their awareness of the snake? How about their concentration? Would they be paying attention to the snake? The couple are then instructed to pretend that each other is a snake! They would then be more likely to pay attention to each other and to remember the attending behavior.

Using Humor. Through the counselor's use of humorous examples of significant issues, clients can sometimes see how they get locked into a negative pattern that can lead to major disagreements. For example, it was upsetting for one husband to have his partner squeeze the toothpaste from the top of the tube. Knowing this, the wife squeezed the toothpaste from the top of the tube anyway, because she wanted to "get back at him" for feeling ignored the night before. The counselor pointed out that the husband "got even" by having a "headache" when he knew his wife wanted to make love. The therapist relayed this message humorously by saying, "to get even, you get a headache from the waist down."

Desensitization. Desensitization is a behavioral technique often used in counseling. In the context of our approach, this technique is used to desensitize couples so that they are not afraid to openly discuss the violence. Through education about violence and its effects, clients are gradually given more freedom or permission to talk about the violence in their own relationship. The counselor also uses direct references to battering, hitting, or being abusive, instead of minimizing the violence by referring to "minor slaps." The violence is openly discussed with the couple in great detail. The counselors analyze a "hit." The clients are asked to describe the hit: open handed, fist, knuckle, back hand. They are asked to describe how the punch was thrown. The goal is not to have the couple minimize the severity of the behavior but to encourage an open dialogue between the couple about the violence. This helps destroy the "secret," the conspiracy of silence that exists in most battering relationships. Desensitization techniques are also used as part of the approach for anger management. This method involves relaxation training within a step-by-step approach of dealing with anger.

Rational-Emotive Techniques (RET). Many abusive men often see their violent behavior as the result of some event. This, of course, results in excessive blaming of others, an often-cited characteristic of the violent male (Gondolf & Russell, 1987). Presentation of the ABC principles of RET is often effective in helping the couple take responsibility for their behavior. The counselors must be well versed in this approach, since they will usually be met with resistance by the couple. It is helpful to have the clients present a specific incident when some event "caused" them to react by becoming angry or losing control. Some batterers comment that anyone would behave as they had, given similar circumstances. The counselors point out that there is no universal reaction to any incident. The man's reaction is a choice, either learned over time or selected spontaneously. For example, the man may be told, "Not all people slap others who call them names; there are other options. You don't hit everyone who you argue with, do you?"

Most couples are unaware of the many irrational beliefs that they have concerning themselves, their families, and the world in general. Cognitive restructuring through education and awareness training is one way to focus on these belief systems. One abuser defended his violence by informing us that he survived being whipped many times by his father. Another case concerned a woman who felt her husband was not affectionate. She indicated that the only physical contact they had was during intercourse. The husband's response was "I've always been this way; guess I'll always be this way." In situations like these, clients are confronted about these beliefs. Through cognitive restructuring, communication training, and education, clients can achieve a more realistic view of themselves and others. For example, one woman believed "If he loved me he would spend all of his free time with me instead of wanting to go hunting." The irrational belief was that she was basing his love on whether he spent all his free time with her.

Clients can change the way they think, feel, and respond by becoming aware of what they are telling themselves and, when it is negative, learning to change it to positive self-talk. For example, someone may believe that "I'm a failure; I can't do anything right." This person can stop, analyze the negative thinking, and change it to a positive message by saying, "Yes, I blew it this time, but no one is perfect. I don't have to be perfect" (rational thinking); "I've done a lot of successful things. I'll do the best that I can."

At times, clients think too much about "shoulds," "oughts," or "musts," and feel like failures if they fall short of these standards. They also apply these faulty thinking patterns to their spouses and children, for example, "I ought to just do what he wants so there won't be any trouble." This type of thinking isn't healthy for the individual or the relationship. Most likely, no matter what she does, there will always be something she hasn't done. Helping clients to become aware of this type of thinking and to consciously make a change is the key to changes in behavior and feelings about themselves.

We help clients distinguish between high-priority issues and low-priority issues that get blown out of proportion. A husband might be upset about his wife's being 5 minutes late getting home. His response is to hit her when she walks in the door. If the timing is right, the counselor might really exaggerate this issue. For example, the therapist might say, "Man, Joe, I can see why you're upset. Five minutes late! You're sitting home worrying, and she's probably out gallivanting around! She probably even stopped off at the motel on the way home. How could she do this to you after all you do for her?" This could go on and on. The goal is to help the client see how he reacted to such an issue.

Evaluation

Shupe and Stacey conducted an extensive independent follow-up of couples who had participated in our program (Riza, Stacey, & Shupe, 1985). Their results showed that 1 year after counseling, 78% of the women surveyed reported less or no violence and 79% remained married to their partners. In addition, findings showed that all of the couples surveyed would recommend our program to others. In a pilot study of a sample of couples, responses to various measures and questionnaires were collected prior to entering treatment and at the completion of the program (Geffner, Kreager-Cook, Sharne, Crawford, & Persinger, 1987). The results indicated significant improvement in self-esteem, communication and marital satisfaction, and a reduction in violence, stress, and hostility.

Ending domestic violence is the obvious goal for all of us who are working in this field. It appears to us that it is time to integrate and unite those utilizing various approaches, since most methods provide important information and various of them may be successful with certain people. Some abusers volunteer for treatment on their own, whereas others may not even participate with court mandates. Similarly, some battered women find shelters empowering, whereas others merely use them as emergency stops before returning to their abusive husbands. The intent of the person seeking therapy is probably a strong predictor of the outcome of the treatment. The advantage of a conjoint psychoeducational approach and other couples' interventions (Geller & Wasserstrom, 1984; Neidig & Friedman, 1984) is that for couples who do participate, the family system can be changed. This preserves the family and leads to a more mutually satisfying relationship without abuse, which is often what both the husband and the wife desire.

This approach should also reduce the likelihood of the intergenerational perpetuation of violence, since new roles, attitudes, and communication are established that affect children as well. However, research is still needed to verify these long-term effects on the couple as well as the children. As stated previously, there are cases where a conjoint approach is not feasible; in these situations, utilization of other methods for the battered woman and the abusive man are required. However, to eliminate any method or technique without research evidence seems counterproductive. Our approach will, we hope, add to the repertoire of the various practitioners working with violent couples.

References

Bach, G. R., & Wyden, P. (1970). *The intimate enemy*. New York: Avon Books.

Bandura, A. (1973). *Aggression: A social learning analysis*. Englewood Cliffs, NJ: Prentice-Hall.

Barling, J., & Rosenbaum, A. (1986). Work stressors and wife abuse. *Journal of Applied Psychology, 71*, 346–348.

Beck, A. T. (1979). *Cognitive therapy and emotional disorders*. New York: New American Library.

Bograd, M. (1984). Family systems approaches to wife battering: A feminist critique. *American Journal of Orthopsychiatry, 54*, 558–568.

Clarke, J. I. (1978). *Self-esteem: A family affair*. New York: Harper & Row.

Cook, D., & Frantz-Cook, A. (1984). A systemic treatment approach to wife battering. *Journal of Marriage and Family Therapy, 10*, 83–93.

Dell, P., & Goolishian, H. (1981). Order through fluctuation: An evolutionary epistemology for human systems. *Australian Journal of Family Therapy, 2*, 175–184.

Douglas, M. A., & Colantuano, A. (1987, June). *Cluster analysis of MMPI scores among battered women*. Paper presented at the Third National Family Violence Research Conference, University of New Hampshire, Durham, NH.

Ellis, A., & Harper, R. A. (1975). *A new guide to rational living*. North Hollywood, CA: Wilshire Book Co.

Ganley, A. (1981). *Court-mandated counseling for men who batter*. Washington, DC: Center for Women's Policy Studies.

Geffner, R., Franks, D., Patrick, J. R., & Mantooth, C. (1986, August). Reducing marital violence: A family therapy approach. In R. A. Geffner (Chair), *New approaches for reducing family violence*. Symposium conducted at the annual meeting of the American Psychological Association, Washington, DC.

Geffner, R. A., Jordan, K., Hicks, D., & Cook, S. K. (1985, August). Psychological characteristics of violent couples. In R. A. Geffner (Chair), *Violent couples: Current research and new directions for family psychologists*. Symposium conducted at the annual meeting of the American Psychological Association, Los Angeles, CA.

Geffner, R., Kreager-Cook, S., Sharne, K., Crawford, C. M., & Persinger, A. (1987, August). Effectiveness of a couple therapy program for reducing marital violence. In R. Geffner (Chair), *Effectiveness of different treatment programs for reducing spouse abuse*. Symposium presented at the annual meeting of the American Psychological Association, New York, NY.

Geffner, R., Rosenbaum, A., & Hughes, H. (1988). Research issues concerning family violence. In V. B. Van Hasselt, R. L. Morrison, A. S. Bellack, & M. Hersen (Eds.), *Handbook of family violence* (pp. 457–481). New York: Plenum Press.

Geller, J. A., & Wasserstrom, J. (1984). Conjoint therapy for the treatment of domestic violence. In A. R. Roberts (Ed.), *Battered women and their families: Intervention strategies and treatment programs* (pp. 33–48). New York: Springer.

Gelles, R. J., & Cornell, C. P. (1985). *Intimate violence in families*. Beverly Hills, CA: Sage.

Goldenberg, I., & Goldenberg, H. (1985). *Family therapy: An overview* (2nd ed.). Monterey, CA: Brooks/Cole.

Gondolf, E. W., & Russell, D. M. (1986). The case against anger control treatment programs for batterers. *Response, 9*, 2–5.

Gondolf, E. W., & Russell, D. M. (1987). *Man to man: A guide for men in abusive relationships*. Bradenton, FL: Human Services Institute.

Hamberger, L. K., & Hastings, J. (1986). Personality correlates of men who abuse their partners: A cross-validation study. *Journal of Family Violence, 1*, 323–345.

Hershorn, M., & Rosenbaum, A. (1985). Children of marital violence: A closer look at the unintended victims. *American Journal of Orthopsychiatry, 55*, 260–266.

Hotaling, G. T., & Sugarman, D. B. (1986). An analysis of risk markers in husband to wife violence: The current state of knowledge. *Violence and Victims, 1*, 101–124.

Hughes, H. M., Rau, T. J., Hampton, K. L., & Sablatura, B. (1985, August). Effects of family violence on child victims and witnesses. In M. Rosenberg (Chair), *Mediating factors in adjustment of child witnesses to family violence.* Symposium presented at the annual meeting of the American Psychological Association, Los Angeles, CA.

Jackson, D. D. (1965). The study of the family. *Family Process, 4,* 1–20.

Keeney, B. (1983). *Aesthetics of change.* New York: Guilford Press.

L'Abate, L., Ganahl, G., & Hansen, J. C. (1986). *Methods of family therapy.* Englewood Cliffs, NJ: Prentice-Hall.

Mantooth, C. M., Geffner, R., Franks, D., & Patrick, J. (1987). *Family preservation: A treatment manual for reducing couple violence.* Tyler, TX: University of Texas at Tyler Press.

McKay, M., Davis, M., & Fanning, P. (1983). *Messages: The communication book.* Oakland, CA: New Harbinger.

Neidig, P. H., & Friedman, D. H. (1984). *Spouse abuse: A treatment program for couples.* Champaign, IL: Research Press.

Pagelow, M. D. (1984). *Family violence.* New York: Praeger.

Riza, W. R., Stacey, W. A., & Schupe, A. (1985). *An evaluation of the effect of the Family Preservation Program in Tyler, Texas* (Vol. 35). Arlington, TX: University of Texas at Arlington, Department of Sociology, Anthropology, and Social Work, Center for Social Research.

Rosenbaum, A., & O'Leary, K. D. (1981). Marital violence: Characteristics of the abusive couples. *Journal of Consulting and Clinical Psychology, 49,* 63–71.

Rosenbaum, A., & O'Leary, K. D. (1986). Treatment of marital violence. In N. Jacobson & A. Gurman (Eds.), *Clinical handbook of marital therapy* (pp. 385–405). New York: Guilford Press.

Satir, V. (1967). *Conjoint family therapy* (Rev. ed.). Palo Alto, CA: Science and Behavior Books.

Satir, V. (1972). *People making.* Palo Alto, CA: Science and Behavior Books.

Sedlak, A. J. (1988). Prevention of wife abuse. In V. B. Van Hasselt, R. L. Morrison, A. S. Bellack, & M. Hersen (Eds.), *Handbook of family violence* (pp. 457–481). New York: Plenum Press.

Steinfeld, G. J. (1986). Spouse abuse: Clinical implications of research on the control of aggression. *Journal of Family Violence, 1,* 197–208.

Steinfeld, G. J. (1987). *Spouse abuse, an integrative interactional model: Contracts and levels of intervention.* Unpublished manuscript.

Straus, M. A. (1979). Measuring intrafamily conflict and violence: The conflict tactics scales. *Journal of Marriage and the Family, 41,* 75–88.

Straus, M. A. (1980). Victims and aggressors in marital violence. *American Behavioral Scientist, 23,* 681–704.

Straus, M. A., & Gelles, R. J. (1986). Societal change and change in family violence from 1975 to 1985 as revealed by two national surveys. *Journal of Marriage and the Family, 48,* 465–479.

Tolman, R. M., Beeman, S., & Mendoza, C. (1987, June). *The effectiveness of a shelter-sponsored program for men who batter: Preliminary results*. Paper presented at the Third National Family Violence Research Conference, University of New Hampshire, Durham, NH.

Walker, L. E. (1979). *The battered woman*. New York: Harper & Row.

Walker, L. E. (1984). *The battered woman syndrome*. New York: Springer.

Watzlawick, P., Weakland, J., & Fisch, R. (1974). *Change: Principles of problem formation and resolution*. New York: W. W. Norton.

6

Second-Order Systemic
Work with Violent Couples

Gerry Lane
Tom Russell

Introduction

Throughout this chapter references will be made to the systemic
movement, first- and second-order cybernetics, and first- and second-
order change. The following definitions will assist the reader in
understanding our use of these terms. *The systemic movement* refers
to the shift in thinking and practice among therapists from viewing
the individual client as the unit of service to viewing the larger client
system as the unit of attention. The larger client system can then be
viewed as an autonomous construct comprised of interactions among
those people who participate in that unit. Most recently, the systemic
movement reflects a growing shift from thinking based on notions of
power and control, pathology and dysfunction, and objectivity toward
that based on notions of organizational coherence, self-healing tau-
tology, and a less hierarchical interaction between therapist and
client. Therefore, the focus of treatment is the conversational exchange between the client system and the therapist regarding the
relational interactions among those involved, keeping in mind that
the therapist is always a part of that domain also.

First- and second-order cybernetics refers to the two basic developments of family therapy and practice. First-order cybernetics describes models of family therapy based on notions of the hierarchy between the therapist and client, with the therapists being in a one-up, expert position. These models assume objectivity and place a great deal of emphasis on the use of power tactics to create change within the client system. Second-order cybernetics refers to a shift away from these ideas to family therapy models more concerned with mutual exchange between therapist and client and emphasizing more egalitarian methods of exchange. These models do not presume that objective truth on the part of the therapist is possible.

First- and second-order change refers to the way in which change is viewed and the way in which change occurs. First-order change is viewed as resulting from the conscious intent on the part of the therapist to impose certain specific instrumental changes upon the client system. Many structural maneuvers fit this description. Second-order change refers to changes that occur within the client system out of exchanges with the therapist, but not because the specific change was consciously contrived by the therapist. These changes can be described as having evolved out of the therapy conversation but not having been caused or created by the therapist. These changes can be described as creative solutions emerging from within the client system.

Recent developments in systemic theory and its application are changing and expanding the boundaries of traditional family therapy thought and dogma. The systemic movement and second-order cybernetics place previously held beliefs about therapy, the therapist, the client, and objective reality in italics with a question mark. This chapter will explore some of these concepts in a most controversial context: couples' violence. The discussion of the application of these concepts in this context elicits a plethora of responses, ranging from curiosity and fascination to outrage and fury. However, many clinicians who work within this context are now searching for different ways of responding to couples who remain together and are violent. These clinicians are searching because they have witnessed couples who haven't responded positively to more traditional interventions held out as the protocol for treating couples who are violent. Some of these traditional approaches may work within a social control model of therapy in which a victim/victimizer dichotomy is emphasized. The application of systemic concepts as a way of eliciting curiosity and triggering changes is offered as an alternative to social control models of therapy. This application places the couple in a new context under a positive connotation.

We want to state emphatically that we support strategic social change whenever it can be accomplished. There is no question that there is an increasing need for more safe shelters for the abused woman who is able and ready and willing to leave. There is a need for the whole social structure to be reorganized so as to make it possible and easier for the abused spouse to be able to leave the violent situation with economic and emotional support. Continued advocacy in these directions is essential. Working toward such change is an unquestionable necessity in dealing with violence-prone couples. However, we are not proposing an either/or solution to treatment of these couples; We are proposing a both/and solution. It is essential that the reader keep the both/and frame in mind or else lose sight of the dilemma from which, in part, this work has emerged. What can be done with violent couples who remain together is the major dilemma to which we are referring.

Second-Order Family Therapy

Initially, family therapy thought and practice was a radical departure from mainstream psychiatry. It shifted the focus from the belief that pathology resided in the individual to the belief that pathology resided within the family system. As family ideology has evolved, it has remained couched in the language of dysfunctional systems, for most family therapists. A small group is emerging that has vigorously abandoned the notion of pathology altogether. These people are sometimes referred to as minimalists, constructivists, and/or second-order systems practitioners.

Recent developments in systemic theory and practice offer new hope and possibilities for clinical work with violent couples. A shift to a second-order cybernetic paradigm forces the therapist to leave behind the most strategic and controlled tactics of traditional family therapy. The therapist begins to view his or her observations as subjective and therefore becomes more curious about the family's beliefs and presuppositions about the world. Any description of reality is therefore observer-inclusive and cannot be separated from one's own ideology.

Shift in Paradigms

The most influential theorist in relation to the systemic paradigm and our own clinical work is the late Gregory Bateson. In the last decade of his life, Bateson laid down the crucial framework for shifting to a new way of viewing the world of form and pattern. Bateson presented the concept of immanent mind, in which he described the living world as a process of interlocking sequences that evolve through time and cannot be controlled through conscious purpose (Bateson, 1979). In an unpublished interview with Bateson conducted by Bradford Keeney, Bateson described the difficulty in shifting to the systemic view:

> It isn't that simple ever, any of it. Now I suspect that there are better reasons than just rigidity and stupidity for not changing paradigms. I think that if one didn't have that extra bit of rigidity there, one's whole paradigmatic structure would fall to pieces very soon. I'm sure that's what people are really afraid of, it's that total way of thinking about anything which will fall to pieces if they let the paradigm go.

As we moved into the systemic paradigm, we had to experience our own premises. Bateson discussed in his book *Mind and Nature* (1979) the concept that difference is information. He describes the micronystagmus of the human retina as an example of this. This simply means that the retina is kept constantly moving, which allows us to view stationary objects; however, what we actually see, according to Bateson, is only the outlines, which we fill in with our own presuppositions and premises. In a similar view, the Chilean biologist Humberto Maturana describes human beings as existing only through language (Maturana, 1985; Maturana & Varela, 1980). Therefore, we are forced to examine the language we are constructing in our clinical realities.

We experienced this shift in paradigm as particularly difficult when we entered into the domain of clinical work with violence. We were acutely aware that, nationally, the trend in working with violence was to adopt a conceptual frame based on a victim/victimizer dichotomy. However, we believe this view perpetuates the symmetrical, adversarial relationship between men and women. It is important to recognize that it developed in reaction to the victim-blaming stance—the view that the abused party in a relationship provokes the abuse, which has long characterized the legal and psychiatric professions' responses to domestic violence. To us, neither the victim/victimizer nor the victim-blaming conceptual frameworks are useful ways of approaching domestic violence.

In our thinking and clinical work, Bateson's concept of binocular vision is crucial. He used the analogy of two eyes, each giving a monocular view of what goes on and together giving a binocular, in-depth view. This double view is the relationship. Following this concept, one can never separate victim from victimizer, dominance from submission, aggressiveness from passivity, and so on. Each description is one half of an interactional pattern, not a personality characteristic residing in an individual. Therefore, when therapists make a distinction of victim or victimizer, they are separating a pattern and viewing both halves of the recursive process without taking into account the relational context.

Bateson used the story of aggression in lions to demonstrate this concept. He described how a lion's stalking a zebra is quite different from the aggressive behavior of two lions who are vying for females or territory. When a lion stalks a zebra, it makes itself very, very small and moves quite slowly as it moves in for the kill. The lion expends as little energy as possible in this context, which quickly ends in the death of the zebra. When two male lions are vying for territory or females, they act in an opposite manner. Each lion tends to make itself extremely large and expends a tremendous amount of energy in attempting to back the other lion down. This becomes a pattern of mutual exhibitionism, with the most common result being one lion's retreating without having to shed blood. Both of these stories show lions being "aggressive"; however, the behavior shown by the lion in relation to the zebra is the exact opposite from the story of the two lions vying for territory. In a linear sense, both stories describe aggression; however, when one shifts to the systemic view, one can see in the first relational context that the lion and zebra were in a complementary dance of predator/prey. In the second relational context, the lions were in a symmetrical struggle, with each attempting to control the relationship. These two descriptions given by Bateson, by way of Konrad Lorenz's (1963) work on aggression in animals, have had a deep and lasting impact on our thinking about violence in the couples we see.

The couples we see with severe, repetitive, one-sided violence generally show extremely rigid dominant-submissive complementarity. In these cases, each spouse has swallowed a contextual pattern of violence of some form in their family of origin. Often these couples describe themselves as being deeply in love. Violence and love are learned and were merged together at a deep premise level through repetitive early childhood experiences. In order to trigger change in these more severe rigid patterns, we believe that one has to disrupt the premises that support the patterns of violence.

In our experience, couples who's relationship has evolved into a symmetrical pattern of violence often have more episodes of fighting than couples in a complementary pattern; however, there are less severe outcomes. The couple is constantly in opposition to each other and only shift to brief moments of complementarity after an incidence of violence. The act of hitting serves the function in these couples of deescalating the arguments and triggering the ritual of making up. During these peace-making rituals, couples tend to show a great deal of affection, and many describe these periods of complementarity as the moments that hold them together. We have found in our work with symmetrical violence that the therapist's intervention should attempt to introduce complementary peace-keeping rituals into a couple's overall symmetrical pattern.

Power and Control

We approached working with these violent couples in a systemic model with some apprehension. We were acutely aware that the national trend in working with violence was to adopt a social control model of therapy that emphasized a victim/victimizer dichotomy. The major emphasis of this type of therapy is the social control agent's assuming a one-up position in order to separate the couple, usually by encouraging the woman to go to a battered woman's shelter. The men were either left alone to deal with the court system, or in some cases, they were mandated to a group composed of other "victimizers." We view this trend as emerging from a hierarchical stance of power and control (Hoffman, 1985) that perpetuates the symmetrical, adversarial relationship between men and women. We viewed this social control model of therapy as having developed out of and in reaction to the machismo that is the pervasive view of the male-dominated hierarchical professional structure (legal, religious, psychiatric). Such professionals adopted a victim/victimizer view, but the "victims" tended to be blamed. Both the "victim/victimizer" and "blaming the victim" stances have evolved from an epistemological premise that we do not share (Bateson, 1972).

The central mobilizing factor that allowed us to begin testing the systemic model in couple violence was the failure of the "victim/victimizer" model with the couples we were seeing who had been referred by the court. Time after time, we saw couples who had had much exposure to social control agents who, in our view, were operating from an instructional interaction (Maturana & Varela, 1980) perspective. By "instructional interaction" we are referring to actions taken by a person (helper, teacher, therapist, etc.) on behalf of another person based upon the premise that one can unilaterally determine and/or control how another person will respond to information given. This process can be viewed as an attempt to place little packets of information into the heads of other people (Hoffman, 1985). An example of this is when a therapist "instructs" a "victim" to leave the "victimizer." This has sometimes resulted in a frustrated therapist who then diagnoses the victim as having a masochistic personality disorder. Meanwhile, the violence continues. Our staggering observation was that these instructional interactions did very little to disrupt the recursive pattern of violence. It was also our observation that these interventions were based on the premise of power and control. To quote Gregory Bateson, "What is true is that the idea of power corrupts . . . Power corrupts most rapidly those who believe in it and it is they who will want it most" (Bateson, 1972, p. 333). The paradox is that the agents of social control, operating from a premise of power and control, reinforce this (in our view) false epistemology in these couples' domains.

Neutrality/Nonblaming Stance

The Milan Associates, who have done important work within the systemic perspective, see neutrality as "a specific pragmatic effect that his/her total behavior during the session exerts on the family (and not his intrapsychic position)" (Selvini, Boscolo, Cecchin, & Prata, 1980, p. 11). This nonblaming stance has had a profound effect on the couples we have seen. By the therapist's not blaming or imposing a solution on the couples, a new context and opportunity is created for the couple to begin to view themselves differently. This difference can be described as a shift toward a metalevel circular view. Boscolo has described this phenomenon "as system becoming more intelligent about itself" (Boscolo, personal communication, 1983). We agree with Maturana, who states that "there is no one way that the system is," that "there is no absolute objective family" (Maturana, 1985, p. 36). Thus, each person's view of the relationship is different and is valid. Therefore, by not blaming, one is respecting the validity of each partner's view of the relationship. "Furthermore, understanding this gives the therapist freedom to allow the system to transform, to disintegrate, to become something else, without the belief that what happens is his doing, or that he must help the family become what it should be" (Maturana, 1985, p. 42).

Positive Connotation

Positive connotation is an essential aspect of Milan/systemic work. We have found Peggy Penn's description of positive connotation to be the most clinically useful one (Penn, 1985, p. 270). She describes positive connotation as "a technique that describes positively the current organization of the system." She goes on to say, "Blaming in any form is omitted, and instead a perception is offered that defines positively the family's dilemma, regards it as context bound, and implies that contexts themselves are relative and changeable."

In the *Family Therapy Networker* interview with Salvador Minuchin, he discusses Milan/systemic work. He states, "Some of the people who use this method seem to believe that only positive connotation is appropriate at any point: abuse, family violence, whatever" (Minuchin, 1984, p. 28). It is our position that one never positively attributes violent behavior. In recent discussions of our work with Luigi Boscolo, he concurred with our position of never positively attributing violence (Boscolo, 1985, personal communication). Therefore, how is positive connotation used in a pragmatic way with these couples?

In our work with these couples, our initial interaction is the introduction of the context marker, which is "We will only see you once as a requirement of the court; if we meet again, it is up to you." This interaction places the therapy system under a positive connotation without positively connoting the violence. Although this may seem subtle, our experience is that it has a profound effect on eliciting curiosity, which we view as the seed of transformation. It is our observation and premise that for most of these couples, curiosity is a strange and discontinuous event. Webster's defines curiosity as "an eagerness to know, an inquisitiveness." The couple come expecting the therapist to blame and to prescribe what should be done, who should do what, and when. These couples have experienced this time after time with various "social systems." When the therapist does not take one of these control positions, this event triggers self-observation or curiosity. For these couples to become minutely self-observing is the beginning of a possible transformation. Thus, the goal of therapy is the amplification of this curiosity.

Relationship to the Court System

Many violent couples who come to treatment have been mandated to do so by a court system. In our work, many of the couples who came to us for treatment were referred in this manner. It was our belief that the first order of business was to clarify our position with the court system.

We view our relationship with the court itself as a complementary one, a relationship based upon differences. We do not see therapy with the couple as a diversionary process, nor do we see it as an adjunct to the judicial process. We carefully consider what evaluative information, if any, is provided to the court. Any such information that is given to the court is done only after the information is shared with clients and then only with their approval. We do not provide diagnostic material in the form of mental illness labeling to the court. The function of the court referral is to provide the couple an opportunity to engage in a process that may provide them with "information that may make a difference" (Bateson, 1972).

Simply put, criminal behavior is the business of the court, not therapy. Therapy may make a difference once that process has run its course. We agree with Thomas Szasz about the demedicalization of therapy. "It is not a 'disease' about which there is a 'cure'" (Szasz, 1984, p. 47). Such a proposition is a very dangerous one. Therapists can easily find themselves in the role, however unintentionally, of using mental illness terms "to incriminate innocent people and excuse guilty ones." We must avoid participating in the "Therapeutic State" (Szasz, 1984).

We do not see our primary role with these couples to be that of a social control agent. That is not to say that social control is not absolutely important in situations like this. The danger as we see it is the blurring between the therapist's role and the role of the social control agent. We are concerned when couples no longer know the difference between a social control person and a therapist. The court systems and the criminal justice systems in America often are confronted with violent couples. However, sometimes they lack enough evidence and information to prosecute the batterer. They often turn to mandated therapy as a social control process as well as a quasi-punishment. There is a danger in that type of process becoming a quasi-punishment and a game. The game occurs when the couple come to therapy because they are mandated. They let the therapist in on very little of their lives, because their dilemma is if they tell the therapist too much, they are afraid the therapist will cooperate with the criminal justice system and therefore prosecute them.

The court's initial position was that it would mandate a certain number of sessions, thereby determining length of treatment. This did serve the function of establishing the initial connection in the therapeutic system. However, our position was that in order to work in a second-order systemic model (B. Borwick, personal communication, 1983; Selivni, Boscolo, Cecchin, & Prata, 1980), the therapist must shift from a hierarchical position of control and power (Hoffman, 1985) to a more egalitarian position. Therefore, we had to shift the therapy from a mandated context to a nonmandated context. The court's primary need at that time was to mandate therapy for these violent couples. Our stance with the court was that we would only see these couples once, under a mandate. Work beyond the first mandated session would then be of a confidential and voluntary nature between the couple and the therapist. This was accomplished in negotiations with the court.

We look at couples who come to us, and if we determine that imminent life-and-death issues are primary, then our role is not to do therapy with these couples. We will shift to a role of social control agent to facilitate an appropriate referral elsewhere to ensure the safety of both partners. However, we draw a clear distinction between what we do and what role is assumed by agencies of social control.

Therapy Approach

In our work we attempt to observe interactional patterns and elicit historical premises and causal attributions (Howe, 1984) that in our view maintain the recursive pattern of violence. We emphasize our concern about the violence and underscore its potentially grave consequences without blaming, in a causal fashion, either partner. We do this through circular questioning and future questioning (Penn, 1982, 1985). We communicate to each partner his or her responsibility for the violent behavior and for remaining in a violent relationship. For example, we might ask, "If this violence in your relationship continues, who will die first?" We might follow up with such a question as "If one of you kills the other and the other is in prison, how will your children be taken care of?" Still further, we might ask, "If one of you is dead and the other in prison, and your children grow up without you, who will they blame for not having parents?" We try not to impose our maps or solutions onto the couple in regard to their dilemma.

Violence is the use of physical force to regulate shifts in interactional dynamics in a relationship. In the purist sense, we view violence in couples as communication about their relationship. Violent behavior is a dangerous and powerful message that frequently occurs as a crescendo in the couples' symmetrical dance. As stated previously, the message of violence for couples who are intimately involved is embedded in their recursive interactional patterns.

It is quite important from our systemic perspective to see the communication of violence as connected to the couples' deeply held premises about how one should live intimately with another. These deep premises about love, control, and punishment were programmed through early childhood contexts and are central to the cocreation of violence in adulthood.

Interventions

In the development of systemic treatment, much attention has been given to the design and form of interventions. These interventions have taken the forms of paradox, symptom prescriptions, and therapeutic rituals, to name a few. In our work, primary attention is given to designing interventions of a circular form. We have coined the term "circular replication" to describe this kind of intervention (Lane & Russell, 1984). We view the symptomatic behavior bringing the couple in for treatment as a message embedded in a larger circular pattern. Circular replication is a nonjudgmental comment on the larger pattern, of which the symptomatic behavior is only a part. By mentioning this pattern in a neutral and curious manner, the therapist provides a chance for the couple to step outside of their patterns and observe them for the first time. We assume that one can never fully observe or describe the actual circularity present in a client system. One can present an observed replication of it.

Circular replication is introduced at the end of the session as part of a final commentary. One function of reserving the circular replication as a part of a final commentary is that of creating a perturbation. In doing so we are connecting the observed behavioral pattern with the observed operating premises. We view circular replication as a distinct type of final intervention. We view the circular replication as having the potential for shifting the couple's paradigm.

It is not our intent to elicit a specific "right" solution. The observer does not have a belief in objective reality and of how one should be. The therapist who views his or her interactions with the client system as perturbations has no expectations of the system except that it will interact with his perturbations and evolve in its structurally determined manner.

In the following case example, we will be discussing in detail our interventions in this most complex of problems. The transcript of the session below involves a consultation we provided to a couple at the request of their therapist. Gerry Lane interviewed the couple, while Tom Russell served as consultant, observing from behind the one-way mirror. Through ongoing commentaries of the edited interview material we highlight the thinking behind our questions, methods, and interventions.

Transcript of a Consultation Session

> Therapist - Gerry Lane
> Consultant - Tom Russell

THERAPIST: Well, I guess where I would like to start is how you got here, to the Center.

HOWARD: My therapist recommended it. (Pause) I told her that we were having some problems that sometimes include violence and . . . uh . . . she recommended it . . .

THERAPIST: She thought Louise should come with you, too?

HOWARD: Uh, yeah.

THERAPIST: Did you agree with the therapist that it was good to come?

LOUISE: I talked to her on the phone.

THERAPIST: (To Louise) Did you ever see this therapist with Howard?

LOUISE: No.

THERAPIST: Do you have an individual therapist also?

LOUISE: No.

THERAPIST: Okay, so what is the situation? I know the therapist suggested that you come, Louise, but how would you describe why you're here?

LOUISE: Uh . . . I'm here because the fighting we're having at home is not acceptable to me and I'm afraid and I don't want to get hurt and I'm tired of things breaking . . .

THERAPIST: Have you been physically hurt?

LOUISE: Yeah.

THERAPIST: How badly?

LOUISE: (Pause) I don't know how to describe how badly . . .

THERAPIST: Have you been to the hospital?

LOUISE: No, just black and blue.

THERAPIST: Mainly where? Face? Arms?

LOUISE: I don't know. (Pause)

THERAPIST: Is this the first time you've told an outsider?

LOUISE: Yeah, especially someone I don't really know.

THERAPIST: Exactly, exactly.

LOUISE: So I'm not . . . and it's really warm in here (laughing).

THERAPIST: Have the police been involved in this at all?

LOUISE: No, no.

THERAPIST: Okay.

LOUISE: I think more things have broken than me.

THERAPIST: But you've been hit.

LOUISE: Yeah.

THERAPIST: And that's an issue for you, and I'm sure it's an issue for Howard.

HOWARD: Yeah, it is an issue.

Commentary: We always begin the interview with a violent couple by first assessing the level of violence and the couple's explanation of why they have come to the therapist. This is done before exploring the interactional patterns between the couple.

THERAPIST: How would you describe things between yourself and Louise now?

HOWARD: I would say that things are generally good, but when they're bad that's a real problem. I mean if we have a fight, I can say she did this wrong, or she can say I did this wrong. But when it gets out of control, I'm hitting her and hurting myself. I punched a wall and hurt myself. It just isn't acceptable on any level. If, aside from that, things are very good . . . I mean that's a little bit preposterous.

THERAPIST: Oh, no, not really.

HOWARD: So I feel, and I'm pretty sure that Louise feels, that basically we have a good marriage. And yet we absolutely have to deal with this issue of violence.

THERAPIST: How would you describe the violence, Howard? What's it like? What's going on between the two of you when you feel the escalation, when things start to really heat up?

HOWARD: I think typically we're arguing about something either we could deal with or is trivial. And we'll tend to feel that the other is being unreasonable. Typically, I'll get to a point where I'll feel that she is provoking me beyond what I can deal with and something happens.

THERAPIST: Yeah, so you kind of keep going up and up with each other to a point you, Howard, will say something. Louise, you come back—is that how it operates? Or, Louise will say something; you'll come back with something?

LOUISE: Sometimes it's faster than that.

THERAPIST: Yeah, how fast?

LOUISE: (Laughing) I think it's more than sometimes. Things go on for a long time, and Howard gets really angry, and he doesn't get angry a little bit at a time. Then something really trivial can make things explode. So it doesn't mean that we've been having a fight for an hour.

THERAPIST: Yeah, okay. Things have built up so something trivial can come up.

HOWARD: The last time that we had something like this, we were talking, and I didn't answer her sufficiently. I turned to leave the room, and she said something to me. I turned around, and I hit the door with my elbow, and it put a hole in the door. I don't think I really hit you, but I had my hands on her, and it was just a really bad scene. It leaves both of us feeling terrible.

THERAPIST: Do you see the incident the same way, Louise? How would you describe what happened? I guess this was the last incident?

LOUISE: Yeah, that's what happened. We talked about it since then.

THERAPIST: How do you explain that Howard loses his temper like this?

LOUISE: How do I explain it?

THERAPIST: Yes, what's your explanation?

LOUISE: (Pause) I don't really have an explanation.

THERAPIST: How does that feel? You feel puzzled?

LOUISE: Terrible! (Then laughs.)

THERAPIST: Terrible, okay. So you must have several different ideas that you play around with about what triggers this in the relationship. I would be interested in hearing those, if you have any, and I'm sure you do.

LOUISE: I'm not sure I understand your question.

THERAPIST: Your ideas about what triggers this in the relationship.

LOUISE: I think Howard feels really powerless sometimes. So I think that this is a real power play. I think that he's really angry at a lot of things, and I am just who he gets angry at. 'Cause he doesn't really get angry at anybody else particularly, and I think that's a problem.

Commentary: At this point, the therapist is eliciting the multiple maps from which the couple is operating in regard to the identified problem. Through this questioning, new maps are being cocreated that link the violent behavior to larger interactional patterns.

THERAPIST: When he gets angry at you do you feel he's really angry at you or angry at something else?

LOUISE: Angry at something else.

THERAPIST: And how do you respond when he's angry at you but not really angry at you?

LOUISE: It's hard!

THERAPIST: Do you ever get angry with him? Do you get back?

LOUISE: Yeah, but not like this.

THERAPIST: [To Howard] How does she do it? How does she get angry back at you? What does she do?

LOUISE: I talk.

HOWARD: She criticizes and complains. I mean, there are times when one can go on indefinitely over some trivial thing. I feel that what she says about me also goes for her, but her means are verbal. She will, if she's anxious or if she's uptight, she will lash out at me verbally and sometimes will continue for a long period of time.

THERAPIST: When Louise is going at you, how do you deal with it? Do you withdraw, do you fight back, argue back, criticize? What do you do?

HOWARD: I think I've begun to notice that I do tend to escalate that. If she criticizes me, I'll say something nasty back. I think probably she's better at verbal fighting than I am. I tend to think she beats me up verbally. To some extent, I withdraw. Sometimes I find myself talking, saying things to her, to myself.

THERAPIST: Like what?

HOWARD: Like "Oh yeah, you're so good at doing things, you know I didn't put the dishes in the drain right. But I see how you wash dishes too, so what are you complaining about," I'm saying to myself, which I don't know if I should say that. It tends to be an escalation, you know. That's not such a great thing to do, if she complains about me, I complain about her. It's head on.

THERAPIST: So when you're in this kind of pattern, things are kind of moving up on the ladder. How do you all stop it? How is it deescalated? Is that when you really lose your temper?

HOWARD: It gets to a point where sometimes I feel like the only way I can stop her is to totally humiliate myself, apologize, say I'm sorry, no matter what I think about it.

THERAPIST: Is this before or after you lose your temper?

HOWARD: Before.

THERAPIST: Before, okay.

HOWARD: Before . . . sometimes I try and do that. Sometimes I say no, I'm not going to do that. Why should I apologize for something I don't feel is my fault?

THERAPIST: But you feel compelled . . .

HOWARD: Well, I feel that maybe that will placate her.

THERAPIST: Will it stop it, when he apologizes like that?

LOUISE: (Laughing) He doesn't apologize.

THERAPIST: Do you know what he is talking about?

LOUISE: See, I think what happens is . . .

THERAPIST: Wait, before you go on, he says he feels kind of humiliated . . .

LOUISE: I think he feels all that.

THERAPIST: You never see it?

LOUISE: I don't think it necessarily is going on. I think if I say things, he feels attacked. So then he feels like it goes on but I don't get any clue that the first thing I said registered. What could be going on could be 5 minutes, and he could feel like it was an hour. So if I say, "You didn't do whatever," he doesn't say anything, so I'll say, "I'd really like it if you did whatever this way." He still doesn't say anything. So I'm starting to feel really frustrated. So I don't think it's like your analogy so much, that it's both of us building. To me it comes up from outer space. Like we were talking about these windows the other day. I was saying something, and he was leaving the room. I said, "Don't leave yet, I haven't finished," and he slammed into the door, you know. Like this was out of the blue, as far as I was concerned. I don't know where it came from. I didn't feel like there had been any long harangue.

HOWARD: Yeah, I agree with that.

LOUISE: And when I see it coming I hide, I run. I try to get anywhere away.

HOWARD: I don't totally agree with that.

THERAPIST: So when he slams the door, say, raises his voice, then what do you do?

LOUISE: I say, "Try to calm down."

THERAPIST: Are you afraid at this point?

LOUISE: Yeah (quietly).

THERAPIST: So it frightens you.

HOWARD: At that point I had totally lost my cool.

THERAPIST: But you hadn't gone after her at that point?

HOWARD: Did I? Did I immediately go? (Looks at wife) I can remember yelling at her to stop talking, and she kept talking. I said shut up, and she kept talking and she kept talking. It's like I get the feeling no matter what I do, calm, angry, totally out of control, once we're in that situation she won't shut up. She'll just keep coming after me. And if I did "X," I should have done "Y." If I do "Y," I should have done "X."

Commentary: At this point, we would describe the couple's dominant pattern as symmetrical. By symmetrical we mean behavior that elicits similar behavior from another. This is a competitive process. This can be a game without end until something occurs that shifts the relationship from symmetrical to complementary. Violence often serves this purpose.

LOUISE: But I wasn't saying anything. See, that's the problem. I think that sometimes it's that I'm not saying anything. I really do.

THERAPIST: But somehow you hear her when she's not saying anything.

HOWARD: I think she doesn't have any qualms at all about criticizing me seven times before breakfast, and to her it's just the normal state of affairs.

THERAPIST: [To Louise] To you maybe that's showing concern or affection.

LOUISE: Yeah and I wasn't. I think a lot of things I say . . . he thinks I'm criticizing him, and maybe we're just talking about whether to leave the windows opened or closed. It was more like it was going to rain and what should we do, and I didn't see that necessarily as criticism.

THERAPIST: In some sense you don't feel like he listens to you.

LOUISE: I feel like he doesn't hear it.

THERAPIST: And you're saying the same thing, that you're feeling like sometimes she doesn't listen to you.

HOWARD: [Nods silently.]

Commentary: Our observation is that this issue of listening/not listening fits with Luigi Boscolo's description of communication patterns in symmetrical relationships. In a recent conversation (L. Boscolo, personal communication, 1987), he described how in such relationships, one person will begin to speak, usually in a critical manner, and the other will hear only the first few words. At that point, the other begins thinking about how he or she will respond without hearing the other's idea fully. Consequently, these couples often complain about the lack of communication. We see a recursive pattern in the therapist's ability to maintain curiosity through circular questioning and the couple's ability to evolve new ideas, explanations, and premises.

THERAPIST: What do you do to keep the peace or bring the peace back after one of these blow-ups? How do you make up?

HOWARD: [Pause] In a more normal situation when things don't go totally out of control?

THERAPIST: Let's say they go totally out of control, you grab her, you hit her. What's the process of making up?

HOWARD: We're separated for an hour or some period of time.

THERAPIST: Do you leave?

HOWARD: I leave or she leaves.

THERAPIST: Who leaves the most?

HOWARD: I can remember both of us leaving.

THERAPIST: So you both of you . . .

HOWARD: [Pause] We clean up. I apologize. I feel terrible.

LOUISE: I feel terrible.

HOWARD: She feels terrible. She says, "We can't do this." I say, "You're right, we can't do this."

THERAPIST: At that moment, is she open to the apology? Does she accept it after the hour's separation? She says she feels bad, and you can come back. You apologize. Do you feel she moves close to you at that moment?

HOWARD: Yeah, at that point I feel that she loves me and if she didn't love me, she wouldn't accept it.

THERAPIST: So hold it here. So one of the ideas you have is that if she didn't love you, that she would not accept this. In some way this validates the relationship for you. It's like this is a way that I know that we're in love. And you have a marriage because she accepts this. She doesn't like it.

LOUISE: She doesn't really accept it. [Laughing]

THERAPIST: He feels you accept it.

LOUISE: I know. That's part of the problem, that's a problem.

Commentary: We see in this sequence how the violence serves to disrupt the escalation between the couple. In other words, the violence stops the fight, and this appears to be a paradox. However, this is understandable when one understands that this event allows for a new context within which a different kind of fit can emerge. This new fit is often described as being more complementary. We see the violence setting into motion peace-keeping rituals that temporarily stabilize the relationship. The dilemma for these couples is that they become addicted to the violence as a way of regulating the oscillation between symmetry and complementarity. In other words, after a violent act, the couple move into a peace-making ritual where they show tremendous love and affection. This is the cement that holds them together until the next escalation. This is a deadly pattern.

During the next segment of the session, the interview shifted to the exploration of premises and narratives in each spouse's family of origin. Howard described his family as emotionally cool, with only rare expressions of overt anger. However, when verbal anger was expressed, it was quite dramatic, with long periods of tension following the outbursts. He reported that his parents had a highly complementary relationship, with his mother consistently following his father's directives. The underlying premise appears to be that a wife should comply with her husband's demands.

In Louise's family, there was a continuous uproar of verbal battles. She described constant symmetrical escalations between her and her sisters and her and her parents. The fighting in her family appears to have been a process of connecting that never resulted in violence. The premise that appears to have evolved in her family is that to be in love is an opportunity to express anger and difference safely.

During the first break in the session, the team discussed the difference in each family of origin's premise about the meaning of anger and how it should be expressed. There was also discussion about how Louise was unable to see her part in the interaction that perpetuated their repetitive pattern. The team began to view the violent act as serving the function of testing their loyalty to the relationship. The transcript picks up after the return from the break.

THERAPIST: My colleague wanted to find out a little more, Howard. You
              said earlier in the interview, when you come back you feel
              very accepted. In between these incidents where you lose

	the temper, is there ever a period where you have doubts about the relationship or her feelings toward you?
HOWARD:	I don't think I ever doubt that she loves me. The complaint I tend to have against Louise is that she's nagging me, to put it in a general term. And I wonder how she can expect things to be really wonderful and terrific at 7:00 when at 6:30 she's nagging me. So I sometimes wonder if it's more important to her to ventilate her anxiety. I never seriously doubt her love.
THERAPIST:	After things heat up, you go away for a while. There's a nice period when you come back after you apologize.
HOWARD:	No, it's not a nice period.
THERAPIST:	It's not a nice period?
HOWARD:	It's not like I feel "Oh, great, she loves me."
THERAPIST:	No, no, no.
HOWARD:	It's that, well what can I say, the tension has been released to some degree.
THERAPIST:	In your mind, she's not nagging you.
HOWARD:	No, that's not really true. Louise almost always has something to say.
THERAPIST:	Is there a difference between something to say and nagging in your mind? Or are they both the same?
HOWARD:	No, they're not both the same. I was saying nagging to just put things simply.
THERAPIST:	Louise, what would happen if the two of you didn't escalate like this in the relationship, if things didn't get this intense? Do you think the two of you would drift apart? Because it seems like this is when both of you vent some frustration about what has happened in the relationship. We realize that sometimes Howard, in your opinion, just blows up for nothing, but usually, you agreed earlier, that things kind of build. What would happen if the two of you didn't have this pattern, this ritual? Or if this pattern continued, what do you think would happen in 6 months?
LOUISE:	I don't know.
HOWARD:	I think it would destroy our marriage.
THERAPIST:	Who would leave, who would take the first step if it continued?

LOUISE: I don't think it would destroy our marriage. I think we would like to think it would.

THERAPIST: Okay, that's interesting.

LOUISE: You know what I mean, we'd say, if we're intelligent people then we would, but I don't think that we'd let it go on for 3 years.

THERAPIST: But that's interesting because I think you're really being straight on an emotional level when you say you don't think this would destroy the marriage. My impression is that Howard knows that.

HOWARD: I know it would destroy our marriage, and it would destroy my life.

LOUISE: I don't think it would. I think if it would, you'd stop. That's what I think part of the power is.

Commentary: During the final commentary to the couple, after the second break, the consultant, Tom Russell, was invited to come into the room with the couple and the therapist. This is seen as a variation on Tom Andersen's (1987) use of the reflecting team, which allows the team to present their hypotheses and views of the couple's dilemmas directly in front of the client system. The transcript picks up after the return from the break, later in session.

THERAPIST: Why don't you start, Tom. I want to hear what you're thinking.

CONSULTANT: Well, I guess I'm struck by the fact that this has, in the words you used, "come out of the closet." The problem with the violence has been brought out into the open in a way that it can be looked at differently, differently in terms of the two of you being seen as a couple here and having a chance to exchange with other people and other people exchange with you about that. That seems to me a real nice addition to whatever has been going on for Howard in terms of what he's been trying to struggle with with his therapist, and Louise's struggling with it vis-à-vis not being here, but struggling with it indirectly. This really makes it very different.

THERAPIST: Yeah. One of the things we discussed outside of the room, that I want to discuss in front of Louise and Howard, is the difference in style in the families of origin: how they handle temper, how they handle anger. In Louise's family, that was a way to connect, to be together. Everybody was yelling, it was normal, and nothing happened. No one separated, no one threw any punches.

CONSULTANT: They maintained being a family, being close in that way.

THERAPIST: And one lives in a situation like that. They don't learn how to sense when things are getting out of hand because they've never had that experience. And it's almost hard to believe that that could happen.

CONSULTANT: Well, I think when something is a problem, our styles develop a radar to that. My impression is that in Louise's family there was no need to develop radar. It was a way of being a family and being close. My sense, is that in Howard's family that may have meant something very different. And then the two of them coming together, it almost is a conflict of loyalties, which, at this point in time, may be sending up all these signals that there is this clash of philosophies going on.

THERAPIST: Well, in Howard's family they were serious. My impression was that when they were yelling it was a way . . .

CONSULTANT: To do something.

THERAPIST: It was a way to stop something. Of course people complied more, other than Howard and his father. They seem to be able to argue some and have some closeness there. So he has had some experience. He and his father were able to argue, and it didn't destroy the relationship.

CONSULTANT: That might be something that can grow, that can really be built on.

THERAPIST: We don't want to burden you with a lot of ideas right now, you can only hear so much, but we think you're at a nice place to start couples' therapy. What we've done today is a consultation that will be used with your therapist who begins to work with you. We feel that many couples we see with violence in their relationship are not ready to start couples' therapy. With you, we think it's time. And we think you may have already made some important changes just by getting here.

CONSULTANT: I think the only thing I want to add is a real sense of commitment I see here, of how strong the connection between the two of you has been.

Commentary: In this dialogue, we are highlighting the positiveness of the couple's willingness and desire to deal openly with the violence in their relationship. We are also highlighting the positiveness of the "observed love" between this couple, which they have both expressed. However, we are not in any way noting any positiveness in the violence. We are connecting the couple's premises in regard to dealing with difference, specifically anger and violence, that evolved out of their families of origin. We view this type of feedback as a circular replication.

THERAPIST: Now, there is one thing we'd like to experiment with before you come back and see your therapist here. We would like you to have a couple of meetings, twice before you come back. What is today?

LOUISE: Wednesday.

THERAPIST: Wednesday. Say Thursday and Sunday, have these meetings. In the first meeting, Louise, we'd like you to talk to Howard and Howard only to listen. We'd like you to let your mind wander and just fantasize what your family would have been like if they had dealt with their anger and conflict more like Howard's family had dealt with it. We'd like you to only listen, Howard. And, Louise, you go as long as you need to go. Howard, you only listen. Then we'd like you to switch and Sunday Howard you talk to Louise about how things would have been different in your family if they'd handled the conflict and anger and yelled and screamed like they did in Louise's. We realize this is just an exercise in fantasy, but we'd like you to do this. Then when you come back, we'd like you to share these fantasies with the therapist. We think this will help Louise begin to work with you. There is one other thing we want you to begin to think about, Howard. That is how can you help Louise learn when you are beginning to lose your temper, beginning to get to the point where you're going to hit her. She doesn't have the experience to really know when this is beginning to happen.

CONSULTANT: The radar is not there with Louise right now.

THERAPIST: We'd like you to begin to think about how you can begin to help her develop her radar. Because you have more experience in your family with this.

CONSULTANT: And it may be what he's helping her learn about is when he needs a time-out.

THERAPIST: Yeah.

HOWARD: Actually, that's just what came to mind. We've talked about having a code word and I was thinking . . . a code blue time-out.

CONSULTANT: But Louise doesn't have that radar because of her experience in her family. There was no reason for her to develop that.

CONSULTANT: So this is something we'd like you to think about. Do you have any comments or ideas, based on anything we have said at this point, that you'd like to share now?

LOUISE: I don't have that much experience with his family other than his mother, and she doesn't get angry. That's a big problem. I mean she does, she has ulcers.

THERAPIST: This is what we want. We realize this is fantasy.

HOWARD: What you've been saying makes me really think, 'cause I've noticed Louise says my mother is such a sweet lady, and she is, but Louise doesn't notice my mother is being a bit more aggressive.

LOUISE: She doesn't say anything.

CONSULTANT: It's a different language than Louise learned.

THERAPIST: We have to add something to the ritual, Tom. That is, after Louise fantasizes about it, then in the same meeting, Howard, you come back and correct her fantasy by showing her the way it was.

CONSULTANT: But let her fantasize first.

THERAPIST: And then in the next meeting, Louise, you come back and when Howard fantasizes about your family you let him know your interpretation because there are so many different ways of looking at a family.

LOUISE: Yeah, we had very different families.

THERAPIST: So we'll let you meet with your therapist, and she'll let you know when to come back.

LOUISE: We appreciate your time.

THERAPIST: Well, we wish you well, and we think things can work.

Commentary: In prescribing this ritual, it is of little consequence in our minds whether the couple performs the ritual or not. However, the couple's thinking about the ritual can have a hypnotic, disorienting effect on loosening their fixed reality of themselves, which usually appears linear. This allows a triggering of a new construction of reality by the couple, independent of the therapist.

Evaluation

In clinical work, much attention is often given to outcome studies that attempt to predict, define, and measure the effect of therapy in relation to change. The premise that supports this type of research is based upon a belief in cause and effect, specifically, that the therapist causes a particular change in a client. Our belief is that a therapist can sometimes trigger changes in certain premises that support certain behaviors. When this occurs, one often sees new behaviors emerge that can't be predicted, directed, or controlled. Neither can these new behaviors be said to be permanent. Human systems are constantly evolving through time. Traditional research is only a punctuation of reality as seen by another at certain points in time.

The concept of change in therapy has also been connected with the idea of success. Success is a subjective judgment along the continuum of change that varies in definition from observer to observer. In our work with violent couples, we define change or success when the interaction in the therapy system can be observed as having triggered a change that can be described as a deescalation of the violence. The definition is then viewed as a behavioral one.

Language is important in our working definition of change and success. We have not used the word "caused." The concept of "triggering" is much more acceptable and fitting in this observer-inclusive process of therapy, which is never objective but rather always subjective. Our belief is that we can never fully know or control outcome; we can only make our observations. Therefore, we would not say that "we" or "something" caused certain changes. We would describe the phenomena as a "triggering."

Another issue that often emerges in conversation about therapy and change is the notion of success and permanency. Is this change permanent? We could never describe such changes as permanent, because human systems are always in the process of evolving/changing. We can only describe changes in terms of observed behavioral changes at certain points in time in the evolution of the human system.

It is our observation that the domain of violence as it relates to therapy seems to elicit in some people much higher expectations for change and permanency than other areas. We are always having doubts about whether or not the violence is over. But at the same time, you can never guarantee that any problem is finished forever. If you remove a cancerous tumor, another may come back. If you have the flu one year, there's no guarantee that it may not happen again. And no one expects a guarantee; however, in this field people are always asking, "Can you guarantee that there will never be violence?" How do you know that it's cured? That is one of the problems of thinking within the medical model about these conditions that exist between human beings. If you are approaching the problem with the premise that there is a cure, then you're always going to be asking, "Is this taken care of?" As systemic thinkers and therapists, we hold the idea that people are always evolving. We don't always know in what direction they will evolve.

Perhaps the high expectation for change and permanency of therapeutic interventions with couples' violence occurs because working with these couples triggers in us all our own personal premises about violence. These personal or self-premises about violence connect to broader social and cultural premises. We often experience deep personal discomfort when such triggering occurs. It is no wonder that such triggering of deep personal premises often elicits such responses of control and punishment, which can become a part of the process of therapy.

In order for a therapist to shift to a second-order model, she or he has to have an experience of hitting bottom, similar to that of an alcoholic. The therapist must face his or her inability to directly change or control other human beings.

Our work and studies of violent couples have been of a qualitative rather than quantitative nature. With this background, we will share some findings based upon the follow-up we have done with approximately 40 violent couples with whom we have worked in couples' therapy. Six months after the end of therapy, we made follow-up calls on the couples. We asked how things were going, were they still together, and were there reoccurrences of violence. In approximately 60% of the cases, the women provided follow-up information to us; in the other 40% the men gave us the information. Of the couples sent to us by the court, 60% chose to return after the first session, when the court mandate was no longer guiding them. Couples were seen for an average of 3 to 10 sessions. Seventy percent of the couples reported no further incidences of violence 6 months after the end of therapy. Approximately 40% of the couples ended up separating by the second or third session, or within 6 months following therapy. Many of these couples had never separated previously. We believe that our nondirective, nonjudgmental approach, which elicits a couple's curiosity and anxiety about their violent patterns, triggered for them the opportunity to make choices in their lives.

Conclusion

Second-order systemic thinking can open up the possibilities of new realities for therapists working with couples with violent patterns. For many couples, violence serves the function of regulating closeness, distance, symmetry, and complementarity. One of our observations with couples in complementary relationships, in which one spouse is abusing and the other spouse is always being hurt, is that these couples describe themselves as being deeply in love, and there is very little anxiety about the violence. During the period of closeness following the violent episode, both partners truly feel, on a deep, cognitive level, that the violence will never occur again. These are the couples that have the most possibility for continued violence. This is what we call "dangerous love"; their love blocks them from seeing their pattern and having any insight into the possibility for further violence. Through circular replication, we attempt to disrupt or trigger a change in the premises that support the patterns of violence. We begin to feel better about couples when their anxiety heightens and they start to be anxious about the future.

We are not proposing a panacea for treating violent couples. The more involvement we have with these ideas with these couples, the more aware we are of the duality of love and violence in human beings and mankind as a whole. We think it presumptuous to believe that one can think of eradicating violence at the level of the couple and the family without the same attention being given to violence on the larger level of culture and nation against nation. The two are recursively connected.

References

Andersen, T. (1987). The reflecting team: Dialogue and metadialogue in clinical work. *Family Process*, 26(4), 415-428.

Bateson, G. (1972). *Steps to an ecology of mind*. New York: Ballantine Books.

Bateson, G. (1979). *Mind and nature*. New York: E. P. Dutton.

Hoffman, L. (1985). Beyond power and control: Toward a "second order" family systems therapy. *Family Systems Medicine, 3*, 381-396.

Howe, G. (1984, November). *Changing the family mind*. Paper presented at the Fourth Annual Symposium on Family Therapy, University of Tennessee, Knoxville, TN.

Lane, G., & Russell, T. (1984). *Circular replication: A system intervention*. Paper presented at the Fourth Annual Symposium on Family Therapy, University of Tennessee, Knoxville, TN.

Lorenz, K. (1963). *On aggression*. New York: Harcourt Brace Jovanovich.

Maturana, H. (1985). An interview with Humberto Maturana. *Family Therapy Networker*, 9(3), 32-43.

Maturana, H., & Varela, F. (1980). *Autopoiesis and cognition*. Dordrecht, Holland: Dreidel.

Minuchin, S. (1984). An interview with Salvador Minuchin. *Family Therapy Networker*, November/December, 26-68.

Penn, P. (1982). Circular questioning. *Family Process, 21*, 267-279.

Penn, P. (1985). Feed forward: Future questions, future maps, *Family Process, 24*, 299-311.

Selvini, Palazzoli, M., Boscolo, L., Cecchin, G., & Prata, G. (1980). Hypothe-sizing-Circularity-Neutrality. *Family Process, 19*, 73-85.

Szasz, T. (1984). An interview with Thomas Szasz. *Family Therapy Networker*, July/August, 25-66.

IV
Integrative Approaches

7

Eclectic Approaches in Working with Men Who Batter

Alan Rosenbaum
Roland D. Maiuro

During a recent conversation, a respected colleague of ours suggested that marital aggression was rooted in a need for control. "Men," he said, "use aggression to control their female partners." We agreed. Control is certainly an important factor in the dynamics of marital violence. His treatment approach, well known and effective, focused on helping abusers relinquish control and share power with their spouses. Several weeks later, we discussed the same topic with the director of a treatment program for wife abusers, who stated that "poor impulse control" and "defective self-concept" were the critical factors. We agreed. Abusers are certainly impulsive and often have poor self-esteem. Her treatment program, which focused on these factors, was, she claimed, very successful. Sometime later, one of our graduate students, well aware of these previous conversations, reported on a workshop she had attended. The model presented at the workshop conceptualized marital violence as a couples' problem and suggested that communication between spouses was the critical factor. Conjoint couples' counseling was suggested as an effective intervention for violent couples. Again, we could agree. Violent marriages were typically very discordant. Abusive husbands rarely expressed themselves to their wives, and communication between spouses in violent couples is often defective and reciprocally negative. Understandably eager to find the answer to a difficult and socially significant problem, the student critically pointed out our simultaneous endorsement of three apparently different perspectives and reflected, "Well, they all can't be right!"

Except in this case they all *can* be right, and we can legitimately agree with all three and probably with several others as well. The problem is that each sees a unitary cause of marital aggression and fails to acknowledge the potential contributions of the factors being championed by the others. There is general agreement that marital violence cuts across all ethnic, racial, religious, education, and socioeconomic strata, yet we insist on seeking commonalities that explain all of the variance. The evidence suggests otherwise. Many, but not all, abusers come from violent family backgrounds (Stark & Flitcraft, 1987). In many cases the husband can be singled out as the perpetrator, but a number of studies have emerged that suggest that spousal abuse and violence is often mutual (Steinmetz & Lucca, 1987). Substance abuse appears to be involved about half the time (Byles, 1978; Fagan, Stewart, & Hansen, 1983). Many abusers have poor impulse control, but many others appear to be overcontrolled (Hershorn & Rosenbaum, 1985). Marital discord is prevalent among abusive couples, but in a more recent prospective investigation, the mean score for the aggressive group was in the satisfactory range on a quantitative measure of marital satisfaction (O'Leary, Arias, Rosenbaum, & Barling, 1985). The safest conclusion would appear to be that there are numerous routes by which husbands come to be wife abusers and a multitude of variables that increase the likelihood of violence. Consequently, one could make a good argument for treatment programs that approach marital aggression in an eclectic fashion.

If marital aggression is multidetermined, intervention strategies will be differentially successful depending on the dynamics operative in any given case. Individual or couple counseling formats offer opportunities to tailor the content of therapy to meet the specific needs of the client(s). However, many practitioners cite advantages to group modalities (e.g., peer confrontation, vicarious learning, social support, economic service delivery) and favor group therapy over individual therapy (Ganley, 1981; Jennings, 1987). Logistically, group approaches to treating marital violence, especially time-limited group approaches, must provide a standard package that accommodates the needs of as many of the participants as possible. Providing a variety of approaches and strategies within the structure of the treatment program increases the likelihood that each of the participants will resonate to, and benefit from, some aspect of the program. The Men's Educational Workshop at the University of Massachusetts Medical Center and the Harborview Anger Management Program at the University of Washington School of Medicine are offered as specific examples of integrative or eclectic group treatment approaches to domestic violence.

Domestic Violence: Definitional Issues

Since domestic violence is a multidisciplinary problem, there are a variety of ways to define it. Within the criminal justice system, domestic violence is subject to definition by applicable laws and criminal sanctions. Domestic assault, simple assault, battery, assault with a deadly weapon, kidnapping, unlawful imprisonment, menacing, and trespassing are some of the most common crimes involved in such cases (Goolkasian, 1986). For clinical purposes, domestic violence can be defined regardless of formal criminal proceedings. It is a form of assaultive behavior that occurs between intimates, usually in the context of a cohabiting relationship. In this chapter, the terms domestic violence, battering, and spouse abuse are used interchangeably.

Most clinicians working in the area of spouse abuse acknowledge the importance of adopting a broad and multifaceted definition of domestic violence (Ganley, 1981; Sonkin & Durphy, 1982). A precise definition would encompass all behaviors that exert *physical* force to injure, control, or abuse a family member or intimate. These behaviors may include simple assault, such as hitting, shoving, kicking, or battering with objects or weapons. Some cases also involve forced sexual activity in which physical contact is preceded by threats, beating, or the use of weapons (e.g., marital rape). Violence may also take the form of property destruction or be directed toward pets.

Some writers have also incorporated nonphysical acts into the definition of domestic violence (e.g., "psychological battery," Ganley, 1981). These behaviors include threatening, coercive, demeaning interchanges that are terrorizing in nature or emotionally abusive. Although clinical researchers may legitimately question the labeling of nonphysical acts as "battering" or "violent" on semantic, conceptual, epidemiological, or empirical grounds, abusive behaviors are often concomitant to physical acts of violence (Fagan et al., 1983). As such, psychologically abusive acts should be recognized as associated features and part of a behavioral cluster that surrounds and revivifies acts of actual physical violence.

Guiding Principles for Treatment of Spouse Abusers

We use the phrase "guiding principles" as opposed to "theoretical model" because model implies a typical pathway or singular etiology. It should be borne in mind that the guiding principles are merely generalities that provide the rationale for the structure of treatment. Some of the principles are empirically derived, whereas others have evolved from either our own clinical work with domestic violence or published descriptions of other treatment programs (e.g., the Spouse Abuse Educational Workshop of Frank and Houghton, Rockland County, NY, 1982).

1. *Abusers do not enjoy being abusive.* Marital aggression most often comes under public scrutiny when an episode is particularly heinous or the injuries are unusually severe or result in a homicide. These same characteristics, which contribute to the newsworthiness of an incident, tend to portray the batterer in the most unsympathetic light. This is understandable, and public disapproval is clearly appropriate in cases of domestic violence. However, such stories promote a picture of the typical batterer as a misogynist or sadist. Although the sociopathic brute who enjoys inflicting pain on his spouse surely exists, he is in the minority according to most accounts provided by professionals who work directly with battering men. Moreover, unless court mandated, such individuals will rarely request or comply with treatment.

The more typical batterer is unhappy with his life and his behavior. Even the batterer who believes it is his right or duty to discipline his wife (and children) is often unhappy with himself and his familial relationships. His marriage is likely to be unsatisfactory; his wife and children often dislike and fear him. A recent study conducted at the Harborview Anger Management Program revealed that a large percentage of domestically violent men experience clinical levels of depression concomitant to their anger and aggression (Maiuro, Cahn, Vitaliano, Wagner, & Zegree, 1988). Batterers in treatment groups frequently express feelings of being trapped and wishing things could be otherwise. As one batterer expressed it, "I wish I could do things over again. . . . I mean not just stop now but wipe the slate clean . . . make it so none of this had ever happened."

Dealing with these issues is important but difficult. Aggressive behavior is deplorable, and changing social attitudes from tolerance and legitimization of domestic violence to censure and disapprobation has been an arduous (and ongoing) process. It is necessary to communicate this disapproval of aggressive behavior without being depreciatory of the men themselves. Both the Men's Workshop and the Harborview Anger Management Program deal with this by discriminating "what they do" from "who they are." Their abusive behavior is reviled; they are accepted as worthwhile individuals. Experience with the Men's Workshop indicates that between intake assessment and the start of a group, there is an approximately 50% drop-out rate; however, once a group commences, the drop-out rate drops to below 20%. This may indicate a loss of the less serious, less motivated clients, but it may also be attributed in part to providing the men with social support and acceptance, in contrast to the loathsomeness they feel and the rejection they expect from others. Although the men may not specifically articulate this, they often remark that the group is "not as bad as they thought it would be" or express sorrow that the group must end.

There is also some therapeutic gain from this conceptual schema. Differentiating the behavior from the person shifts the therapeutic focus from personality change to behavior change. We often hear batterers attempting to explain (excuse) their behavior (and incidentally why therapy is a waste of time as well) by saying, "it's just the way I am. I'm just an aggressive person." Reframing this as the need to change what they do rather than who they are seems a more manageable and realistic goal, perhaps increasing the likelihood that they'll give it a try.

2. *Violence has harmful immediate and long-term effects on every member of the family.* Although the wife is the most obvious victim, all members of the household are negatively affected by spousal violence. Although the findings are equivocal, there is considerable evidence that children display concurrent behavioral and emotional difficulties (Wolfe, Zak, Wilson, & Jaffe, 1986). There is

also support for the concept of the intergenerational transmission of marital aggression (Stark & Flitcraft, 1987), suggesting a serious long-term consequence. Delineating the potential damages to the children engendered by the occurrence of interpersonal violence often provides an important impetus for change.

The negative impact on the wife seems obvious, but apparently not so to the batterer. When asked how the violence affects the wife, many batterers fixate upon their own plight or attempt to justify their actions by citing the "provocation" they experienced. Some of the men respond by saying that they never thought about it. When asked to "think about it," they will often experience discomfort. Depersonalization of the victim is an important part of the dynamics of interpersonal violence. Conversely, empathy for another human being or family member is an effective inhibitor of aggression. Although they express difficulty in identifying with the wife/victim, batterers can often recall an incident where they were subjected to feelings of pain, fear, shame, humiliation, and powerlessness. In such cases, generalizing these feelings to the wife can be an effective aggression control strategy. To facilitate this process, the Harborview Anger Management Program encourages a broadened concept of victimization in which perpetrators are viewed as victims of their own behavior. Ideally, this reframing of the problem can provide a bridge to improved understanding of the plight of others in a situation that is invariably pressured with perceptions of blame, guilt, and condemnation. In those cases where empathy is difficult to establish, this type of reframing can be used to appeal to the perpetrator's self-interest to avoid further punishment and self-damaging consequences.

3. *Batterers often have negative attitudes toward women, which contributes to the occurrence of aggression in marital relationships.* Much as been written about the sociocultural influences on marital aggression. Devaluation of women and other minority groups has surely contributed to the permissibility of aggression directed toward them. On a more personal level, negative stereotypes of women as nagging, demanding, critical, and so forth, are frequently suggested by batterers as justifications for aggression. The devaluation of others is also a common strategy for bolstering one's flagging self-regard. The self-esteem deficits of batterers have been adequately documented (Goldstein & Rosenbaum, 1985). Individuals who feel they don't measure up to their peers may be easily swayed to violence against a variety of less potent targets.

4. *Abusers generally lack nonviolent alternatives for express-ing themselves or for achieving desired goals within their marital relationships.* A general lack of assertiveness skills has been identi-fied by clinicians as a possible area of dysfunction in domestically violent men (Ganley, 1981; Saunders, 1984; Sonkin, Martin, & Walker, 1985; Steinmetz, 1977). Rosenbaum and O'Leary (1981) reported that abusive husbands were less able to assert themselves to their wives than nonviolent husbands, in either maritally conflicted or maritally satisfied relationships. Maiuro, Cahn, and Vitaliano (1986) similarly found maritally aggressive men to have assertive-ness deficits. Their research indicated that skill deficits were particu-larly notable in the area of request behavior, which includes the expression of needs and wants in a positive and growth-oriented fashion. They also demonstrated that the assertiveness deficits were significantly and inversely related to the amount of anger and aggres-sion that the men expressed.

Other investigators have noted that batterers sometimes expe-rience status incompatibility in relationship to their wives, suggest-ing the possibility of real or perceived intellectual inferiority. In a recent study of power needs and assertiveness in domestically violent men, Dutton and Strachan (1987) found that a high need for power combined with deficits in assertive behavior differentiated violent men from maritally satisfied, nonviolent controls. The violent group was also observed to be lower on assertiveness skills than a maritally distressed group, supporting the idea that such deficits play an important role in determining violent behavior. Taken together, these factors suggest that batterers may be at a verbal disadvantage in discussions and arguments with their wives. In fact, batterers in treatment will often contend that they cannot hold their own in verbal battles with their wives and may even try to justify the aggression as "the only way I could shut her up." Viewed in this way, aggression may be conceptualized as an equalizer that negates the wife's verbal advantage. This becomes even more important to the husband with traditional or authoritarian values, who believes in the importance of the man's always being right and always being in charge.

5. *Abusers are frequently saddled with traditional, patriarchal notions that men are expected to be dominant, omniscient, omnipo-tent, and infallible.* Distorted or unrealistic views of the husband's role in a marital relationship, often modeled after those portrayed in

the husband's family of origin, sometimes compel the batterer to try to do or be more than he is able. Batterers are frequently unable to ask their wives for help with tasks that they feel are "the man's job." It is a sign of weakness or failure to be wrong in front of one's family—even worse, to admit being wrong in an argument with one's spouse. A frequent problem implementing time-out procedures involves the husband's perception of leaving an argument as "loss of face" or "backing down." Reframing such self-restraint as the more difficult and admirable behavior may minimize the self-esteem damage and increase the probability of successful use of the technique.

6. *Marital aggression is an individual's problem, most commonly the man's. Marital discord is a couple's problem.* It is unconscionable to compel spouses to remain married when one or both are subjected to violence. It is inadvisable to suggest that violent couples remain together when vows to honor and protect have been broken. However, it is clear that marital aggression and discord are interrelated in a circular fashion. Each must be dealt with in a different way, but both must be dealt with if a couple plans to remain together. It seems reasonable to provide assistance to aggressive couples who have chosen to remain together.

Herein lies one of the most politically delicate issues confronting clinicians working in this area. Profeminist adherents are concerned that providing marital therapy to violent couples will place the wife in jeopardy. The logic of the argument is that marital therapy is often distressing. Couples are encouraged to raise sensitive issues and to communicate frankly. En route to learning constructive strategies for interacting with each other, spouses often miss the mark, overreact, and say things they don't mean. Such learning points produce conflict and disequilibrium, which may further potentiate the expression of aggressive behaviors by the husband toward the wife. A second reason concerns the message to the couple that is tacitly expressed by conjoint marital therapy structure, namely, that marital violence is a couple's problem.

On the other hand, proponents of couples' counseling models (Mantooth, Geffner, Franks, & Patrick, 1987) argue that couples are free to decide whether they will remain together, and if they so choose, for whatever reasons, it is worthwhile to help them maximize the quality of their relationship. Most practitioners would readily agree that violence is not a couple's problem (i.e., the husband is solely responsible for his aggressive behavior). One could reasonably argue that conjoint therapy need not reinforce mutual responsibility for violence but, rather, may present an opportunity for differentiating the abuser's responsibility.

Moreover, many of the commonly employed strategies are even more effective if the wife is an informed, cooperating participant in treatment. For example, the time-out is one of the most popular components of intervention programs for batterers. Rosenbaum (1986), reporting on follow-up assessment of group completers, identified the time-out as the most frequently employed aggression control strategy. One impediment to the successful use of time-out involves the spouse's reluctance to allow the batterer to exit from the argument. Often this is due to her concern that the conversation will not be resumed and the issue will not be resolved. Educating the wife as to the importance of the time-out (combined with providing assurance, in the form of the husband's promise, that the discussion will be resumed as soon as the danger of aggression has abated) and soliciting her cooperation (in addition to suggesting that she, too, utilize the strategy when she feels things reaching the flash point) increases the likelihood of safe, successful implementation of this technique.

The decision of whether to involve the wife in treatment is a difficult one. One way of reconciling the two positions is to treat the batterer's aggression, individually or in a group, prior to providing couples' counseling. This clearly sends the message that the aggression is the man's problem and that it must be dealt with before any marital reconciliation can be attempted. It also allows time for the wife to make decisions about whether she wishes to remain in the relationship. If she does decide to remain with him, it provides an additional margin of safety since it gives the therapist(s) an opportunity to assess whether the aggression is controlled sufficiently to permit conjoint therapy to commence. Both the Men's Workshop and the Harborview Anger Management Program take this approach. The batterer must complete a course of evaluation and treatment before couples' counseling is considered. If the leaders are comfortable with the batterer's progress, and if the spouse has made the decision to remain in the relationship, only then is a referral to marital therapy offered as part of a comprehensive treatment plan.

7. *Batterers have often learned their abusive behaviors from their parental role models.* Much has been written about the intergenerational transmission of violence, beginning with Straus's char-

acterization of the family as a breeding ground for violence. Speculation regarding the mechanism of this intergenerational transmission has often focused on social learning explanations, more specifically, vicarious learning. Social learning theory postulates that modeling is more probable if the model is rewarded for the behavior. Many abusers grew up in households where the father ruled by violence or the threat of violence, thus establishing aggressive behavior as an effective control strategy. The Men's Workshop takes the position that violence is a learned behavior and that learning has occurred in at least two ways: modeling and direct reinforcement (i.e., being rewarded by the power and control it affords an otherwise ineffectual individual). More important is the corollary of this principle, that is, if violence is learned, it can be unlearned.

It is necessary to distinguish between short-term gains and long-term consequences. The delay-of-reinforcement gradient suggests that immediate reinforcement is more powerful than delayed reinforcement, other attributes of the reward being equal. Research on certain high-potency reinforcers suggests that immediate reinforcement takes precedence even over delayed negative consequences of high magnitude (e.g., immediate sexual gratification may exert a more powerful influence on behavior than the long-term threat of AIDS). In terms of marital aggression, the immediate reinforcement afforded by violence (e.g., feelings of power and control, winning an argument, getting one's way, getting back at or hurting someone who has offended you in some way) can outweigh the negative longer-term consequences (e.g., loss of love, negative effects on children, defective marriage, legal consequences, loss of self-esteem).

The Men's Workshop approach addresses both aspects of learning. A developmental perspective is taken in which the negative feelings many of these men had for their own fathers are discussed. Interestingly, many batterers can describe fistfights with their fathers that occurred in an effort to protect their mothers, and most can relate feelings of hatred, fear, and contempt for their fathers. The men are encouraged to pair or associate their personal abuse with their own abuse of their wives and to thereby make the negative consequences of such behavior more salient.

Being psychoeducational in nature, the group also attempts to educate the men regarding alternatives to violent role models. The advantages and disadvantages of "being the master of the house" and of constantly forcing things to be done their way are critically discussed. The men are encouraged to try out compromise strategies of "shared control" as an alternative to perpetuating the negative reciprocity inherent in "win-lose" power struggles. Once the negative reciprocity is broken, the resulting improvements in the marital relationship can positively reinforce the husband for behavior that shares power and control.

8. *Batterers must take responsibility for their aggressive behavior.* As part of their behavioral-emotional and attitudinal behavior change, batterers must acknowledge that the locus of control for spousal aggression is within them. Disavowal of responsibility for the aggression comes disguised in many forms. One of the most common forms involves the notion that the men are provoked to violence by the wife/victim. Men often complain that their wives "make them do it," "hit them first," or engage in some other type of behavior such as nagging, being a poor housekeeper or inadequate mother, refusing their sexual advances, or spending their hard-earned money. Although mutual abuse is an undeniable reality in many cases of domestic violence, therapy can help differentiate provocation from justification. If the husband is unhappy with his wife, he has other, nonviolent options, such as leaving the relationship or asking his wife to join him in couples' counseling.

Another form of irresponsibility involves attributing aggression to some distinguishing agent, most commonly alcohol or drugs. Although it may be true that these substances contribute to impaired judgment, this does not relieve the batterer of responsibility. In a recent study, Maiuro, Vitaliano, Cahn, and Hall (1987) compared domestically violent men who abused alcohol at the time of their offense to a demographically matched comparison group that did not abuse alcohol. Although some differences were found in the strength of the relationship between anger indices and aggressive behavior in these groups, both groups evidenced significant problems with anger, hostility, depression, and coping deficits, regardless of alcohol use. If a domestically violent man is indeed an alcohol or drug abuser, he needs specialized treatment for both spousal abuse and substance abuse. However, in most cases of alcohol abuse, the batterer is choosing to drink and is engaging in a behavior he knows is likely to increase the probability of poor impulse control and aggression. The choice to drink or use drugs becomes his responsibility.

In general, "losing control" has become an all-too-convenient fiction and a classic method for reattributing responsibility. The popularity of the colloquialism "He's out of control" suggests that control is something easily lost. In the majority of spouse battering incidents, the perpetrator is in control, and in fact, violence is often a way of gaining control in the relationship. This is exemplified by the batterer's frequent refrain: "It was the only way I could get her to stop nagging me" ("shut up," etc.). Perhaps the most important goal of the Men's Workshop is to dispel notions of loss of control and to reframe aggression as a control strategy. One of the reasons for the effectiveness of the time-out technique is that taking a time-out destroys any illusion of spontaneity. It is more difficult to disavow responsibility and claim loss of control if one takes a few moments to contemplate one's actions.

Applications and Interventions

The Harborview Anger Management Program and the Men's Educational Workshop both represent eclectic approaches to dealing with the male batterer. They have a number of commonalities and a few differences. Since the Men's Workshop has been described elsewhere (Rosenbaum, 1986; Rosenbaum & O'Leary, 1986), the Harborview Program will be described in greater detail.

Harborview Anger Management Program Rationale

The Harborview Anger Management Program approaches domestic violence as a community mental health concern ("Helping Angry and Violent People," 1987). From this perspective, domestic abuse is viewed as a serious behavioral-emotional problem characterized by poor regulation of emotions and a failure to adapt to community standards of conduct. Anger is identified as a primary focus of treatment, not because it is the sole component and determinant of domestic violence (Gondolf, 1985) but because it is one of the most proximal and powerful motivating events preceding the act of assault. Indeed, in a recent comparative study, we found the levels of anger and hostility in domestically violent men to be similar to those evidenced by men who were generally assaultive toward nonintimates or both intimates and nonintimates (Maiuro, Cahn, Vitaliano, Wagner, & Zegree, 1988). Although all forms of anger expression and violence do not necessarily involve mental or psychological disorders, expressions of anger and violence that endanger intimates and loved ones are clearly maladaptive in a civilized culture. Individuals who are dangerous to self and others have been recognized as a public health problem (Koop, 1987) and are being mandated to treatment in increasing numbers.

Concerns are sometimes raised that the labeling of domestic violence as a mental health problem will somehow "excuse" the behavior as a form of insanity or underappraise the prevalence of the problem as the concern of a select, disturbed population. In a similar fashion, attention to indivdual psychological and biological factors is sometimes construed as being incompatible with a focus upon the sociopolitical factors that shape the permissive atmosphere for the occurrence of violence toward women and children and the lack of sanctions for such behavior. Since a community mental health approach encompasses public health and social systems concepts, neither of these concerns need to be the case. The use of mental health concepts to help explain and intervene in domestic violence cases need not be employed or viewed as "excuse" making. Indeed, such concepts may be useful for understanding victims (cf., Battered Woman's Syndrome—Thyfault, Bennett, & Hirschorn, 1987; Walker, 1983) as well as offenders. Moreover, a community mental health approach is congruent, rather than incompatible, with the recognition of sociopolitical, and economic factors as determinants of interpersonal violence.

Approximately 70% of domestic violence referrals to the Anger Management Program come from the criminal justice system. The remaining 30% are either referred by other clinics and social service agencies or self-referred. These cases are assigned to a specialized group therapy program that meets weekly for a minimum of 22 weeks. Each group consists of 12 to 16 people and is led by a male and a female therapist. Spouses, mates, and family members are encouraged to attend select meetings when appropriate. Attendance is strictly monitored, and patients who miss more than two sessions must start over. As a result, the drop-out rate can be as high as 30% to 40%. Pre-and-post assessments are conducted on a systematic basis to evaluate the status and progress of each case and to create a data base for program evaluation.

Harborview Program: Treatment Techniques and Components

Assessment and Diagnosis. It has been our experience that individual psychological factors play a major role in determining an aggressive response. People vary considerably in terms of their responses to stress, conflict, and perceived threats to personal esteem and control. A variety of psychological, biological, social, and environmental factors can increase the likelihood that someone will respond in an irritable and violent fashion. Although the vast majority of spouse abusers may not evidence chronic mental disorder of psychotic proportions, there are data to suggest that many have significant psychological problems that help potentiate violent outbursts when the men are threatened or under stress.

In an early study of 23 domestically violent men taken into custody, Faulk (1974) found approximately 65% to have a diagnosable psychiatric disorder. The most commonly identified problems included depression and delusional jealousy, with anxiety, personality, and post-head-injury syndromes and dementias also represented.

In a comprehensive review of existing research on domestically violent men, Hotaling and Sugarman (1986) concluded that the data pointed toward serious and enduring patterns of maladjustment in batterers, with many cases appearing to evidence some form of personality disorder. In a cross-validated study of 198 spouse abusers, Hamberger and Hastings (1986) found that 88% of the men evidenced discernible psychopathology when systematically assessed with the Millon Clinical Multiaxial Inventory (MCMI), the Novaco Anger Scale, and the Beck Depression Inventory. Schizoidal/borderline, narcissistic/antisocial, and dependent/compulsive disorders were particularly represented. In evaluating well over 1,000 cases of domestic violence to date, we have uncovered a broad spectrum of diagnosable profiles in batterers. In accord with the findings of previous investigators, we have found many meeting the criteria for personality disorders, various types of depression (Maiuro et al., 1988), impulse control disorder, unresolved learning disabilities or attention deficits, alcohol abuse (Maiuro, Vitaliano, & Cahn, 1987), cyclic mood or arousal disorders, adjustment reactions, organic personality syndromes, and, to a lesser extent, formal thought disorder.

The Harborview Anger Management Program places a great deal of emphasis upon the initial assessment phase of treatment.

Having an eclectic focus, the program assumes no single etiology or profile on an *a priori* basis, and a broad data base is collected on each client. Given the social undesirability of interpersonal violence and the legal duress that many clients face, care must be taken to ensure satisfactory levels of trust and predictability in the therapeutic relationship as part of the assessment process. Checks should be conducted on test-taking attitudes if psychometric or self-report indices are employed, and multiple sources of information should be gathered to help ensure a reliable and comprehensive evaluation. The multiple sources of information obtained by the Anger Management Program routinely include all relevant offense history (police and victim reports on both instant and prior infractions of all types), comprehensive mental health data through psychiatric interviewing, extended interviewing with respect to anger dyscontrol and the violence history, a battery of psychometric indices (e.g., MMPI, Beck Depression Inventory, anger/hostility measures, assertiveness measures, and coping profiles), as well as reports from the spouse, friends, or relatives.

A broad-based assessment allows difficult questions regarding the spouse abuser's violence profile, diagnostic status, relative probability of dangerousness, and amenability to treatment to be addressed with a greater degree of confidence. Information relevant to adjunctive dispositions, such as alcohol and drug treatment, parenting skills, and couples' therapy/counseling, is also collected. Comprehensive assessment data also provide a basis from which to discuss the spouse abuser's problems and can help communicate the therapist's desire to understand the determinants of abusive and violent behavior in the individual case. Feedback is provided to all clients in a psychoeducational and prescriptive fashion to provide a rationale for treatment and to enhance the client's interest and involvement in the rehabilitation process.

Socioenvironmental reengineering. Although individual psychological, and in some cases biological, factors are emphasized in a mental health evaluation, a community or public health approach also attends to the socioenvironmental force field surrounding the abuser and the victim. In this regard, we consider referral to the Harborview Anger Management to be an *adjunctive* measure to criminal justice proceedings in cases of interpersonal violence, rather than an alternative or substitute for such proceedings. Since September of 1984, Washington State has enjoyed the benefit of a domestic violence prevention act that mandates arrest in cases of spousal assault. This provision was a collaborative effort resulting from years of education and consultation provided by family violence service providers and women's support groups to law enforcement and legislative leaders. The statute not only permits the immediate removal of the perpetrator from the home environment but also allows the imposition of a restraining order to further protect the safety and well-being of the victim. In the city of Seattle, an advocate is made available to the victim through the City Attorney's office (Family Violence Project), and a referral is made to the women's shelter network.

In the course of prosecution of the case, the judge will often mandate evaluation and treatment of the perpetrator in addition to customary fines and punitive consequences. Such a disposition not only requires that the offender seek rehabilitative services with a specialized provider (an option that many, if not most, would be reluctant to pursue), it also allows for probationary monitoring of the case. Probationary monitoring can enhance rehabilitative efforts inasmuch as the treatment provider is able and willing to provide information regarding compliance and the presence or absence of high-risk behavior. The Harborview Anger Management program openly acknowledges limits to the privilege of confidentiality to all prospective clients who present with any type of violent behavior. The criminal justice system is not simply regarded as a referral source but as a collaborative resource in decreasing the likelihood of further violence. This approach is not only consistent with a public health model but is also designed to decrease the social isolation and privacy that numerous researchers have associated with domestic violence (Straus, Gelles, & Steinmetz, 1980).

Self-Awareness Training: Anger Cues. As in the case of the Men's Workshop, the Harborview Anger Management Program makes use of psychoeducational techniques in its approach. Clinic staff believe that the seemingly uncontrollable and unanticipated episodes of violence perpetrated by many patients can be explained by the patients' poor sense of their own emotions. The program has developed a videotape that describes a variety of dynamics related to anger and assaultive behavior (Maiuro, Eberle, Muscatel, & Donovan, 1981). Clients view the videotape in a group setting and are encouraged to compare their own experiences to those illustrated in the vignettes. Clients are also taught cognitive, behavioral, and physiological signals related to anger and impending loss of control. Therapists then have each client develop a personal definition of emotional cues to help them recognize and short-circuit an aggressive response in the early stages of arousal.

Management of Arousal/Mood Problems. It has been documented that high levels of arousal can impair human performance during complex problem-solving tasks such as interpersonal conflict and emotionally laden encounters. Once the self-awareness training has occurred, many clients can employ a variety of arousal reduction strategies, such as progressive muscle relaxation, imagery, and deep-breathing exercises. Other clients may employ more naturalistic techniques, such as going for a walk or listening to soothing music. Such "self-control" techniques can help increase the probability that the client will be in a controlled state of body and mind that is conducive to rational problem solving.

However, as most experienced clinicians will testify, there are clients for whom such techniques are difficult to implement or for whom they are ineffective. This may be particularly so in cases where chronic hyperarousal (e.g., hypomania, mania, attention deficit, type A personality) or unipolar or bipolar affective instability exists. In such cases, it can be useful to seek the consultation of a psychiatrist who is familiar with aggressive behavior problems in order to discuss the advisability of psychopharmacological intervention. In those less frequent cases in which a formal thought disorder of a psychotic nature is suspected, a medications approach should be considered the treatment of choice, with psychotherapeutic interventions as an adjunctive measure.

Cognitive Restructuring. Spouse abusers often experience distorted views and attitudes toward their partners and the act of violence that precipitated their entry into treatment. Dehumanizing attitudes and labels for victims (e.g., "bitch," "the little woman," "dumb broad," "a woman's place is . . .") that result from sex role stereotypes and objectification (or "thinging") must be confronted. The abuser must be educated regarding the hostile dynamics and violence-facilitating properties of such attitudes and behavior. Refocusing the client's attention to specific areas of conflict in behavioral terms (e.g., "I feel angry and left out when you don't tell me where you're going") can help break these habitual ways of thinking.

Many cases, particularly those referred by the criminal justice system, are often characterized by denial and minimization of problems, and projection of responsibility (Maiuro, Sandberg, Cahn, & Vitaliano, 1988). Perpetrators often have a developmental history of abuse or abandonment, with a resulting negative bias with respect to the intentions of their partners. Poor self-esteem, tied to such histories or to current failures and frustrations, often creates a heightened sense of vulnerability and a tendency to perceive threat where it may not exist.

In such cases, a rational-emotive approach can be useful (Ellis, 1977). In such an approach, clients learn to critically examine the antecedent events related to their abusive behavior, their personal beliefs and attitudes about those events, and the emotional consequences that directly result from those beliefs and attitudes (ABC technique). When conducted in a group process format, abusive clients can gain insight into their own role in generating their emotions and behavior and can restructure their perceptions and thinking in a manner conducive to rational problem solving rather than violence.

Assessment and Enhancement of Feelings Repertoire. Clinicians working with domestically violent males have long recognized their tendency to immediately transform feelings of hurt, insecurity, and fear into anger and violence (Ganley, 1981; Sonkin & Durphy, 1982). The Anger Management Program employs a number of structured exercises to help spouse abusers recognize and label a more flexible range of emotions and feelings. These exercises are designed to help the men develop alternatives to anger and to desensitize them to emotions that may have been socially or developmentally conditioned and anxiety provoking.

"Time-Out" Training with Mate or Significant Other. Studies of interpersonal problem solving between abusers and their mates indicate that a form of "negative reciprocity" often occurs, which personalizes and escalates the conflict rather than resolves it (Deschner, 1984; Margolin, John, & Gleberman, 1988). In those cases where the spouse or mate is available and willing to participate in the abuser's treatment (and such involvement is not contraindi-

cated by basic safety concerns), training both partners in the appropriate use of time-out techniques can be useful. The use of such techniques is particularly important in those phases of treatment when other self-control skills are not well developed, or in the inevitable situation when conflict resolution skills may be tested and overwhelmed. Careful attention must be given to the possibility that the technique will be used in a passive-aggressive fashion, in which the partner's concerns are cut off or avoided. The purpose of the technique is to provide a behavioral safety valve to decrease the likelihood of continued abuse and an opportunity for de-arousal to promote rational problem solving.

Skill Training: Conflict Resolution. According to social learning principles, the use of aggression to resolve conflict is a learned behavior. Whether an individual engages in this behavior or not is a function, in part, of whether alternative nonviolent behaviors are in the repertoire. Bandura (1973) observed that individuals who commit acts of violence often lack appropriate conflict resolution skills and resort to more primitive and physical ways of acting and responding. During the therapy sessions, participants reenact with the therapists a scene that triggered extreme anger. Another therapist coaches the patient through the reenactment, which is videotaped for use in subsequent discussion. Clients have an opportunity to practice arousal reduction techniques and to employ conflict resolution strategies such as "I" language, identification of problems in behavioral terms, active listening and restatement, negotiating possible solutions, and contracting for change. In this manner, the clinic program serves as a sheltered laboratory in which clients can participate in desensitizing exercises and learn nonviolent ways of coping with stress and conflict. To enhance generalization, clients are given a list of problem-solving tips to carry with them as cue cards for real-life encounters. Examples of such problem-solving tips would include selecting and sticking to one issue, using "I" language to express feelings, and asking for things in positive and behavioral terms.

Skill Training: Assertiveness-Aggressiveness. A wealth of general resource materials exists for helping spouse abusers develop better assertiveness skills (cf. Alberti & Emmons, 1982; Lange & Jakubowski, 1976). In our experience, the assertiveness deficits fall into two general domains, namely, skill deficits and discrimination problems in which the individual confuses assertiveness with aggressiveness. Skill deficits can stem from a lack of cognitive skills for implementing the behavior or from performance anxiety that results in an inhibition or avoidance of the behavior. Our clinical research program suggests that domestically violent men may have relatively little difficulty defending their rights and territory but significant problems in positively expressing their wants and needs in a socially appropriate and growth-oriented manner (Maiuro, Cahn, & Vitaliano, 1986). The Anger Management Program assertiveness component includes feedback on assessment results, therapist modeling, skill training, discrimination training regarding noncoercive and nonabusive communication styles, and videotaped role play practice.

Skill Training: Effective Communication. Once the basic conflict resolution skills have been developed, emphasis is placed upon stylistic attributes such as nonverbal gestures, eye contact and gaze, verbal intonation, and physical posturing and proximity. It is entirely possible for a client to deliver a conflict resolution strategy in a hostile, controlling, and overbearing fashion. As in the case of other skill-training components, the Anger Management Program makes extensive use of videotape technology during treatment sessions to focus on these issues. Such technology allows clients to see themselves as other people do (often a dramatic and powerful experience) and does much to remove the treatment process from the realm of verbal feedback and debate.

Reassessment

As a part of the treatment process, clients receive feedback regarding change or the lack of change in their clinical profiles. This feedback is based on postassessment with the same test battery employed at the beginning of treatment, as well as on observations made by other clients, spouses or significant others and the group leaders. If sufficient changes have occurred to significantly reduce the likelihood of further acts of violence and abuse, the client is considered graduated from the program. In other cases, a mixed profile of selective change in some areas with no change in other areas may be observed. In those cases, adjunctive treatment in the form of individual or further group therapy may be recommended. If no significant change has occurred, or a high-risk profile continues, the client is invited to repeat the program or to seek treatment elsewhere, to lower the risk of violence. In all cases, the referral source is notified of the client's treatment compliance, general outcome, and our recommendations.

Men's Workshop Program Rationale

In the Men's Workshop, the batterer is conceptualized as an unhappy, ineffectual, and socially isolated individual seeking alternatives to violence. Laboring under traditional role expectancies learned in his family of origin and reinforced by the sociocultural media, he seeks dominance in his marital relationship. Lacking adequate verbal acuity or other nonaggressive conflict resolution skills, he resorts to physical aggression to achieve his desired goals. The use of aggression further contributes to his defective self-image, alienates him from his wife, and increases the probability of the negative marital interactions that elicit aggressive responses. The batterer does not know how to break out of the negative behavioral cycle in which he is trapped. This dynamic further contributes to his sense of being unable to control his aggressive behavior.

The Men's Workshop is structured as 7 90-minute sessions, ideally led by a male-female coleader team. Six of the 7 sessions divide into two conceptual units of 3 sessions each. The first unit focuses on attitude change, the second unit on behavior change. The seventh session was added after several years of group operation and involves inviting the female partner to attend the group. A review of batterer programs several years ago revealed wide variability in the structure of men's groups (Rosenbaum, 1986), some being open-ended, some closed, and the number of sessions ranging from as few as 5 or 6 to as many as 50 or more. It was felt that batterers, being a resistant population, would be more likely to participate if a program was of shorter length. Hence, a closed ended, 6-session format was established, with the caveat that the program was the beginning of the change process. One goal of the group, therefore, was the development of an individualized continuation plan tailored to the specific needs of each participant. The continuation plans have typically involved individual psychotherapy, drug or alcohol counseling, and, if there is an intention (on the part of both partners) to remain in the relationship (and if it is deemed to be safe, at least to the extent that safety can be reasonably assured), marital therapy. The goal of the seventh session is to educate the female partner as to the goals and strategies of the group, to enlist her cooperation in the techniques being employed (such as allowing and supporting the husband's use of the time-out, and suggesting that she might use it herself when she senses the situation escalating toward aggression), and discussing the continuation plan with her.

In contrast to the Harborview Anger Management Program, most participants of the Men's Educational Workshop have been voluntary self-referrals. The majority are participating under pressure from the spouse, usually in the form of a threat of separation or legal consequences. The absence of a court order to participate is another reason for the more time-limited structure of the workshop as compared to lengthier programs such as Harborview's.

Men's Workshop: Treatment Techniques and Components

Participation in the workshop begins with the intake evaluation, which involves an interview with the batterer. If the couple is cohabiting and the woman feels comfortable with attending, she is also interviewed. Assessment of the aggression incorporates the four forms of violence identified by Ganley (1981). The wife is interviewed privately, and her safety is assessed. She is given appropriate referrals to sheltering, legal, therapeutic, and social services. She is further advised to exercise her legal options if her safety is threatened.

Both the Harborview program and the Men's Workshop employ a male-female coleader team. We believe this leadership structure serves several purposes. Since the primary referral problem involves violence toward women, it is important to draw out and observe the men's reactions to female figures. The presence of both a male and a female leader can sometimes reveal a pattern of differential responding in the participants, which can be used for diagnostic and therapeutic purposes.

From a process perspective, the coleaders can also provide a model of a couple in which power is shared equally. Care must be taken to ensure that the coleaders model an egalitarian relationship, taking turns starting and ending sessions, sharing duties within the group, and participating equally. The use of a female coleader also provides a model of a woman in a professional role. This role stands in contrast to the narrow or negative opinion that some batterers have of women and helps them to confront these destructive attitudes. Additionally, the presence of a female coleader can short-circuit the development of an "all-male" camaraderie, which can sometimes reinforce sex role rigidity and macho attitudes toward violence and victimization.

The first three sessions comprise the attitude-change component of the program. The goal of these sessions is to communicate the concepts articulated in the guiding principles. These include (1) recognition and acceptance of responsibility for one's aggressive behavior; (2) discussion of the negative effects of aggression on every member of the family, including the husband; (3) discussing the legal implications of assaultive behavior; (4) viewing aggressive behavior as a choice made by the aggressor in consideration of the consequences; (5) discussing negative attitudes toward women; and (6) examining the controlling aspects of aggression.

These principles are taught using examples provided by the participants. The following example illustrates how this process is used to deal with the secondary gains of aggressive behavior:

Context: The husband is explaining how violence is an effective means to an end.

LEADER: So what you're telling us is that hitting your wife is the only way you can get things your way?

BATTERER: Well, it works, doesn't it?

LEADER: I don't know what you mean by working.

BATTERER: Well, after I hit her, things get done my way.

LEADER: So it has an immediate positive result.

BATTERER: Yeah.

LEADER: Well, what happens afterward?

BATTERER: What do you mean?

LEADER: Well, how does your wife treat you later on?

BATTERER: She doesn't treat me very well, I guess.

LEADER: How long does it take for her to get over it?

BATTERER: Well, she doesn't talk to me for days, and even when she starts talking, she's not very friendly.

LEADER: Would you say you're happy with your relationship?

BATTERER: Not very. How happy can you be when your wife is so cold to you? She never seems happy, and we don't do much together.

LEADER: Do you have a good sexual relationship?

BATTERER: No.

LEADER: Do your kids seem to be happy?

BATTERER: No . . . We have a lot of problems with them . . . They're very disrespectful.

LEADER: To you?

BATTERER: To both of us. We don't have much of a family . . . you know . . . we don't do a whole lot together . . . as a family.

LEADER: It sounds like hitting hasn't really gotten you what you want, has it?

Sessions four through six comprise the behavior change component of the workshop. The participants have, it is hoped, begun to accept responsibility for their violent behavior and have been convinced of the importance and the possibility of positive change. The focus is on two interrelated types of strategies: those aimed at short-circuiting the development of anger (e.g., communication skills, cognitive restructuring) and those aimed at aggression avoidance (e.g., recognizing anger cues, taking a time-out, relaxation, stimulus control tactics) if the former fail. These techniques have been discussed in the description of the Harborview program. Their implementation is similar in the Men's Workshop.

One additional strategy that we have found useful involves stimulus control. With this technique, batterers have been asked to identify rooms of the house and times of the day or days of the week when aggression is most probable. We are familiar with the notions that the kitchen is the most violence-prone room of the house, followed by the bedroom, whereas the bathroom is the least violence-prone room. This has been translated into a strategy of avoiding arguments in those "hot spots." Similarly, it has been argued that couples should avoid arguments during "hot times" such as weekends or evenings. Although such strategies may have a transient effect, it is unrealistic to assume that problems and arguments will disappear if the couple stay out of those rooms or avoid each other at those times.

We have extended and modified this strategy by asking the men to identify the characteristics that distinguish arguments that eventuate in aggression from those that remain nonviolent. Several factors have emerged. Many batterers report standing up to be a very common precursor to aggression. This makes practical sense, as it is more difficult to strike somebody from a sitting position. It also is supported by Laird's work on the relationship between body position and emotion (Laird, 1974). According to this model, an individual assuming an angry or aggressive pose is more likely to feel anger and act aggressively. We instruct Workshop participants to remain seated during arguments or heated discussions with their spouses and to use standing up as a cue to take a time-out. They are also advised to discuss this strategy with their spouses (at a time when they are not in conflict) since if the wife stands up, it may increase the chances that the husband will also stand up. If either spouse stands up, the couple should use this as a cue to terminate the discussion. A second factor that has been associated with aggression is prolongation of the argument. The men commonly report that the probability of an aggressive response increases as the length of the argument and the number of topics being discussed increases. Couples are advised to try to keep their arguments time limited and focused on a single topic.

In keeping with the psychoeducational character of the workshop, the participants are provided with copies of *Aggress-less* (Goldstein & Rosenbaum, 1982), a self-help manual that reiterates and reinforces the techniques that the men have been taught. Written for the psychologically naive reader, this book is readily understandable and seems to appeal to the batterers we have treated. In addition to the techniques that have already been mentioned, the book introduces the skills of negotiation, contracting, self-control, and calming others.

Program Evaluation

The Harborview Anger Management Program and the Men's Workshop are both committed to clinical research and have attempted to address the issue of efficacy through ongoing program evaluation. The inclusion of an evaluation component addresses the clinical needs of the individual and the public safety concerns of the community. It also provides a basis for evolving our understanding of the spouse abuser and the determinants of interpersonal violence.

The Anger Management Program's effectiveness in treating men who commit domestic violence was presented to the American Psychological Association in August of 1987. Sixty-five men with independently documented histories of assaultive behavior completed the treatment program and were assessed on a pre-and-post basis. The treated group was compared to a naturally occurring waiting list sample (dictated by limited treatment resources for indigent and low-income perpetrators in the Seattle area). The waiting list comparison sample was similar to the treated sample on demographic, offense, and clinical variables. Waiting list subjects received minimal treatment consisting of a diagnostic evaluation, orientation to the program, follow-up contact to assess violence potential and clinical status, monthly reports of compliance to the referring agency, and probationary monitoring in those cases referred by the courts (approximately 60%). Crisis intervention was available to all participants on an as-needed basis, and the men's female partners had access to Seattle's women's shelter network.

The study results indicated that men who completed the program had significantly lower levels of anger, depression, and aggression and demonstrated more adaptive patterns of coping than they did prior to treatment. No such improvements were found in the matched sample of men who received minimal treatment over the same time period. Further evaluation of a follow-up sample indicated that the changes in the treatment group had persisted at the end of 1 year. Formal collection of recidivism data through the courts and the legal system is now in progress.

Based on follow-up data coming at least 6 months and up to 3 years from men who had completed the Men's Workshop, Rosenbaum (1986) reported a recidivism rate of approximately 12%. This is probably an overly optimistic estimate of the effectiveness of the workshop since it is based on participant self-report and a very small sample.

Outcome investigations of batterer programs are essential but problematic. The first issue involves the specific definition of battering employed by the investigator and the use of appropriate instrumentation to assess the target behavior(s). Although there are a number of measures available for assessing spouse-specific and general aggression, for example, the Conflict Tactics Scale (Straus, 1979), the Buss-Durkee Hostility Inventory (Buss & Durkee, 1957), and the Brief Anger-Aggression Questionnaire (Maiuro et al., 1987), many studies still appear to rely upon interview and questionnaire methods with unknown psychometric properties. Program evaluation efforts could benefit from the development and use of standardized measures, particularly in the area of psychological abuse.

Another issue deals with the selection of an appropriate outcome criterion. Rosenbaum (1986) required cessation rather than reduction of aggression, but this standard varies across studies. Other investigators (e.g., Maiuro et al., 1987) suggest that change should be defined more comprehensively to include attitudinal, emotional, and coping variables as well as overt behavioral aggression variables.

A related issue concerns the selection of an informant for outcome data. Self-report by the batterer may not be reliable in a significant number of cases. However, confirmatory information from victims may not be accessible or available. Although desirable, official criminal records may be an incomplete estimate of actual offending. Although one could reasonably argue that all of these data have some degree of validity, it is probably fair to say that biased outcomes may be obtained if data are drawn from only one source. The use of multiple sources of outcome data can help balance these effects and simultaneously lend insight into our methodology for assessing change.

Although the term "spouse abuse" is frequently used in battering research, inspection of demographic data often reveals that many of the participants are not legally married to their partners. Even among those married, a significant number may be separated. Such differences present measurement issues that should be addressed for purposes of comparability. Confidentiality issues must be also addressed if the batterer is involved with a new partner who may be unaware of his prior history of relationship aggression.

Finally, to adequately evaluate the impact of intervention programs, research designs are needed that include follow-up data as well as initial outcome results. The follow-up period must be of a length sufficient to avoid capitalizing on the "honeymoon period" of nonviolence that often coincides with participation in a treatment program. Although the use of a strict behavioral aggression measure may appear to be a suitable and conservative criterion, it should be pointed out that in many abusive relationships, violence is a serious but relatively infrequent phenomenon. This can create statistical analysis problems due to the low base rate. Rosenbaum and O'Leary (1986) have suggested that follow-up intervals of at least 6 months posttreatment should be employed before judging an intervention successful.

Large-scale controlled studies are necessary in order to better evaluate the effectiveness of spouse abuse programs. Attention should also be given to comparative designs to address what happens in cases that are not effectively helped. Most batterer programs, including those presently described, have reported drop-out rates of 30% to 50%, suggesting that we are not serving a large portion of the population in need. The work performed to date appears promising, but many questions remain unanswered.

References

Alberti, R. E., & Emmons, M. L. (1982). *Your perfect right: A guide to assertive living* (4th ed.). San Luis Obispo, CA: Impact Publishers.

Bandura, A. (1973). *Aggression: A social learning analysis.* Englewood Cliffs, NJ: Prentice-Hall.

Buss, A. H., & Durkee, A. (1957). An inventory for assessing different kinds of hostility. *Journal of Consulting and Clinical Psychology, 21,* 343-349.

Byles, J. A. (1978). Violence, alcohol problems and other problems in disintegrating families. *Journal of Studies on Alcohol, 39,* 551-553.

Deschner, J. P. (1984). *The hitting habit: Anger control for battering couples.* New York: Free Press.

Dutton, D. G., & Strachan, C. E. (1987). Motivational needs for power and spouse-specific assertiveness in assaultive and nonassaultive men. *Violence and Victims, 2*(3), 145-156.

Ellis, A. (1977) *Anger: How to live with and without it.* Secaucus, NJ: Citadel Press.

Fagan, J. A., Stewart, D. K., & Hansen, K. V. (1983). Violent men or violent husbands? In D. Finkelhor, R. J. Gelles, G. T. Hotaling, & M. A. Straus (Eds.), *The dark side of families: Current family violence research* (pp. 49-67). Beverly Hills, CA: Sage.

Faulk, M. (1974). Men who assault their wives. *Medicine, Science, and the Law, 14,* 180-183.

Frank, P. B., & Houghton, B. D. (1982). Confronting the batterer: A guide to creating the spouse abuse educational workshop. New City, NY: Volunteer Counseling Service of Rockland County.

Ganley, A. L. (1981) *Court-mandated counseling for men who batter: A three-day workshop for mental health professionals.* Washington, DC: Center for Women's Policy Studies.

Goldstein, A. P., & Rosenbaum, A. (1982). *Aggress-less: How to turn anger and aggression into positive action.* Englewood Cliffs, NJ: Prentice-Hall.

Goldstein, D., & Rosenbaum, A. (1985). An evaluation of the self-esteem of maritally violent men. *Family Relations, 34,* 425-428.

Goolkasian, G. A. (1986). *Confronting domestic violence: A guide for criminal justice agencies*. Washington, DC: National Institute of Justice.

Gondolf, E. W. (1985). Anger and oppression in men who batter: Empiricist and feminist perspectives and their implications for research. *Victimology: An International Journal, 10*, 311-324.

Hamberger, L. K., & Hastings, J. E. (1986). Personality correlates of men who abuse their partners: A cross-validation study. *Journal of Family Violence, 1*, 323-341.

Helping angry and violent people manage their emotions and behavior: Harborview Anger Management Program. (1987). *Hospital and Community Psychiatry, 38*, 1207-1210.

Hershorn, M., & Rosenbaum, A. (1985). Children of marital violence: A closer look at the unintended victim. *American Journal of Orthopsychiatry, 55*, 260-266.

Hotaling, G. T., & Sugarman, D. B. (1986). An analysis of risk markers in husband and wife violence: The current state of knowledge. *Violence and Victims, 1*, 101-124.

Jennings, J. L. (1987). History and issue in the treatment of battering men: A case for unstructured group therapy. *Journal of Family Violence, 2*, 193-213.

Koop, C. E. (1987, September). *Healing interpersonal violence: Making health a full partner*. Keynote address at the Surgeon General's Northwest Conference on Interpersonal Violence Report, Seattle, WA. Washington, DC: U.S. Public Health Service.

Laird, J. D. (1974). Self-attribution of emotion: The effects of expressive behavior on the quality of emotional experience. *Journal of Personality and Social Psychology, 29*, 475-486.

Lange, A., & Jakubowski, P. (1976). *Responsible assertive behavior*. Champaign, IL: Research Press.

Maiuro, R. D., Cahn, T. S., & Vitaliano, P. P. (1986). Assertiveness and hostility in domestically violent men. *Violence and Victims, 1*, 279-289.

Maiuro, R. D., Cahn, T. S., Vitaliano, P. P., Wagner, B. C., & Zegree, J. B. (1988). Anger, hostility, and depression in domestically violent versus generally assaultive men and nonviolent control subjects. *Journal of Consulting and Clinical Psychology, 56*, 17-23.

Maiuro, R. D., Eberle, J., Muscatel, K., & Donovan, D. (1981). *Anger management* [Videotape]. Seattle: Instructional Media Services, University of Washington.

Maiuro, R. D., Sandberg, G., Cahn, T. S., & Vitaliano, P. P. (1988, April). *MMPI profiles in domestically violent men: Court-referred versus self-referred samples*. Paper presented at the annual meeting of the Western Psychological Association, San Francisco.

Maiuro, R. D., Vitaliano, P. P., & Cahn, T. S. (1987). A brief measure for the assessment of anger and aggression. *Journal of Interpersonal Violence, 2*, 166–178.

Maiuro, R. D., Vitaliano, P. P., Cahn, T. S., & Hall, G. N. C. (1987, July). *Anger and hostility in alcohol abusing versus non-alcohol abusing domestically violent men.* Paper presented at the Third National Family Violence Research Conference, Durham, NH.

Mantooth, C. M., Geffner, R., Franks, D., & Patrick, J. (1987). *Family preservation: A treatment manual for reducing couple violence.* Tyler, TX: East Texas Crisis Center.

Margolin, G., John, R. S., & Gleberman, L. (1988). Affective responses to conflictual discussions in violent and nonviolent couples. *Journal of Consulting and Clinical Psychology, 56*, 24–33.

O'Leary, K. D., Arias, I., Rosenbaum, A., & Barling, J. (1985). *Premarital physical aggression.* Unpublished manuscript, State University of New York, Stony Brook, NY.

Public health problem of violence receives epidemiologic attention. (1985). *Journal of the American Medical Association, 254*, 881–892.

Rosenbaum, A. (1986). *Group treatment for abusive men: Process and outcome. Psychotherapy, 23*(4), 607–612.

Rosenbaum, A., & O'Leary, K. D. (1981). Marital violence: Characteristics of abusive couples. *Journal of Consulting and Clinical Psychology, 49*, 63–71.

Rosenbaum, A., & O'Leary, K. D. (1986). Treatment of marital violence. In N. Jacobson & A. Gurman (Eds.), *Clinical handbook of marital therapy* (pp. 385–405). New York: Guilford Press.

Saunders, D. G. (1984). Helping husbands who batter. *Social Casework, 65*, 347–352.

Sonkin, D. J., & Durphy, M. (1982). *Learning to live without violence: A handbook for men.* San Francisco: Volcano Press.

Sonkin, D. J., Martin, D., & Walker, L. (1985). *The male batterer: A treatment approach.* New York: Springer.

Stark, E., & Flitcraft, A. (1987). Violence among intimates: An epidemiological review. In V. B. Van Hasselt, R. L. Morrison, A. S. Bellack, & M. Hersen (Eds.), *Handbook of family violence* (pp. 293–318). New York: Plenum Press.

Steinmetz, S. K. (1977). *The cycle of violence.* New York: Praeger.

Steinmetz, S. K., & Lucca, J. (1987). Husband battering. In V. B. Van Hasselt, R. L. Morrison, A. S. Bellack, & M. Hersen (Eds.), *Handbook of family violence* (pp. 223–246). New York: Plenum Press.

Straus, M. A. (1979). Measuring intrafamily conflict and violence: The Conflict Tactics (CT) Scales. *Journal of Marriage and the Family, 41*, 75–86.

Straus, M. A., Gelles, R. J., & Steinmetz, S. (1980). *Behind closed doors: Violence in the American family.* New York: Doubleday/Anchor.

Thyfault, R. K., Bennett, C. E., & Hirschorn, R. B. (1987). Battered women in court: Jury and trial consultants and expert witnesses. In D. J. Sonkin (Ed.), *Domestic violence on trial: Psychological and legal dimensions of family violence* (pp. 55-70). New York: Springer.

Walker, L. (1983). The battered woman syndrome study. In D. Finkelhor, R. J. Gelles, G. T. Hotaling, & M. A. Straus (Eds.), *The dark side of families: Current family violence research* (pp. 31-48). Beverly Hills, CA: Sage.

Wolfe, D. A., Zak, L., Wilson, S., & Jaffe, P. (1986). Child witnesses to violence between parents: Critical issues in behavioral and social adjustment. *Journal of Abnormal Child Psychology, 14,* 95-104.

8

Integrating Feminist and Social Learning Analyses of Aggression: Creating Multiple Models for Intervention with Men Who Batter

Anne L. Ganley

Introduction

In the past few years there has been a proliferation of programs designed to intervene in situations of domestic violence. These programs have emerged out of a pressing need to stop the spread of domestic violence in current and future generations. With limited resources and often in isolation from one another, these programs have created effective strategies and brought relief to countless women, children, and men. Some of these intervention programs are based on a myriad of competing but incomplete theories about the nature and cause of this violence. In some programs, the practitioners apply to domestic violence cases counseling theories that were never conceptualized to address violence. Other intervention programs claim no theoretical roots in the design of strategies, or they claim an eclectic approach, borrowing techniques from different theoretical models without reflecting on the theory behind those techniques. Other programs struggle to be congruent with a particular theory or theories. Some programs are more successful than others in ending the violence.

If we are to increase the effectiveness of interventions and if we are to attempt to replicate effective programs, we must examine the theoretical bases of our successes and failures. We need an integrated, comprehensive theory of domestic violence to guide practice and to foster relevant research. From my perspective, an integration of two theories, a feminist analysis of domestic violence and the social learning analysis of aggression, fills this need.

A Historical Perspective

Historically, the reality of domestic violence has been documented since the beginning of written records. However, its identification as a human problem worth addressing is not as constant. The acknowledgment or lack of acknowledgment of domestic violence as a problem seems to parallel the status of women in various societies (Dobash & Dobash, 1979; Gage, 1893). When domestic violence was recognized as a problem, intervention strategies varied according to how the problem was defined and what was considered its cause.

For example, in United States, the oft-derided Women's Christian Temperance Union (WCTU) was founded to deal in part with the abuse women and children were experiencing at the hands of drunken husbands and fathers. The founders mobilized a social movement against alcohol. This intervention strategy reflected their conceptual framework that alcohol caused the abuse. After some initial success, the movement proved to be ineffective in stopping either the use of alcohol or the violence against women and children.

During the same period, the Tlingit people, native to southeast Alaska, defined wife beating as a serious crime against the community because all members of the community were highly valued and necessary to tribal survival. In the rare cases when wife beating did occur, the whole community came together for a potlatch where the abuser's clan made restitution to the victim's clan in material goods. The consequences for such violence were expensive to the batterer and highly visible (Fortune, 1987). Wife battering was a rare occurrence in this community. Such community action seemed to deter future incidents.

In these two examples, domestic violence was acknowledged as a problem, but different understandings about the cause led to different intervention strategies. Furthermore, the examples raise the possibility that the success of a particular intervention may partly be dependent on successfully delineating cause(s) of the problem.

Currently, domestic violence is recognized as a significant problem in the United States and Canada. In the last 15 years, due to the persistent efforts of the battered women's movement (Schechter, 1982), domestic violence is now viewed as a crime throughout both countries. It has become grounds for both criminal and civil legal action (Lerman, 1983) as the legal system has joined with battered women to stop the violence. Services for victims, community education, interventions for perpetrators, and research are increasing. Although the problem is commonly acknowledged, there is less consensus about the cause(s). This partially explains the variety of interventions currently used.

Counseling as an Intervention for Domestic Violence

Counseling as a specific intervention for domestic violence is a relatively recent phenomenon. For years, counseling theories and practice ignored domestic violence. It was not discussed in the literature until 1964, when the intrapsychic theories viewed the violence merely as a symptom of individual pathology. Too often the domestic violence was considered a symptom of the victim's pathology (Snell, Rosenwald, & Robey, 1964) rather than a symptom of the perpetrator's pathology. Within this violence-as-symptom perspective, therapeutic efforts were misdirected at "curing" the available patient (usually the victim) of a mental disorder, in the belief that the perpetrator's violence would then disappear. The next set of therapeutic interventions to emerge was a variation of the notion that violence is merely a symptom of something else. But this time the violence was considered a symptom of a dysfunctional relationship or family rather than of a dysfunctional individual. Although this shift in perspective was viewed as a major breakthrough, since it emphasized the current interactions of the family members rather than individual personalities, intrafamily and intrapsychic conceptualizations of violence actually have the same theoretical flaws.

Alternative frameworks for understanding the occurrence of domestic violence have been developed. These frameworks name the violence as the problem and not merely as a symptom (Adams, 1988; Bograd, 1984; Brygger, 1986; Edleson, 1984; Ganley, 1981; Goldner, 1985; Hilberman & Munson, 1978; Walker, 1979, 1984). Furthermore, they view domestic violence as a problem fostered by social norms and institutions (Pence, 1983; Schechter, 1982). Many interventions evolved from this reconceptualization, and they focus on different dimensions of domestic violence. Some programs include counseling components, whereas others do not; some focus on the victim, some on the perpetrator, and some on both. The interventions developed by battered women's programs in the United States and Canada emphasize the lethal nature of domestic violence. These programs concentrate on the priority of the victim's safety and her right to control her own life. In implementing these goals, many of these programs also address the social systems (law enforcement, the legal system, religious institutions) that perpetuate domestic violence. Other battered women's programs, some traditional mental health systems, and some men's programs focus on altering the violence of individual perpetrators of abuse, using a variety of techniques and approaches (Currie, 1983; Donnenwerth, 1986; Emerge, 1980; Ganley, 1981; Ganley & Harris, 1978; Pence & Paymar, 1986; Sinclair, 1985; Sonkin & Durphy, 1982). Research measuring the effectiveness of these and similar programs is appearing as they stabilize over time.

To be effective in ending domestic violence, we must be willing to struggle with the varying theoretical frameworks, not just for the sake of abstract debate but for the sake of developing a consistent, reliable, comprehensive theory that will allow us to explain, predict, and eliminate violence within (as well as outside) families. As practitioners we must be willing to explicate our theoretical framework so we do not use the right technique for the wrong reason or the wrong technique for the right reason. Either may result in partial success or partial failure, which sometimes is conveniently interpreted as the client's "resistance" or "not being ready for change" rather than as a failure in our assumptions and theoretical framework. Connecting theory and practice is important; in the case of domestic violence, partial success or partial failure can result in death.

What follows is an integration of a feminist analysis of domestic violence with a social learning analysis of aggression (Bandura, 1973,

1979). These two analyses have been the most fruitful in my work with both victims and perpetrators of domestic violence. The integration of the two analyses views violence as having individual, family, and social determinants. The integration offers more than interpretations or dynamic descriptions of human behavior. Starting with a clear definition of battering, I will give a brief overview of the most salient aspects of the two theories as applied to domestic violence. In addition, I will discuss some of the counseling approaches based on these analyses.

The Problem: A Definition of Battering

The definition of any problem becomes crucial to the development of solutions for that problem. It guides the selection of the goals and the strategies of intervention. In this chapter and in the domestic violence work that I do, I define the primary problem of domestic violence in terms of the violence that occurs.

This violence may be called wife beating, domestic violence, woman abuse, spouse abuse, marital assault, conjugal violence, or battering. The differences in labels reflect either intentional or unintentional efforts to emphasize or deemphasize gender issues, the marital nature of the violence, or the attribution of responsibility for the violence. Regardless of what it is called, I define this battering as "assaultive behavior occurring in an intimate, sexual, theoretically peer, usually cohabitating relationship" (Ganley, 1981). Battering is defined both by the behaviors that are occurring and the context in which they occur.

Behaviorally, battering to an observer looks like the stranger-to-stranger violence of simple assault, assault and battery, harassment and menacing, property damage, arson, robbery, sexual assault, and homicide. However, it occurs in a relationship where victim and offender are "family" to each other. They may be legally married, separated, or divorced. In the growing evidence of courtship violence, the couple may be or may have been only dating. Given the intimate context of the violence, battering has some similarities to other types of violence found in families: child abuse, sibling abuse, and abuse of the elderly. However, unlike these types, in domestic violence both victim and perpetrator are adults who are in a supposedly peer relationship where neither has a legitimate role in disciplining of the other. The intimate family context influences how both perpetrator and victim relate to and are affected by the violence.

Unlike stranger-to-stranger violence, the assaults are repeated against the same victim by the same perpetrator (Ganley, 1987). These assaults may occur in different forms: physical, sexual, psychological, and the destruction of property/pets (Ganley, 1981). There is the "hands on" battering where the offender has physical contact with the victim's body: physical or sexual assault. In both physical and sexual battering, there are a range of behaviors. The physical may include shoving, pushing, scratching, biting, back handing, slapping (open or closed fist), choking, burning, use of weapons (household objects, knives, guns), beating, and so on. The assaults may or may not result in physical injury. Sexual battering, like physical battering, covers a range of behaviors: pressured sex, coerced sex (forced to do particular kinds of sex, to have sex with third parties, in front of children, etc.), and sex accompanied by physical violence. Sexual battering, like physical battering, may result in physical injury or emotional damage or both.

In "hands off" battering, the perpetrator has no contact with the victim's body; the assaults are carried out through psychological battering and the destruction of property/pets. Psychological battering includes activities typically associated with brainwashing: threats of violence (against the victim, others, and himself), *repeated* attacks against self-esteem, coercing victim to do degrading things (e.g., lick a line across a kitchen floor with her tongue), and excessive controlling of the victim's activities (e.g., access to money, friendships, sleeping and eating habits, holding a job, being an autonomous person). In the destruction of property/pets, even though something else is damaged, the attack is still meant for the victim. It is her clothes that are torn, her pet cat that is strangled, gifts that he has given her that are burned, or even his favorite object that he damages and then says, "Look what you made me do."

Too often the lethal nature of battering is ignored. Victims are maimed and killed every day by battering, and these battered women are not the only victims. There are the children who directly experience the battering through the physical and sexual violence directed at them or by witnessing the violence directed at their mothers. In addition, there are the other victims of spouse abuse: those who attempt to help (e.g., lawyers, police, family members, etc.) or the innocent bystanders who just happen to be in the path of a perpetrator battering his partner (e.g., the perpetrator who murders his wife and six other residents in a building by setting fire to an apartment complex). Any definition of the problem has to take into consideration the lethal and widespread impact of the behavior.

Battering is a *pattern* of behavior, not isolated individual events. One form of battering builds on another and sets the stage for the next battering episode (Ganley, testimony before Attorney General's task force on domestic violence, 1984). The central form that shapes the pattern is the physical or sexual violence (Ganley, 1981). It is this physical expression of the battering that gives power to the psychological battering. The victim of psychological battering has learned, like prisoners of war, that psychological torment or controlling behavior can be backed up by a physical assault. The power of "hands off" battering in damaging the victim comes in part from the physical or sexual violence that has preceded it. Therefore, I make a distinction between *psychological battering* where there is always the spoken or unspoken threat and actual occurrence of physical battering, and *emotional abuse* where there is no credible threat of violence since the perpetrator has not been physically or sexually violent in the past.

Psychological battering and emotional abuse may look the same to an outside observer. Both are carried out in the same way, and both are damaging to a relationship. However, psychological battering and emotional abuse occur in different contexts. With emotional abuse as defined above, there is damage but no immediate threat to life. With psychological battering, there is always the possibility of physical assault. They are somewhat different problems, requiring different interventions. The strategies developed by specialized domestic violence programs are based on an awareness of this difference between troubled families where there is no violence and troubled families where there is battering. Given the atmosphere of terror and coercion that results from "hands on" battering, interventions for all forms of battering must always take into consideration both the lethal nature of the violence and its impact on victims and perpetrators.

Battering in its multiple forms constitutes a pattern of *control*. Although there is discussion among practitioners about the meaning of that control (Ganley, 1981; Pence & Paymar, 1986; Serum, 1982), there is growing consensus that the battering pattern functions to establish domination or control in a relationship. Battering may be done intentionally to inflict suffering. For example, the man may physically punish a victim for thinking/behaving in a way that is contrary to the perpetrator's views. Or battering may be done simply to establish control in a conversation without intending harm. Regardless of the intent, the violence has the same impact on the victim and on the relationship. It establishes a system of coercive control (Ganley, 1981; Okun, 1986; Pence & Paymar, 1986; Serum, 1982). This effect of the violence is useful in understanding victims, perpetrators, and their interactions with each other and with others. For example, the meaning of certain transactions between couples will differ depending upon whether or not these exchanges are occurring in a relationship where there is violence.

Without intervention, battering increases in frequency and severity. This does not necessarily mean that the physical violence will escalate. Sometimes it stabilizes or even decreases as the psychological battering increases. In any individual's pattern, there will be shifts in the forms of violence most commonly used; however, the overall increase can be seen if the entire pattern of control is assessed.

Feminist Analysis of Domestic Violence

There is no single, unified feminist analysis of domestic violence. There are multiple perspectives among feminists who are discussing and writing about various types of violence against women. The differences and connections surface as the complexities of these issues are addressed. However, there are some commonalities found in the feminist literature. Fundamentally, a feminist analysis attends to the realities of gender (maleness and femaleness) and patriarchy (the institutionalization of a power differential based on gender). In its application specifically to domestic violence, a feminist analysis requires the acknowledgment of the differences between victim and perpetrator. It also highlights the issues of gender, power, and social systems, as well as how the interactions among the three result in the deadly reality of battering. These aspects of a feminist analysis are the most salient ones to an understanding of domestic violence and the development of effective interventions.

Definitions of Victim and Perpetrator

There has been a growing move away from using terms such as victim and perpetrator, particularly by family or couples' therapists. While the reasons for this vary according to the theory, the loss of those terms can blur reality and obscure the vision of what needs to happen to end violence. A perpetrator is a person who "brings about or carries out or commits a crime" (Webster's Ninth New Collegiate Dictionary). Physical assault and most types of battering behaviors are crimes. A perpetrator is the one who performs this act. A victim is one "who is acted on and is usually adversely affected by a force or agent; one that is injured, destroyed, or sacrificed under any of various conditions; one that is subjected to oppression, hardship or mistreatment" (Webster's Ninth). A battered woman is injured, destroyed, and subjected to oppression and mistreatment. There is a victim of battering, and there is a perpetrator. Although there may be a small percentage of cases where both parties are physically assaulting the other, these sometimes prove to be situations where the victim is attempting to defend herself from the attacks of the perpetrator (Saunders, 1986). To avoid serious errors, a very careful assessment must be done of the battering pattern before a couple are identified as engaging in "mutual battering."

Even for practitioners who use the terms and acknowledge the differences between victim and perpetrator, there is controversy about perpetrators being perceived as victims. Some counselors would argue that since some perpetrators were victims of violence as children in their families of origin, they are "victims." Even though they may have been victims as children, that does not make them victims of their abusive behavior as adults. Although interventions with perpetrators may need to address the historic victimization some of them experienced, such interventions should not relieve perpetrators of the responsibility for what they are doing to their partners in their adult relationships. Sometimes perpetrators are characterized as victims because they suffer the loss of intimacy in the relationship or experience self-inflicted damage during assaults on the victim. Although perpetrators' battering may be very self-destructive, that does not make them victims of their own abuse. Victims are people who suffer due to a force or agent outside of themselves. A perpetrator may suffer from his battering of another, but the act of violence is internally located and within his control.

If we lose sight of the difference between victim and perpetrator, we treat both as if they were the same, as if they had the same power to end the violence. Both may have power in their lives, but their power is not equal. The perpetrator always has more power to change his own behavior than a victim has to change *his* behavior. In certain battering relationships, the perpetrator has even more power to change his behavior than the victim has to change her own behavior. In battering relationships, the power of each adult to determine his or her own life and to have influence in the couples' relationship is not equal. In our studies of hostage or prisoner of war situations, we acknowledge a power differential between guard and prisoner. The power of the guard, partly enforced by access to and use of weapons, limits the behavior choices of the prisoner. This same dynamic occurs in battering relationships. The power differential is in part determined by the perpetrator's use of the violence itself and in part due to his being male in a patriarchal culture. Given this power differential, perpetrator and victim have different needs as well as different access to resources for intervention.

Gender

From a feminist perspective, domestic violence is one of the manifestations of male violence against women and children. The gender reality of domestic violence is evidenced in the statistics. In United States and Canadian incidence studies reviewing violence in its most extreme form of homicide, it is men who are the most violent, against other men as well as against women. This statistical finding has been true for as many years as such statistics have been kept. In studies of homicides against intimates, once again it is men who more frequently kill their female partners than vice versa (Jones, 1980). Although there may be debates in the nonhomicide literature about women being just as likely candidates as men for being spouse batterers, the reality of shelters, police reports, and emergency rooms clearly indicates that women are much more likely than men to be physically abused by their partners. In a comprehensive and historic review of the literature, Dobash and Dobash (1979) present the gender issue of domestic violence as being one of male violence against women. This is not to say that there are not some women who batter either male or female partners. Feminists acknowledge this minority and have taken the lead in raising issues related to female perpetrators and male victims and battering in lesbian relationships (Lobel, 1986). However, the statistics speak for themselves: Men are more likely to be the perpetrators and women are more likely to be the victims. Although acknowledging the exceptions to the trend, feminist analysis views the gender issue as a crucial link between understanding and ending the violence (Schechter, 1982; Walker & Browne, 1985).

Power

The issue of power makes gender a primary issue in domestic violence. A feminist analysis clarifies the interactive effect of gender and power, both in its physical and social dimensions. Some authors equivocate about whether or not one gender is more aggressive than the other (Dutton, 1988) but acknowledge that men are more physically powerful and cause more injury/death than do women. The state of Washington rewrote its mandatory arrest with probable cause law for domestic violence partly to reflect this fact. When the original law went into effect, police departments were arresting a small but significant number of women. In some cases, the women were arrested as the sole perpetrator; in other cases, both the man and the woman were arrested, leaving it to the courts to sort out the responsibility for the violence. The legislature changed the law in cases where both parties used physical force. The law was changed to give the police the responsibility to determine the probable primary aggressor in the incident and to arrest only that individual. The police consider the following factors: (1) the intent of the law (to protect victims), (2) the comparative extent of the injuries inflicted (e.g., she scratched him as he choked her) and the seriousness of threats in creating fear of physical injury, and (3) the presence of a history of prior violence, as evidenced by prior calls to police. When the law clarified their duties in responding to domestic violence calls, the police significantly reduced its arrests of women and of both parties (Poort, 1986). To the credit of the law and police departments of such cities as Seattle, arrests in domestic violence calls reflect what a feminist analysis would predict: The majority of domestic violence arrests with probable cause were of men assaulting female victims.

Another illustration of the unwillingness to recognize the interactive effect of gender and power was expressed to me by a colonel during a domestic violence training for the United States Army. He acknowledged that maybe men were more physically aggressive than women but felt that physical aggression was only in reaction to the "power of a woman's tongue." Such a comment, as well as similar ones ("Women are more verbally aggressive, and men's only resource is physical force"), suggests that men's violence is only a defense against women's verbal aggression. First, there is no documentation that women are more verbally aggressive than men or that men only hit when women are verbally aggressive. In fact, one study by Margolin, Gleberman, John, and Ransford (1987) found that physically abusive husbands were more verbally aggressive than their wives (as well as more verbally aggressive than both the husbands and wives in nonviolent maritally discordant relationships). But even if the myth of the powerful female tongue were true, a fist in the face is not equal to a verbal insult. As I pointed out to the colonel, if a women's tongue were more powerful than or equal to physical force, the United States Army would dispense with its armies of male fighters and weapons and commission female soldiers to fight its wars verbally.

The most significant contribution of feminist analysis of gender and power is not in the discussion of physical power but in its focus on the social power of men through social norms and institutions. A feminist analysis reminds us of the well documented difference between men and women in terms of economic, political, and social power, both inside and outside of the family (Dobash & Dobash, 1979; Martin, 1976, Schechter, 1982). These differences are institutionalized in our legal, social service, religious, and economic systems. Consequently, an individual man who batters is supported by each of these systems. Until recently, the legal system sanctioned his behavior, the social service system blamed his victim, the religious system condoned his behavior through silence or teachings (Fortune & Hormann, 1980), and the economic system shut out victims from resources needed for change.

Social Systems

A feminist analysis offers us a systems perspective of domestic violence without limiting the systems perspective to the family system. In addition to the family, feminist analysis considers the impact of other social systems: legal, social service, economic, religious, and educational. Such an analysis looks at the interactive effects among individuals, families, and other social systems. The individual exists within a family that lives in a community, which is another context within society. The violence is the result of what individuals learn as they interact with each other within all levels of systems. Each of the systems, in turn, interact with one another and further influence and shape individuals' behaviors. Battering is not merely the result of transactions between an individual man and his wife but emerges from the past, present, and future interactions of that individual with family, friends, strangers, and every social system that forms the context for those interactions. Feminist theorists, practitioners, and activists have continually called society to task for its contribution to the problem of all forms of violence (Dobash & Dobash, 1979; Pence, 1983; Schechter, 1982). Their persistence is now being reflected (but not always cited) in mainstream theorizing about family violence, as authors now conceptualize all types of violence as being multideterminate (Dutton, 1986, 1988; Finklehor, 1984; Gelles & Straus, 1979; Straus, 1976). Domestic violence as well as other types of family violence is now seen as having roots within the individual, the family, and the culture. Effective interventions must address the dynamics of all three.

Social Learning Analysis of Aggression

While a feminist analysis provides the broad outline for an understanding of domestic violence, a social learning analysis provides a framework necessary to the development of specific interventions. Although Albert Bandura (1973) did not address domestic violence in his landmark book on aggression, his analysis and review of the research on aggression offers a great deal to the field of domestic violence practice, theory, and research. For too long the traditional literature in domestic violence has relied primarily on sociological inquiry, psychological study of personality characteristics, or on fragmented treatment research, while ignoring the social psychology research on aggression. Even in reviews of the major psychological, sociological, and sociocultural theories of family violence (Lystad, 1986), social learning analysis is given only token recognition. With few exceptions (Donnerstein, Linz, & Penrod, 1987; Dutton, 1988; Wiggins, 1983), there has been little attention given to the experimental research on aggression and how it can enhance our understanding of how to intervene in domestic violence.

What follows in this section is a brief review of the most crucial components of the social learning analysis of aggression as it applies to domestic violence. The abbreviated concepts discussed here illustrate the value of that theory and the research based on it for developing interventions for battering. However, to fully utilize a social learning analysis, one must become familiar with information provided in more detailed accountings of the analysis (Bandura, 1973, 1979; Dutton, 1988; Wiggins, 1983), as well as with the feminist critique provided by J. Macaulay (O'Leary, Unger, & Wallston, 1985). In these more complete discussions, a fuller social learning analysis of aggression is revealed. The rich detail of the analysis and the research it has encouraged underscore its usefulness for practitioners and its compatibility with a feminist analysis.

As Bandura (1973, p. 43) points out, a complete theory of aggression must explain how the aggressive patterns of behavior are developed, what causes people to behave aggressively, and what maintains their aggressive actions. Whether trying to understand domestic violence in general or a specific indivdual's battering, the questions remain the same: How are the aggressive patterns developed, what causes those individuals to behave that way, and what maintains those abusive behaviors? Bandura's analysis (Bandura, 1973, 1979; Dutton, 1988) answers those questions by looking at the three major determinants of aggression: (1) the origins of aggression, (2) the instigators of aggression, and (3) the maintaining conditions.

Origins of Aggression

A social learning analysis of aggression would view the origins of battering in terms of biological factors, observational learning, and reinforced performance of the perpetrator within a social context. Although biology does not play a major role in this analysis of aggressive behavior, some biological factors influence what individuals learn and what they can perform (Bandura, 1973, 1979). Certain activity levels, physical structure, and structure limit what types of aggression can be performed. For example, certain physical abilities are required to choke a person. A social learning analysis does remind us that although biology may contribute to one's ability to be aggressive, the performance of such aggression depends on other factors as well: on whether the necessary instigators are present and on the influence of the regulators of that behavior (Bandura, 1979). For example, Dutton (1988) suggests that from a social learning perspective, men may be biologically predisposed to act aggressively since they are endowed with greater musculature than women. This size/strength differential increases the probability of men's physically aggressive behaviors producing their intended effect (e.g., gaining control), thereby resulting in positive reinforcement for their abuse.

According to social learning theory, battering is learned through observation and practice. Observational learning is the primary means by which individuals learn how to perform behaviors: attending to modeled behavior, coding it in symbols, and integrating it by motor reproduction (Dutton, 1988). As applied to domestic violence, this principle is consistent with the finding that witnessing spouse abuse as a child is an even greater predictor of abusing an intimate as an adult than being abused as a child (Hotaling & Sugarman, 1986). Although some behaviors are acquired through trial-and-error experiences, where behavior is shaped into new patterns by its consequences (Bandura, 1973), observational learning is the primary mechanism for most types of aggression.

What the individual learns through observation is more than just the execution of particular behaviors. The rules and regulations of when, where, and against whom to perform those behaviors are also learned by observation. Social learning theory makes the distinction between learning and performance (Bandura, 1973). Being exposed to violence, knowing how to do it, and being able to do it does not mean one will be violent. An individual's use of an acquired behavior pattern like battering depends on (1) the appropriate inducements (see instigators of aggression, below), (2) the functional value, and (3) the reward, or absence of punishment, for performance (Bandura, 1979). What is often overlooked is that these three conditions for aggression are learned along with the actual behaviors. Thus, for an individual to batter, he must have learned which are the "appropriate" inducements, when battering is functional, and what the rewards for this behavior are. The differences in the learning histories of batterers about these three conditions explain the infinite variety we see in battering episodes. If we are to look for causes of battering, we must look to those learning histories.

Bandura (1973) indicates that within modern society there are three major sources for learning aggressive behavior by modeling and reinforcement: (1) the family of origin (as it is embedded in a network of other social systems), (2) the subculture with which the person has repeated contact, and (3) the symbolic modeling provided by the media, which communicates social norms and behaviors. The sources may be historic (what the perpetrator learned as a child) or current (what reinforcements the adult perpetrator observes and experiences). There may be a historic basis (childhood) that established the learning of specific abusive behaviors and a current source (adult peer group) that reinforces the performance of such behaviors.

Looking at the learning histories of individual batterers, one can see the various interplays of the three sources of learning domestic violence. For example, one man who batters grew up in a family where his mother was abused, and when police were called to intervene, they blamed the victim and ignored his father. As he grew up from a child to an adult, he related almost exclusively to a subculture of men who strongly endorsed men's control of their wives and children and who positively sanctioned physical "discipline" of both. He was exposed to the traditional values and violence of the United States through the news media, television, and movies.

One can look at another individual's learning history and see a different combination: no violence in the family of origin but active family reinforcement for violence performed in his peer group; as an adult, identification with a subculture of Marine veterans, some of whom abuse their wives "because that is the way marriage is"; and a strong preference for movies depicting all types of violence. Dutton (1988, p. 46) summarizes what is learned from each of the three sources: "(a) explicit demonstration of an aggressive style of conflict resolution, (b) a decrease in normal restraints over aggressive behavior, (c) desensitization and habituation to violence, and (d) a shaping of expectations." These same factors are learned and reinforced by a perpetrator's experiences in battering his victim (see maintaining conditions).

Instigators of Aggression

"Contrary to popular accounts of aggression as explosive emotional reactions, like other forms of social conduct, performance of injurious actions is extensively regulated by environmental cues" (Bandura, 1973, p. 115).

Aggression, like other social behaviors, does not just happen; there must be an appropriate stimulus (instigator) in the contemporary environment. As Bandura's review of the research indicates, which events will evoke aggressive behavior in humans is not determined by genetics but learned in the environment. A social learning analysis explains why some stimuli elicit aggression, whereas others do not; it further explains why some stimuli elicit aggression from some individuals but not from others. To understand where aggression comes from within a social learning perspective, one must also look at three types of instigators of aggression: aversive instigators, incentive instigators, and delusional instigators.

Social learning theory would view the motivation to batter as a response to either (1) an aversive instigator (to remove a perceived aversive stimulus) or (2) an inducement instigator (to gain an anticipated payoff for an aggressive action) (Bandura, 1973, 1979; Dutton, 1988). Therefore, a man may batter during an emotionally charged argument, or he may batter calmly to maintain control over his wife. (For further discussion of the interactive effects among emotional arousal [sometimes labeled as anger by perpetrators], perception of aversive stimuli, and aggressive behavior, refer to Dutton, 1988.) It is simplistic to discount the role of emotional arousal (anger) in battering (Gondolf & Russell, 1986), just as it is simplistic to treat a perpetrator's anger out of the context of his learning history about gender roles. What constitutes aversive instigators or inducement instigators is shaped by the individual's learning history. Therefore, there can be a great deal of variance among perpetrators, as well as between those who batter and those who do not, regarding their perceptions of what is or is not an "aversive" stimulus. For example, one may view his wife's cutting her hair against his wishes as aversive, whereas another will not.

Either aversive experiences or anticipated consequences can activate a variety of learned responses: dependency, achievement, withdrawal, psychosomatization, self-anesthetization with drugs or alcohol, constructive problem solving or aggression (Bandura, 1973). As Dutton (1988) points out, which response the individual selects will partly depend upon (1) the individual's acquired cognitive appraisal of the aversive event—specifically, whether the individual thinks the event can be controlled or not. An individual's use of aggression or one of the other "active" responses (probem solving or achievement) follows from an appraisal that the aversive event is controllable. The individual's use of withdrawal or one of the "passive" responses (drugs or alcohol abuse or psychosomatization) follows from the appraisal that the aversive stimulus is uncontrollable. The choice of response also depends on (2) the mode of response the individual has learned to use to deal with such events. Certain individuals learn some modes of responses but not others. As Dutton (1988) states, both the appraisal of the event as being controllable and the type of response are acquired through the individual's unique reinforcement history. These appraisals or cognitions are the predispositions that individuals have acquired and use under certain conditions. Sex role socialization contributes to the development of those appraisals. Men and women have different learning histories about the appropriateness of aggression and about their roles in relationships. These different histories shape what they consider to be "instigators" and their choice of responses to them. These learnings may partly explain the gender difference in battering.

Social learning theory suggests that whether or not an individual perceives a particular event as an aversive or an inducement instigator is highly subjective. In some cases, these "subjective" perceptions would be described as being delusional. Bandura (1973) acknowledges that in addition to aversive or inducement instigators, there are sometimes delusional instigators to aggression. He cited the 1970 Weisz and Taylor study of presidential assassins, whose violence can be characterized as having been delusionally instigated by "bizarre belief systems." Bandura (1973) outlines how even these delusions and the choice to be violent stemmed from the learning histories of the assassins.

Dutton (1988) applies a social learning perspective to both those batterers who fit *Diagnostic and Statistical Manual of Mental Disorders* (third edition) (DSM III) diagnosis criteria for conjugal paranoia (persecutory delusions/delusional jealousy) and to those batterers whose beliefs may not be delusional by social standards but who are in conflict with their female partners. As Dutton (1988, p. 53) states, "The instigators of males' aggression may exist on a continuum between 'consensually defined' instigators (such as physical threats or attacks) and delusional instigators." I would add that even the so-called "consensually defined" instigators may vary depending upon who is determining the consensus. What is considered a "legitimate" instigator is truly in the eyes of the beholder, and that is greatly influenced by social systems and cultural views.

Maintaining Conditions/Regulators of Aggression

As stated in the definition, battering is a pattern of behavior consisting of repeated aggressive acts. For counselors developing interventions, a social learning analysis of the maintaining conditions of aggression (Bandura, 1973, 1979; Dutton, 1988) is most useful. According to this analysis, battering, like any aggression, is repeated because it works. It has functional value that is rewarded and not punished. Battering, like any form of human behavior, is regulated by its consequences: either rewards or punishments. The rewards may be (1) tangible ones such as establishing control in male-female relationships (Dutton, 1988; Ganley, 1981; Okun, 1986; Pence & Paymar, 1986; Serum, 1982), the expression of emotional arousal (Novaco, 1975), or getting what is wanted in a particular incident. Or the rewards may be (2) social status ones that come from acting in accordance with sex role standards or from specific rewards from peers. Or the reward may be from (3) the alleviation of the perceived aversive stimulus as the victim tries to accommodate the perpetrator to survive the abuse. The rewards to the perpetrator are many and, according to social learning theory, these rewards only have to occur intermittently for the behavior of battering to become entrenched. The strongest reinforcer of any behavior is intermittent reinforcement. Consequently, battering only has to work some of the time to be repeated again and again.

Aggression is also regulated by negative consequences or punishments (Bandura, 1973, 1979). The punishments may be external. To evaluate the effectiveness of external punishments in regulating aggression, one must consider the benefits derived from the aggression, the availability of alternative means for getting the benefits, the likelihood of punishment, as well as the nature, severity, timing, and duration of the punishment. Obviously, the punishments must outweigh the benefits, and they must be repeated consistently to extinguish the behavior. Even then, because of the power of intermittent reinforcement, battering may return once the negative consequences are no longer obvious.

In theory, battering could be regulated by external punishments. Too often society has expected the victim to be the regulator of the perpetrator's abuse, either through her withdrawing the rewards she inadvertently provides or by her punishing his battering behavior. This approach of having the victim become the regulator of the perpetrator's battering is evidenced in a variety of simplistic suggestions to victims: be more assertive, be less assertive, stay separated from him, lock him out. What such advice ignores is that the victim may not have sufficient power or resources in relationship to the perpetrator to withdraw rewards or enforce punishments and also survive the abuse. The power and resources victims do have are most appropriately concentrated on surviving. Fortunately, social systems, such as some criminal justice systems, are beginning to assume the role of providing negative consequences to the perpetrator for this behavior. And not surprisingly, there has been some documentation of success in this approach (Attorney General's Task Force on Family Violence, 1984). Certainly, social systems meting out negative consequences for this behavior need to be developed further, but other peer groups, religious institutions, and work groups should join in this effort to provide negative consequences for battering.

In addition to the external rewards/punishments, the "internal" rewards/punishments of the perpetrators are a source of reinforcement for the battering behavior. Social learning theory informs us that there are self-regulatory mechanisms for controlling behavior. Through observation and feedback, perpetrators adopt certain standards of behavior and can respond to their own actions in self-punishing ways. There is a great deal of variety among batterers in how they view their own behavior. Bandura's analysis would suggest that domestic violence may occur either because (1) some men see violence as acceptable behavior and are rewarded for controlling their partners, or (2) due to high arousal, anxiety about relinquishing control, and the perceived seriousness of the conflict, some men are violent in spite of their self-constraints (Dutton, 1988). They are able to violate their own standards by altering their evaluative self-reactions. Or "as Bandura (1979) put it, moral (i.e., normally socialized) people perform culpable acts through processes that disengage evaluative self-reaction from such conduct rather than through defects in the development or structure of their superegos" (Dutton, 1988, p. 57).

Bandura (1973) describes the processes that individuals use to neutralize their self-condemnation of their own aggression. He suggests that individuals avoid self-reproach in seven ways:

1. *Justification of higher principles*—"The Bible says I am the head of my wife and she must submit."
2. *Palliative comparison*—"I am not a real batterer because I never used a weapon."
3. *Displacement of responsibility*—"I was so drunk, I didn't know what I was doing."
4. *Diffusion of responsibility*—"It happens in every marriage."
5. *Dehumanizing the victims*—"My old lady deserves everything I dish out."
6. *Attribution of blame to victims*—"She drove me to it."
7. *Minimization and selective forgetting of the consequences*—"I got really mad at her only once."

A 1959 study by Bandura and Walters (Bandura, 1973) reveals how anticipatory self-reproach for repudiated aggression serves as a motivating factor to keep behavior in line. Interventions in specialized programs for batterers (see applications section, below) seek to increase perpetrators' personal responsibility as an antidote to their neutralizations of self-regulation of their abusive behavior.

In addition to delineating these origins, instigators, and regulators of aggression, Bandura (1973) also examined what can change these patterns. Based on his review of the research, he discussed the modification and control of aggression. "Since aggression is largely under situational, cognitive, and reinforcement control, these are the events to which treatment addresses itself, rather than to traits, to presumptive drive forces, or to historical causes" (Bandura, 1973, p. 245). The issues that have the most relevance to changing domestic violence are listed as follows: (1) modeling of alternative coping responses such as listening skills and conflict resolution skills, (2) selective reinforcement in which aggression is not rewarded and nonaggression is rewarded, (3) eliminating fantasized instigators of violent outbursts, (4) developing competencies that provide new sources of rewards, and (5) reducing aversive social conditions that promote violence (e.g., the lower social status of women).

In summary, from a social learning perspective, the learning history of perpetrators as well as the current rewards for battering shapes perpetrators' choices in using battering against their victims. Although past history cannot be rewritten, it can be assessed for information on what needs to be altered in the present or future.

Through a system of new rewards and punishments, both external and internal, nonabusive patterns can eventually replace battering.

Advantages and Disadvantages of an Integration of Feminist and Social Learning Analyses

An integration of feminist and social learning analyses not only brings together two compatible theories but also magnifies the power of each to enhance our ability to bring about change in the lives of families. Both analyses consider the roles of gender, social systems, individual attributes, and family experiences in the development of human behavior. However, a feminist analysis of domestic violence focuses on the impact of crucial variables: gender, power, and social systems. A social learning analysis of domestic violence provides us with the details of how battering is acquired and how it can be changed. Specific aspects of the learning process for aggression are outlined, allowing us to separate the process into components that can be altered to facilitate change. A social learning analysis considers both the variables associated with learning the pattern and the variables associated with a person's willingness to perform aggression. It makes sense out of how individuals or families with seemingly similar characteristics or dynamics may or may not have domestic violence. A social learning analysis can account for an infinite variety of individuals and situations and still provide guidance for interventions at individual, family, and societal levels. This allows us to develop interventions for a wide variety of individuals and communities, rather than forcing individuals or families to fit our theories (Hanks, 1987). Whereas a feminist analysis continually reminds us to work on a social as well as on an individual level, a social learning analysis meets the hallmark of a good theory. It does more than describe dynamics and make interesting interpretations; it allows us to make predictions of behavior based on guiding principles that have been well researched. Consequently, it also provides paradigms for ongoing research, which prevents us from losing sight of our goal of stopping violence.

The major disadvantages of the two theories are also the disadvantages of their integration. A feminist analysis needs more research on the specific interactive effects of gender, power, and social systems. Such research is complex and not easily funded. It requires multilayered research projects (Yllö, 1987, 1988) by those willing to leave behind the now "safe" paths of the already established family violence researchers. As for a social learning analysis of aggression, its complexity can initially be overwhelming. More writings such as Dutton's (1988), which looks at the theory's specific applications to both domestic violence research and practice, are needed to make the theory more accessible to counselors. Furthermore, with the exception of the family strategies for aggressive children developed by Gerald Patterson and associates, little has been written that explores the integration of a social learning analysis of aggression with principles of feminist family therapy.

There needs to be more research on the application of the integration of the two theories to specific individual, family, and community interventions. In reality these disadvantages are not weaknesses of the theories themselves; they are more a comment on where we are in our knowledge base. We are just beginning to integrate theories and to develop comprehensive research projects with multiple, complementary hypotheses.

Assumptions of Intervention Models Based on These Analyses

An integration of feminist and social learning analyses of domestic violence provides a framework from which multiple models of interventions can be designed for individuals, families, and communities. Although different intervention programs may evolve from the same analyses, those using a feminist, social learning framework hold certain assumptions in common. This section provides a brief review of those assumptions.

1. From a combined feminist, social learning perspective, battering is conceptualized as behavior taking place in an interpersonal context but having multiple determinants: individual, interpersonal, and social. These multiple determinants stem from both the current and the historical experiences of the perpetrator. The individual determinants include such things as physical attributes and personality traits. Interpersonal determinants include family of origin, peer group, work associations, previous or concurrent intimate relation-

ships, and current family relationships. Social determinants would be community standards expressed in the responses of social systems: legal, social service, religious, and economic.

These determinants may arise from the perpetrator's individual, interpersonal, and social experiences in the past or in the present. As an example, a specific perpetrator's current battering may have roots in his physical size and personality, the violence and controlling behaviors of his father, his attachment to a peer group of abusive men, his being violent in two previous relationships, his strict adherence to a religious faith that he perceives as giving him unquestioned authority over his family, a community legal system that ignored previous charges of assault by blaming the victim, and his listening to a counselor who emphasizes that his current family is out of control and that "he must learn to take charge."

2. From a feminist, social learning perspective of domestic violence, any intervention model must address all the determinants, rather than focusing solely on one and only paying lip service to the others. For example, it would be a mistake in the previously cited example for the intervention to focus primarily on current family transactions and conflicts as the source of the man's violence without acknowledging the role of his violence in previous relationships or the roles of the social systems in supporting the violence. Even his previous therapy may have inadvertently contributed to his battering by fostering his belief that he should "take charge of the family." The intervention should be based on a careful assessment of all the determinants, and the strategies used should reflect the specifics of that multideterminant framework.

3. From a feminist, social learning perspective, battering is perpetuated by its rewards (or absence of punishments), both internal and external, interpersonal and social. Unless these rewards are altered, the person will not remain battering free. As the previous theory discussion indicates, the rewards of battering are many, and even intermittent reinforcement can cause the habit to become entrenched.

4. Current battering is primarily driven by the cognitions of the person doing the behavior rather than by the actions of the victims. In clinical work, I have been repeatedly amazed by the differences in the so-called precipitating events to the battering. Very different behaviors, events, situations are responded to with violence. And yet there is a great deal of similarity among the

meanings ascribed to those events by the perpetrators. The perpetrator's perceptions or cognitions are based on a wide variety of interpersonal experiences, predating as well as concurrent with the relationship to the victim. The cognitions that precipitate battering are not based primarily on experiences in the current relationship. This fact is most evident in the battering done where the perpetrator has little experience with the victim, such as in dating relationships. It is also evident in long-term battering relationships where the batterer explains his behavior with "*No one* is going to treat me like that" and "*All women* are just alike." His perceptions of the events, rather than the victim's actual behavior, influenced his choice of violence. For therapists to focus exclusively on the transactions in the current relationship assumes incorrectly that the violence stems from those interactions, when a far more powerful elicitor of violence is the perpetrator's own cognitions. Perpetrators are adults, and as adults their cognitions are shaped by a particular learning history. In interventions with batterers, such learning histories must be assessed to clarify how a perpetrator self-escalates in order to be violent and then self-reinforces his actions. Perpetrators can learn to deescalate to nonviolence and to self-regulate their aggressive behavior.

5.   Intervention with an individual's battering involves working directly with that person. One cannot change a batterer's behavior solely by working with a victim. To do so belies the power of that perpetrator. Yet repeatedly I have seen staff who in their work with victims get discouraged that the offender does not change. If the work is with victims, the goals are to assist her to increase her safety and to support her ability to have control in her life. These goals can be reached but may not affect the perpetrator's behavior. If the goal is to stop the perpetrator's behavior, then staff must have contact with that individual.

Some counselors using a systems perspective would suggest that it is possible to change a perpetrator by changing the victim, since changing one member of a system changes the system and consequently other members of the system. Such a system change through work with just one member of the system can occur only when the therapist works with the most "functional" member of a family. In cases of violence, "functional" must be defined in terms of the one most powerful, the offender, to bring about change in the violence. Sometimes some therapists have confused "most functional" with "most willing" to participate in therapy and in doing so have ascribed to victims more power to change perpetrators and the family system than they really have. Victims can and do make changes in their own lives without influencing the perpetrator's behavior. In our interventions, we should clarify for ourselves who is expected to make which changes for what goal and assess whether or not the change agent has the power to bring about the expected change.

6. In keeping with the definition of domestic violence as a pattern of control, the goals of intervention are to stop the battering behavior in all its forms and to realign relationships from being based on the abuse of power to being based on mutuality. This involves a process of empowering victims, as well as of changing perpetrators. When the perpetrator stops the battering, success is only partial and remains fragile unless he also is able to relate in noncoercive ways. This change may occur over a long period of time, with initial success being the end of the violent behavior, but long-term change involves a process where the perpetrator acknowledges his abusive history, demonstrates noncoercive patterns of interpersonal communication, and is able to self-reward these changes rather than depending solely on the reinforcement of others.

7. The interventions with perpetrators based on a feminist, social learning analysis, the role of the therapist in the counseling is multifaceted: directive confronter of old patterns, active model and teacher of new patterns, and positive reinforcer of new behaviors and values. All roles require a clear conceptual framework, good assessment skills, and a willingness to take responsibility for taking an active part in the change process. This is not the type of counseling for counselors who prefer merely facilitating a context for change or, as one therapist described his work, "being the one who merely creates the opportunity for the family to have the conversation." Such a stance may be therapeutic on some issues but not in cases of family violence. Such a passive or indirect role for the counselor seems to ignore the power of the violence and its embeddedness in individuals and our culture.

8. Using a feminist, social learning analysis of domestic violence requires that the counselor take a active role in the community, as well as in counseling. Domestic violence is a social problem that cannot be altered by the highly individualistic process of therapy. If counselors are committed to assisting clients in being violence free, then some of their work must occur in the community. The exact nature of that counselor role in the community will vary greatly from

counselor to counselor. For some it means legislative work, for others, coalition work on a particular task; for some it is research to refute victim-blaming theories, for others, working on boards of shelters. For most, it is being a community activist as well as a practitioner.

9. And most basically, a feminist, social learning analysis presumes that the guiding principle of any intervention in domestic violence is the safety of the victim. Battering is lethal; interventions can and do increase risk to victims; this risk must be monitored before, throughout, and after the intervention process. (Counselors should read Hart's 1988 book on accountability, for a discussion of such monitoring.)

Application of Feminist, Social Learning Analyses to Models of Intervention

An integration of feminist and social learning analyses leads to the development of many different types of interventions for domestic violence. Some interventions may be directed at entire communities (Pence, 1983; Pence & Paymar, 1985), or individuals, and some are directed at a particular sector of society, such as specialized training for clergy. Some may be directed at a part of the social structure. For example, California law requires police department policies on domestic violence and domestic violence training for police. Some interventions may have counseling components, and some may not.

A feminist, social learning analysis reminds us that counseling is only one type of intervention that may bring about change in a perpetrator. Change may also occur due to other interventions, such as arrest, prosecution, probation, confrontation, and monitoring by an individual's church. Furthermore, a feminist, social learning analysis suggests that the success or failure of a particular counseling program has as much to do with the other interventions in the community as it has to do with the content or style of the counseling with the perpetrator. A feminist, social learning analysis acknowledges that counseling is not the exclusive answer for this social problem.

Since this book focuses on counseling interventions with batterers, rather than on the social context in which such programs take place, I will limit this discussion to issues specific to the application of a feminist, social learning analysis of domestic violence to counseling with perpetrators.

Victim Safety and Victim Rights

As discussed previously, any intervention in domestic violence must be done within the context of increasing the safety of the victim. Battering is injurious and at times lethal. The pattern is entrenched, and positive change occurs slowly. Even though a perpetrator is in counseling, he is at risk to reoffend. Consequently, each intervention must be evaluated in terms of its ability to increase or decrease the victim's safety. This should be done prior to, during, and after the counseling (see section on evaluation). Separate interviews with the perpetrator and victim are necessary to make accurate assessments of the violence and to provide victims with information crucial to their survival. In domestic violence cases, standard therapeutic approaches and techniques have to be scrutinized so that we do not cause more harm than good. The procedure developed by shelters and by specialized programs for perpetrators provide models for implementing a process for increasing victims' safety without impinging on their rights as autonomous adults (Emerge, 1980; Pence & Paymar, 1986). What is important is that counselors review their approaches and not merely assume that couneling per se is harmless.

Perpetrator's Accountability

Just as victim safety and empowerment are the central intervention issues for victims, client accountability is the central intervention issue for perpetrators (Ganley, 1981; Ganley & Harris, 1978). A feminist, social learning analysis of battering underscores the necessity for perpetrators to become responsible for their own behaviors. Otherwise, change will not occur. For progress to be made, they must be aware of what they are doing, see it as something under their control, and use their own cognitions as regulators of their abuse. In the face of the minimization, denial, and victim blaming perpetuated by both the individuals and society, perpetrator accountability involves a process extending throughout and following the counseling intervention. Specialized programs implement this by a series of strategies: clear statements of personal responsibility for the battering, consequences for relapses, and accountability for participation in the program (attendance, homework); and avoidance of protecting perpetrators from the negative consequences of their behavior (jail, divorce, limited custody of children). Such programs often encourage the criminal justice system, family, friends, and others to hold the perpetrator accountable for his behavior. For too long, the victims have been held accountable for the perpetrator's behavior, while the perpetrator's accountability has been ignored. In doing so, social systems have colluded with the perpetrator's violence. Although it is appropriate to hold victims accountable for their own behavior, it must be done in a way that gives full recognition to the context of the power imbalance between perpetrator and victim, as well as between men and women in society. Victims have power; but within a battering relationship and within patriarchy, their power and accountability is relative rather that absolute. The perpetrator's accountability is the key to changing his behavior.

Confidentiality

Related to the issue of dangerousness is the question of confidentiality. In no other type of therapy does the issue of confidentiality appear so complex. In this age of litigation, with unclear standards for duty to warn and duty to protect, it behooves all therapists working with domestic violence clients to become knowledgeable about the legal issues and professional standards of confidentiality (Hart, 1987; Sonkin, 1986). Although it is beyond the scope of this chapter for me to summarize those legalities and standards, I do want to comment on confidentiality as a therapeutic issue in domestic violence cases. The question here is, Whose confidentiality should be protected for the benefit of whom?

There is a commonly accepted tenet that counseling requires a guarantee of confidentiality or the process will not occur. The belief is that without this guarantee, clients will not tell a therapist everything important and therefore will not benefit from therapy. Consequently, therapists often view confidentiality as the cornerstone of the therapeutic process and not just as an issue of client rights. Yet there is no research indicating that clients will not tell all without such guarantees of confidentiality. It always surprises me how much clients tell even when they clearly know there is limited or no confidentiality, as in cases of child abuse. Given this reality and the reality of domestic violence, confidentiality as a therapy issue needs to be reexamined.

First, what is confidentiality? As most professional standards indicate, confidentiality is more than an issue of keeping client information secret. Confidential information is and should be shared among a treatment team or used to prevent a suicide or as a teaching tool. Maintaining confidentiality is a matter of judgment based on three criteria: (1) what is told, (2) to whom it is told, and (3) for what purpose. One can violate confidentiality by violating any one or any combination of the three criteria. Therefore, a counselor who discusses client information to the right person (another counselor) for the wrong reason (to impress that counselor at a social gathering) breaks confidentiality as much as the therapist who tells the same information to another client. Clients benefit when relevant information is shared with appropriate people for therapeutic reasons.

Second, in domestic violence cases, another issue of importance is whose confidentiality should be maintained and for whose benefit. As indicated by the previous discussion on victim safety, it is crucial that counselors guarantee confidentiality to victims. A breaking of a victim's confidence could result in injury or death for her. That does not mean that a counselor has to keep secret all information provided by her. It means that her permission must be sought first before any information is given to another agency or to the perpetrator. In getting informed consent, the possible consequences to her of sharing certain information must be explored in terms of her safety. This process empowers the victim and allows her control over the information. Oftentimes after such a consultation, victims are willing for their input to be shared even with the perpetrators, but at other critical times they refuse because the risk to them or the children is too great. For victims, providing them with occasions for confidential discussions separate from the perpetrators and respecting that confidentiality is for their benefit and, in some cases, for their survival. And ultimately, the information given in such sessions will benefit the perpetrators as well since it provides data for accurate assessment and monitoring of progress.

The situation is different for perpetrators. Granting them confidentiality, as it is traditionally practiced, not only endangers victims but also does not benefit perpetrators. Information about program attendance and progress as well as violence potential is needed by victims to assess their own safety (Hart, 1987). It is also needed by others working with the perpetrator, such as probation officers, child protective services, divorce lawyers, and other counselors (Ganley, 1987). It is in the perpetrator's best interest that he be held accountable for his behavior. Thus, it is consistent with the therapeutic goals of the perpetrator that he be granted very limited confidentiality. In keeping with clients' rights, professional standards, and legal issues, this should be explained to clients at the outset of entering the program.

Format for Therapy: Individual, Group, Couples', or Family?

Since the development of specialized counseling programs for domestic violence began in 1978, there has been a great deal of controversy about the appropriate format for counseling perpetrators of battering. This controversy has been based on both theoretical and practical grounds (Bograd, 1984; Edleson, 1984; Emerge, 1980; Ganley, 1981; Goldner, 1985; Pence & Paymar, 1986; Sonkin, Martin, & Walker, 1985). A feminist, social learning analysis of battering would appear to rule out the use of individual, couples', or family therapies on theoretical grounds. A feminist, social learning analysis does not view battering as being an intrapsychic phenomenon or merely the result of couple or family transactions. Such approaches may blame the victim and obscure the gender, power, and social systems issues in the perpetuation of the violence.

Given these theoretical and practical issues, programs using a feminist, social learning analysis have most frequently used group interventions as the format of choice with perpetrators. Most of these specialized programs for domestic violence consist of gender-specific groups, either as the total program or as the primary intervention. Consequently, most of the strategies that have been developed are based upon group models. Individual sessions with the perpetrators are usually limited to assessment. If offered, group or individual sessions for victims are viewed as either totally separate from, supplemental to, or complementary to the perpetrators' groups. If couples' or family counseling is offered, it follows the separate, gender-specific group counseling and is viewed as an addition to the primary intervention.

Perhaps what is needed in the discussion of the appropriate format is to separate the issue of session format from the theoretical assumptions typically associated with those formats. For example, we can, for this discussion, separate doing therapy in a family session from using traditional family therapies in that session. If we can make this distinction between format and process, then a feminist, social learning analysis does not categorically rule out the use of individual, couples', or family sessions for intervention in domestic violence. In fact, some feminist programs use all four formats. A feminist, social learning analysis moves the question of who attends a session from deciding who is responsible for the violence to deciding which format is best for the particular therapeutic task at hand. For example, a couples' session may be the appropriate place for the perpetrator to acknowledge to his partner his responsibility for the battering. A group may be the best place to overcome minimization and denial of the violence.

By making the distinction between session format and theory, we raise the possibility that there may be yet-undeveloped couples' or family interventions for domestic violence that are consistent with a feminist, social learning analysis. And we raise the possibility that these interventions could be implemented in individual, group, couples', or family sessions. In such interventions, the strategies used would not overtly or covertly blame victims, ignore the gender issue, forget the power imbalance, or be blind to the role of social systems in domestic violence. In keeping with a feminist, social learning analysis, the strategies would also address the practical concerns of ensuring victim safety, perpetrator accountability, and appropriate confidentiality. However, even if such feminist, social learning couples' and family approaches are developed, I doubt they would or should ever totally replace the separate group approaches for victims and perpetrators. It is only in such groups that both counselor and clients are confronted with the social supports for domestic violence, and only in such groupings will new norms for nonabusive intimate relationships be developed.

Differential Diagnosis: Who Should Get What Type of Intervention?

As our knowledge about the what, why, and who of domestic violence has increased, so have our questions about the effectiveness of interventions. Specific questions have also arisen about who should get what type of intervention. Due to limited resources and growing numbers of clients (either court mandated or not), there has been a push by society to identify who may or may not benefit from counseling or some other intervention. A feminist, social learning perspective frames that question by asking a series of other questions: Who is capable of and willing to learn to self-regulate abuse, to learn and use alternative coping strategies, and to learn and use noncoercive communication patterns?

Attempts to respond to those questions have resulted in partial answers at best. At times it appears that we do not know enough about either perpetrators or interventions to be able to answer what intervention will work with which person. And in spite of a flurry of research on profiles of perpetrators (Saunders, 1987), the inconclusive and contradictory results suggest that partial answers are all that we will have for the near future.

So who should get what type of intervention? From a social learning perspective, intervention depends a great deal on the person's abilities to learn new material. Programs have admission criteria related to language abilities, toxicity (current alcohol or drug abuse), and cognitive impairment (organic or psychotic). These criteria, when used to exclude individuals from counseling, usually reflect the limited resources of the programs rather than the limited applicability of learning theory for these clients. Once learning abilities are assessed through structured interviews and tests, social learning programs can be developed to intervene on any individual's violence, if there are unlimited program resources.

A more difficult issue in differential diagnosis is the issue of motivation. No instrument has been designed to measure accurately clients' motivation for change. Programs at this stage either take everyone who meets their criteria for ability to learn or have developed their own informal measurements of motivation. Some use some form of written, signed contract between client and program to assess motivation. Such contracts delineate the client's responsibilities in participating in the program and outline criteria for dismissal from the program, such as poor attendance, relapses, or participation. Motivation may be assessed solely on whether or not the person signs the contract. Other programs use verbal reports of perpetrators to measure motivation.

Obviously, differential diagnosis is highly unsophisticated at this point and is primarily used for admission purposes. It could also be used to assess clients' strengths and limitations in order to develop learning programs tailored to their abilities. From a feminist, social learning perspective, differential diagnosis warrants more exploration.

Interfacing with Other Community Systems

Any counseling intervention for domestic violence based on a feminist, social learning analysis automatically requires that such counseling be interfaced with the other social systems in that community. Domestic violence is shaped by the responses of the criminal justice system, the civil court system, social services, religious institutions, the media, and economic systems. That translates into counselors' working with multiple agencies in one or more communities: battered women's shelters, child protective agencies, probation departments, welfare, lawyers and judges, victim advocate services, police, medical services, other mental health agencies, and policy-makers. Effective counseling with perpetrators cannot be done in isolation from the rest of the community. To attempt to do counseling without those linkages is like asking a perpetrator to change without having contact with anyone else. Both violate a basic concept of social learning theory, which states that one is shaped by the learning that takes place in social interactions. Interfacing requires time, persistence, and patience. Collaborative work develops only through effort, but it is an effort with many rewards.

Evaluation of Intervention Programs

The evaluation of the effectiveness of an intervention is an important but often slighted part of the program. The effectiveness or "success" of a counseling program depends upon the goals of the program, how success is defined, and how it is measured. To be consistent with a feminist, social learning analysis, the evaluation of counseling programs for perpetrators must address the definitions of the problem, both its behavioral and functional components. Given the lethal nature of battering, it is important to know whether counseling or any other intervention stops, decreases, or increases the battering. Since battering is a pattern of physical, sexual, psychological, and property/pet assaults, the effectiveness of a program needs to be measured in terms of its impact on all four forms of battering. As a social learning analysis points out, aggression becomes an entrenched pattern, and success in modifying it is partly determined by the development and use of alternative patterns (Bandura, 1973). Consequently, measuring success should also involve an assessment of perpetrators' development and use of noncoercive communication patterns. Since battering is a pattern of control in a relationship, measurements of effectiveness would also need to evaluate whether the perpetrator has shifted the power imbalance in his interpersonal relationship from dominance to mutuality.

Measures used in the evaluation should draw on behavioral observation of the perpetrator both in and out of treatment. These behavioral observations of the perpetrator should be gathered from the victims, the perpetrator himself, counselors, and others having repeated contact with the perpetrator, such as probation officers, family members, and friends. Obviously, a base line needs to be gathered either prior to or initially following entry to counseling. After that, the behavioral information should be gathered at systematic intervals, such as every 3 months while in counseling and every 6 months for a year's follow-up, and every year for 3 years after that. It is predictable that there will be an increase in self-report of battering in the first 3 months, as individuals become better observers and their minimization and denial decrease. After that, there should be a decline if the intervention is successful.

There are multiple issues raised by evaluation processes. As in the counseling itself, victim safety must be considered in the development of assessment procedures. Victim participation in outcome studies should never be coerced and should include referral to victim resources. Victims, perpetrators, and others should be debriefed following the evaluation sessions. Any misinformation about domestic violence offered by the clients should be corrected in these debriefing sessions (Hart, 1987, 1988). Systematic evaluation is time consuming, and it is easy to deemphasize such a process, given increasing case loads. It is better to design a simple system that can be carried out than to design an elaborate one that will be overwhelming and poorly implemented. A well designed evaluation system can be expanded later as resources become available. All outcome studies should describe, both in the design section and in the conclusion, the contextual factors which interface with the counseling to bring about change in perpetrators. Examples of such contextual factors affecting perpetrators' counseling would include descriptions of state and community laws, law enforcement procedures, legal response, and victims services.

To date, outcome studies seem to be studies in "successive approximations." They have had limited definitions of success and incomplete measures of effectiveness, so they most often measure "approximations of success." They have been severely limited by the lack of resources designated for that purpose. As more resources become available, and outcome studies are done more carefully, there can be more client, counselor, and program accountability to victims of battering.

Conclusion

The integration of feminist and social learning analyses has much to offer to practice, theory building, and research in domestic violence. Such an integrated analysis makes sense out of what we now know and what we need to know in the future. It provides us with the opportunity to develop multiple models of intervention for domestic violence. It raises additional questions to be answered and offers suggestions for ways to answer those questions. The integration brings together two compatible analyses, each strengthening the other and both providing perspective on the current maze of seemingly contradictory information about family violence.

In an ideal world, practice or phenomenological experience precedes and informs theory building, which precedes and informs research, which then corrects theory and practice. In an ideal world, this becomes a continuing circle, expanding our knowledge of ourselves as human beings. In the real world of domestic violence practice, theory, and research, we need to remember where we are in the developmental stage of this field. At this point, rather than an ever-expanding circle of knowledge, there seems to be a series of stops and starts, as clumps of information come forward from disconnected pockets of practitioners, activists, researchers, and theorists. This fragmentation does not even seem to be diminished for those individuals who assume all four roles. At this point in our history, we must remember the vision of the circle and be activists in striving toward the interaction of practice, theory, and research. By doing so, our practice, theorizing, and research will contribute to the end of violence in the lives of women, children, and men. And that is the ultimate measure of our work.

References

Adams, D. (1988). Treatment models of men who batter: A profeminist analysis. In M. Bograd & K. Yllö (Eds.), *Feminist perspectives on wife abuse* (pp. 176-199). Beverly Hills, CA: Sage.

Attorney General's Task Force on Family Violence. (1984). *Final report.* Washington, DC: U.S. Attorney General.

Bandura, A. (1973). *Aggression: A social learning analysis.* Englewood Cliffs, NJ: Prentice-Hall.

Bandura, A. (1979). The social learning perspective: Mechanisms of aggression. In H. Toch (Ed.), *Psychology of crime and criminal justice.* New York: Holt, Rinehart & Winston.

Bograd, M. (1984). Family systems approaches to wife battering: A feminist critique. *American Journal of Orthopsychiatry, 54,* 558-568.

Brygger, M. (1986). *Critique of traditional family systems practice.* Paper presented at University of Minnesota symposium, Domestic Violence: Conflicts and New Directions.

Currie, D. (1983). A Toronto model. *Social Work with Groups, 6* (3/4), 179-188.

Dobash, R. E., & Dobash, R. P. (1979). *Violence against wives: A case against the patriarchy.* New York: Free Press.

Donnerstein, E., Linz, D., & Penrod, S. (1987). *The question of pornography: Research findings and policy implications.* New York: Free Press.

Donnenwerth, D. (1986). Unpublished materials presented in domestic violence course, Department of the Army, Academy of Health Sciences, Fort Sam Houston, TX.

Dutton, D. (1986). Wife assaulters' explanations for assault: The neutralization of self punishment. *Canadian Journal of Behavioural Science/Rev. Canad. Sci. Comp., 18*(4), 381-390.

Dutton, D. (1988). *The domestic assault of women: Psychological and criminal justice perspectives.* Boston: Allyn & Bacon.

Edleson, J. (1984). Violence is the issue: A critique of Neidig's assumptions. *Victimology: An International Journal, 9,* 483-489.

Emerge, Inc. (1980). *Organizing and implementing services for men who batter.* Boston: Author.

Finkelhor, D. (1984). *Child sexual abuse.* New York: Free Press.

Fortune, M. (1987). Epilogue: Justice-making in the aftermath of woman battering. In D. Sonkin (Ed.), *Domestic violence on trial, psychological and legal dimensions of family violence* (pp. 218-248). New York: Springer.

Fortune, M., & Hormann, D. (1980). *Family violence: A workshop manual for clergy and other service providers.* Seattle: The Center for the Prevention of Sexual and Domestic Violence.

Gage, M. (1893). *Woman, church & state.* Watertown, MA: Persephone Press.

Ganley, A. (1981). *Court-mandated counseling for men who batter: A three-day workshop for mental health professionals.* Washington, DC: Center for Women's Policy Studies.

Ganley, A. (1987). Perpetrators of domestic violence: An overview of counseling the court-mandated client. In D. Sonkin (Ed.), *Domestic violence on trial, psychological and legal dimensions of family violence* (pp. 155-173). New York: Springer.

Ganley, A., & Harris, L. (1978). *Domestic violence: Issues in designing and implementing programs for male batterers.* Paper presented at meeting of the American Psychological Association, Toronto.

Gelles, R., & Straus, M. (1979). Determinants of violence: Toward a theoretical integration. In W. Burr, R. Hill, I. Nyer, & I. Reiss (Eds.), *Contemporary theories about the family* (Vol. 1, pp. 549-581). New York: Free Press.

Goldner, V. (1985, November-December). Warning: Family therapy may be hazardous to your health. *Networker*, 19-23.

Gondolf, E., & Russell, D. (1986). The case against anger control treatment programs for batterers. *Response to the Victimization of Women and Children, 9*(3), 2-5.

Hanks, S. (1987). *An evolving model of family focused clinical intervention in marital violence.* Paper presented at the Third National Family Violence Research Conference, University of New Hampshire, Durham.

Hart, B. (1987). Paper presented at the Third National Family Violence Research Conference, University of New Hampshire, Durham.

Hart, B. (1988). *Safety for women: Monitoring batterers' programs.* Harrisburg, PA: Pennsylvania Coalition Against Domestic Violence.

Hilberman, E., & Munson, L. (1978). Sixty battered women. *Victimology: An International Journal, 2,* 460-471.

Hotaling, G., & Sugarman, D. (1986). An analysis of risk markers in husband to wife violence: The current state of knowledge. *Violence and Victims, 1*(2), 101-124.

Jones, A. *Women who kill.* (1980). New York: Fawcett.

Lerman, L. G. (1983). State legislation on domestic violence. *Response to Violence in the Family, 6*(5), 1-28.

Lobel, K. (Ed.). (1986). *Naming the violence: Speaking out about lesbian battering.* Seattle: Seal Press.

Lystad, M. (Ed.). (1986). *Violence in the home: Interdisciplinary perspectives.* New York: Brunner/Mazel.

Margolin, G., Gleberman, L., John, J., & Ransford, T. (1987). *Interpersonal factors associated with marital violence.* Paper presented at the Third National Family Violence Research Conference, University of New Hampshire, Durham.

Martin, D. (1976). *Battered wives.* San Francisco: Glide.

Novaco, R. (1975). *Anger control: The development and evaluation of an experimental program.* Lexington, MA: Lexington Books.

Okun, L. (1986). *Wife abuse: Facts replacing myths.* Albany, NY: State University of New York Press.

O'Leary, V., Unger, R., & Wallston, B. (1985). *Women, gender, and social psychology.* Hillsdale, NJ: Lawrence Erlbaum Associates.

Pence, E. (1983). The Duluth domestic abuse intervention project. *Hamline Law Review, 6,* 247–275.

Pence, E., & Paymar, M. (1985). *Criminal justice response to domestic assault cases: A guide for policy development.* Duluth, MN: Minnesota Program Development, Inc.

Pence, E., & Paymar, M. (1986). *Power and control: Tactics of men who batter.* Duluth, MN: Minnesota Program Development, Inc.

Poort, L. (1986). *Seattle Police Department statistics—domestic violence arrests, 1984 and 1985.* Paper presented at Seattle Police Department training on domestic violence.

Saunders, D. (1986). When battered women use violence: Husband-abuse or self-defense. *Violence and Victims, 1*(1), 47–60.

Saunders, D. (1987). *Are there different types of men who batter? An empirical study with possible implications for treatment.* Paper presented at the Third National Family Violence Research Conference, University of New Hampshire, Durham.

Schechter, S. (1982). *Women and male violence: The visions and struggles of the battered women's movement.* Boston: South End Press.

Serum, C. (1982). *A profile of men who batter women.* Paper presented at the conference of the Bozeman Area Battered Women's Network, Bozeman, MT.

Sinclair, D. (1985). *Understanding wife assault.* Toronto: Ontario Goverment Bookstore.

Snell, J., Rosenwald, R., & Robey, A. (1964). The wifebeater's wife: A study of family interaction. *Archives of General Psychiatry, 11,* 107–113.

Sonkin, D. (1986). Clairvoyance vs. common sense: Therapist's duty to warn and protect. *Violence and Victims, 1*(1), 7–22.

Sonkin, D., & Durphy, M. (1982). *Learning to live without violence: A handbook for men.* San Francisco: Volcano Press.

Sonkin, D., Martin, D., & Walker, L. (1985). *The male batterer.* New York: Springer.

Straus, M. (1976). Sexual inequality, cultural norms and wife beating. *Victimology, 1,* 54–76.

Walker, L. E. (1979). *The battered woman.* New York: Harper & Row.

Walker, L. E. (1984). *The battered woman syndrome.* New York: Springer.

Walker, L., & Browne, A. (1985). Gender and victimization by intimates. *Journal of Personality, 53*(2), 179–195.

Wiggins, J. (1983). Family violence as a case of interpersonal aggression: A situational analysis. *Social Forces, 62*(1), 102–123.

Yllö, K. (1987). *Reflections of a family violence researcher.* Paper presented at the Third National Family Violence Research Conference, University of New Hampshire, Durham.

Yllö, K. (1988). Political and methodological debates in wife abuse research. In M. Bograd & K. Yllö (Eds.), *Feminist perspectives on wife abuse* (pp. 28–50). Beverly Hills, CA: Sage.

Epilogue

L. Kevin Hamberger
P. Lynn Caesar

This book has presented feminist, cognitive-behavioral, family systems, and integrative approaches in working with men who batter women. The authors explained their underlying assumptions and theories and the rationale behind their counseling or community interventions. They presented ideas for us to consider when evaluating the success or failure of their particular approaches. This is an important first step in beginning to consider how some interventions may be more helpful than others for particular batterers and/or couples.

The field of domestic violence interventions is still too young for us to know what is effective for particular populations of men and couples. Many batterer programs report high attrition rates (Roberts, 1982) and drop-out rates of 40% to 50% (Pirog-Good & Stets-Kealey, 1985). On the other hand, Lane and Russell (Chapter 6) reported that of the couples sent to them by the court, 60% chose to return after the first session, when a court mandate was no longer guiding them. Our explanations for "attrition" and "drop-outs" need to include therapist and program variables, as well as client "resistance." We need to carefully assess the needs of men and the women they batter and match them with complementary intervention programs. Such careful matching needs to be accompanied by program evaluation designs that take into account the criteria for success as defined by the theory and premises underlying the intervention model.

As the field of domestic violence intervention evolves, there remain key issues and concepts that may require further refinement and definition. For example, Ganley's (Chapter 8) basic definition of battering was cited by various contributors to this book as being consistent with their primary definition. She defined battering as "assaultive behavior [physical, sexual, psychological, or destruction of property/pets] occurring in an intimate, sexual, theoretically peer, usually cohabitating relationship." Adams (Chapter 1) and Pence (Chapter 2) also highlight in their definition of wife beating the pattern of coercive acts that serves to intimidate and undermine the victim.

There were, however, some exceptions to Ganley's definition. Some authors, for example, made clear distinctions between physical, injurious acts of battering and abusive but not physically assaultive acts (e.g., Rosenbaum and Maiuro, and Saunders). Most agreed, however, that both physical and nonphysical acts of abuse need to be addressed in treatment. Nevertheless, the diversity of opinion noted among contributors suggests conceptual divergence within the field that, if not addressed, could (and does) lead to confusion and gaps in communication. At the Third National Family Violence Research Conference, Barnett (1987) pointed out this confusion in defining and conceptualizing battering and called for greater standardization of terms. Such standardization would facilitate communication among those working in the field and encourage replication of research. For the present, until such standardization occurs, it is recommended that all reports of research and practice related to battery clearly define the terms from the authors' perspective in order to facilitate better understanding.

Another area of conceptual confusion is the "perpetrator" and "victim" distinction. For example, Adams, Pence, and Ganley differentiate between the (typically male) *perpetrator* (i.e., violent person) and the (almost always female) *victim* of the violence. Lane and Russell (Chapter 6), in contrast, eschew the distinction altogether in their second-order systems analysis. Yet a third conceptualization is offered by Maiuro and Rosenbaum (Chapter 7), who argue that the perpetrator should also be conceptualized as a victim of his own disordered behavior pattern. Geffner, Mantooth, Franks, and Rao

(Chapter 5) also describe the abuser as frequently a victim of the intergenerational transmission of violence. Furthermore, although Pence rejects the notion that men who batter are victims of their own socialization, she perceives the system that differentially grants one group power over the other group to be a dehumanizing one for both men and women. The man's abusive behavior, however, is seen by Pence as resulting from choice and not from some victimization process.

The issues of choice, responsibility and victimization, when examining our work with batterers, are complex ones. Our perception of batterers as victims or perpetrators will influence how we approach these men in a counseling context. Traditionally, judgmental and confrontational therapeutic stances were antithetical to the basic tenets of psychotherapy. The language of victim/perpetrator is borrowed from criminology and the disciplines of law. Some therapists are not comfortable viewing their position as an arm of the law. Historically, therapy assisted people to open up and explore, rather than control and restrict behavior. On the other hand, experienced clinicians working with domestic violence are aware that they need to take a more active role in helping men examine their violence directly. Colluding with batterers to avoid discussions about violence is not therapeutic either. The question arises, then, whether or not counselors need to become like police officers, attorneys, judges, or probation officers, to help their clients examine violence directly. Or are there other ways to help men examine their violence without feeling judged and penalized by a therapist?

The different conceptualizations of violent men and the women whom they batter appear to represent basic contrasting assumptions about physical violence and may not be easily reconciled. Nevertheless, a framework that may be adopted to identify and standardize at least some aspects of terminology is offered by Ganley. There is much evidence to support that many men who batter were directly or indirectly subjected to abuse as children, typically in their families-of-origin (Caesar, 1988; Hotaling & Sugarman, 1986). Hence, as children they may be said to have been victimized in such situations. As an adult in a current relationship, the person who, historically, was victimized perpetuates his violent acts upon his partner.

Although, as clinicians, it is important to know about a man's previous victimization experiences to assist in understanding the dynamics of his particular situation, Ganley reminds us that it is the present behavior pattern that is (1) the reason for referral and (2) the target of intervention. Furthermore, in addition to helping the man stop his violent behavior, the clinician will be concerned with enhancing the woman's safety. It is suggested, therefore, that some type of clear distinction be made between the one who carries out the violence (e.g., "perpetrator," "men who batter," etc.) and the one at whom the violence is directed (e.g., "victim," "battered women," etc.). Such a distinction (even if it is not made in a second-order systemic perspective) acknowledges a known gender difference in which men are more likely to batter and women are most likely to be battered in intimate relationships.

Issues of Research Methodology

Perhaps the most pressing need in the area of intervention with batterers is for treatment outcome studies. Several authors offered cogent ideas for assessing treatment efficacy, but as pointed out by Saunders (Chapter 4) in his review of cognitive-behavioral approaches, firm conclusions cannot be drawn at this time. Methodological problems form the basis of Saunders's assertion.

Research with batterers is typically clinical research and as such is predisposed to problems not encountered when studying nonclinical populations. First, the clinical needs of the client population are of paramount importance and so, of necessity, methodological design and rigor must be subordinated. For example, it would be "good science" in certain studies of the treatment of problems such as phobias or dating anxiety to compare an active treatment with a "no-treatment" control condition. In studying treatment programs for male batterers, however, the consequences of using a "no-treatment" control condition could have lethal implications. In fact, Hamberger and Hastings (1988b) suggested that it would be unethical, for the reasons given, to employ such a comparison group of violent offenders.

More recently, Maiuro, Cahn, Vitaliano, and Zegree (1987) utilized a "minimal intervention" condition in which men on a waiting list for treatment services were periodically monitored prior to receiving treatment. It would also be appropriate to compare various treatment approaches, as reported by Edelson, Syers, and Brygger (1987). In the Edelson et al. study, duration of treatment was also examined. Since various contributors to the present volume reported treatment lengths from three sessions to 6 months, it is suggested that treatment duration is worthy of study.

The reader is cautioned, however, that when reading reports of comparative treatment studies, one must be careful in interpreting results, particularly if one approach appears superior to another. Within the last few years, numerous researchers have called for conceptualizing batterers as a heterogeneous group. Hence, as knowledge of treatment modalities and batterer characteristics evolves, the goal will be to match batterers/clients to appropriate treatment technologies. In this regard, an area of inquiry that has received much research attention in the field of counseling and psychotherapy, but virtually no application in batterer treatment, is that of client-therapist matching. The failure, to date, of both client-treatment and client-therapist matching may reflect the current state of the art in interventions with men who batter. Without attending to these treatment issues, however, the field runs the risk of adopting the myths of uniformity of client characteristics, therapist characteristics, and treatment types, which Kiesler (1966) warned us about. Failure to consider individual differences and develop flexible treatment technologies could result in the vacuous findings typical of early psychotherapy research, which found that treatment works for some, but not for others. The question is not "Does batterer treatment work?" but "For whom does this treatment approach work, and under what circumstances?"

Another issue that has not been well addressed in treatment outcome studies is the relative contribution of treatment over and above that of other components of a community-wide intervention model as described by Pence. In Ganley's chapter, she cautions us to be mindful of the community context in which we work, when discussing the "efficacy" of our programs, and therefore to be appropriately humble in our claims. Dutton (1986) refers to this as "effect size." In other words, how much does treatment reduce violence after the effects of factors such as arrest and jail time are accounted for?

Other issues, related to those of treatment outcome and individual differences, are those of predicting treatment drop-out and violence "relapse." As of this writing, there are no published studies investigating aspects of negative outcome. As pointed out by Mays and Franks (1985), however, negative outcome (premature drop-out, relapse) may be a fairly specific problem that can be addressed through identification of high-risk clients. Hamberger and Hastings (in press) have conducted discriminant function analyses to predict treatment drop-outs and treatment completers who repeated violence within 1 year of completion. These studies, however, are based upon small samples and require replication, both within and across laboratories.

We must bear in mind that the language of "treatment dropout" and violence "relapse" implies that clients do not fit into a particular program, the outcome of which may already be predetermined based upon the philosophy and objectives espoused by that program. Lane and Russell (Chapter 6) point out that we need to examine our high standards for guaranteed success of our interventions within the context of therapist's discomfort with violence. Furthermore, if clients drop out of a particular program or modality of counseling, we may want to examine both client variables and therapist and program variables to determine how to develop a better match between individual clients and program philosophy. For example, Geffner et al. (Chapter 4) reported that of their clients surveyed who completed their couples' treatment program, all would recommend the program to others. It is probably not a coincidence that Geffner et al. also speculate that more abusive couples would utilize conjoint therapy if it were more widely available, since this is often requested by abusive husbands and battered women.

Therapist/Counselor Training Issues

Before someone undertakes to engage in counseling male spouse abusers, he or she must be informed by aspects of treatment related to the sociopolitical matrix within which battering occurs. This includes knowledge of cultural, historical, and political factors that affect attitudes toward women, gender and power issues, and the sociocultural factors that foster and maintain violence toward and oppression of women.

The counselor working in domestic violence needs to be well grounded in an understanding of the issues central to men who batter and the women whom they beat. For example, a woman's decision to remain with the man who beats her is not reflective of masochistic strivings but may be related to her financial dependence on him, social isolation (enforced by him), a sense of futility provided by dealing with an underresponsive legal and/or social services system, and a myriad of other factors. Similarly, knowledge of batterer characteristics and dynamics may assist in understanding and reacting therapeutically to potentially dangerous behavior patterns. For example, a man exhibiting signs of serious depression may benefit from psychopharmacology concurrent with counseling. Similarly, a man who is abusing alcohol or drugs may require concurrent or prior successful treatment in those areas. Knowledge of batterer dynamics related to minimization of violence, exercise of male privilege, and "ownership" of women are also of critical importance.

There are also ethicolegal issues, some of which apply generally to counseling, but some of which have particular applicability to working with men who batter. Sonkin's (1986) article on "duty to warn" the potential victim should be required reading for all who work with men who batter.

Counselors and therapists who work with male batterers must also be knowledgeable and informed about their specific therapeutic practices and the theoretical orientation that guides such practice. Eysenck (1985) suggests three primary functions of theory in counseling and psychotherapy. The first of these is operationalization of variables. This function relates back to the definition of violence discussed previously. Although difficult to achieve in a general way in an area fraught with multiple conceptual frameworks, it should be possible to specify and define important variables within each framework. A second function of theory is to guide the prediction of specific outcomes of interventions (hypothesis testing), and a third, to permit the testing of such predictions. Pagelow (1988) then suggests that the outcome of such hypothesis testing be integrated back into the program in terms of policy, procedure, and treatment approach.

Hence, we have come full circle. In the introductory chapter, we suggested that theory informs practice, which in turn leads to theory testing and revision of both theory and practice. In this way, we are in agreement with Ganley that we are currently just out of our infancy in the developmental level of this field. Through continuing to integrate theory, practice, research, and research findings, the field will evolve and enhance other efforts toward our goal of the elimination of violence in families.

References

Barnett, O. W., & Hamberger, L. K. (1987, July)). *Methodological issues in batterer research.* Roundtable discussion presented at the Third National Family Violence Research Conference, University of New Hampshire, Durham, NH.

Caesar, P. L. (1988). Exposure to violence in the families-of-origin among wife-abusers and maritally nonviolent men. *Violence and Victims, 3,* 49–63.

Dutton, D. G. (1986). The outcome of court-mandated treatment for wife assault: A quasi-experimental evaluation. *Violence and Victims, 1,* 163–175.

Edelson, J. L., Syers, M., & Brygger, M. P. (1987, July). *Comparative effectiveness of group treatment for men who batter.* Paper presented at the Third National Family Violence Research Conference, University of New Hampshire, Durham, NH.

Eysenck, H. J. (1985). Negative outcome in psychotherapy: The need for a theoretical framework. In D. T. Mays & C. M. Franks (Eds.), *Negative outcome in psychotherapy and what to do about it* (pp. 267–277). New York: Springer.

Ganley, A. L. (1981). *Court mandated counseling for men who batter: A three-day workshop for mental health professionals* (Participants Manual). Washington, DC: Center for Women's Policy Studies.

Hamberger, L. K., & Hastings, J. E. (in press). Counseling male spouse abusers: Characteristics of treatment completers and dropouts. *Violence and Victims.*

Hamberger, L. K., & Hastings, J. E. (1988a, August). *Recidivism following spouse abuse abatement counseling: Treatment program implications.* Paper presented at the meeting of the American Psychological Association, Atlanta, GA.

Hamberger, L. K., & Hastings, J. E. (1988b). Skills training for treatment of spouse abusers: An outcome study. *Journal of Family Violence, 3*(2), 121–130.

Hotaling, G. T., & Sugarman, D. B. (1986). An analysis of risk markers in husband to wife violence: The current state of knowledge. *Violence and Victims, 1,* 101–124.

Kiesler, D. J. (1966). Some myths of psychotherapy research and the search for paradigm. *Psychological Bulletin, 65,* 110–136.

Maiuro, R. D., Cahn, T. S., Vitaliano, P. P., & Zegree, J. B. (1987, August). *Anger control treatment for batterers: Outcome and follow-up.* Paper presented at the meeting of the American Psychological Association, New York, NY.

Mays, D. T., & Franks, C. M. (1985). Negative outcome: What to do about it. In D. T. Mays & C. M. Franks (Eds.), *Negative outcome in psycho-therapy and what to do about it*. New York: Springer.

Pagelow, M. (1988, April). Theory and practice in marital violence inter-vention: Discussion. In L. K. Hamberger (Chair), *Theory and practice in marital violence intervention*. Symposium presented at the meeting of the Western Psychological Association, San Francisco, CA.

Pirog-Good, M., & Stets-Kealey, J. (1985). Male batterers and battering prevention programs: A national survey. *Response*, 8–12.

Roberts, A. K. (1982). A national survey of services for batterers. In M. Roy (Ed.), *The abusing partner: An analysis of domestic battering* (pp. 230–243). New York: Van Nostrand Reinhold.

Sonkin, D. (1986). Clairvoyance vs. common sense: Therapist's duty to warn and protect. *Violence and Victims, 1*(1), 7–22.

Index